The Financial Crisis of Abolition

The Financial Crisis of Abolition

John Schulz

Yale University Press

New Haven and London

Set in Garamond and Stone Sans types by Binghamton Valley Composition.
Printed in the United States of America.

Library of Congress Cataloging-in-Publication Data

Schulz, John, 1947–
    [A crise financeira da aboligco, 1875–1901. English]
    The financial crisis of abolition / John Schulz.
        p. cm.
    Includes bibliographical references and index.
    ISBN 978-0-300-13419-3 (cloth : alk. paper)   1. Finance—Brazil—History—
19th century.   2. Slaves—Emancipation—Economic aspects—Brazil.   I. Title.
    HG185.B7S3813   2008
    331,11'734098109034—dc22

                                                                    2007046586

This paper meets the requirements of ANSI/NISO Z39.48-1992 (Permanence of Paper.
It contains 30 percent postconsumer waste (PCW) and is certified by the Forest Stewardship Council (FSC).
10 9 8 7 6 5 4 3 2 1

Contents

What we need in Brazil, therefore, is a large class of small planters, tradesmen, mechanics, etc, who will be proprietors and taxpayers, and who will be deeply interested in the protection of life and property, the maintenance of schools, the creation of roads, bridges, etc, and the intelligent development of agriculture and skilled industries. Agricultural credit institutions, created for the relief of embarrassed planters, will never accomplish this result.

—*Rio News, January 15, 1888*

Preface to the English Edition

During the years 1893 to 1896, the United States underwent its last major crisis as a debtor country before the twenty-first century. America came close to abandoning the gold standard and risked embarking upon a wildly inflationary monetary policy. The same decade saw crises in many of the world's other fast-developing debtor economies, including those of Italy, Australia, Argentina, and Brazil. Although many of the great capital-importing countries suffered crises during the 1890s, their crises came at different times and as a result of different immediate causes. Unfortunate domestic decisions often created difficulties, even though the international economic conjuncture appeared favorable. Excessive foreign borrowing in Argentina and Australia, silver purchase and agricultural difficulties in the United States, and a trade dispute between France and Italy all provoked severe internal distress. Although global business cycles can hardly be ignored, national policies largely determined how the international situation impacted upon individual economies.

The crisis in Brazil in the 1890s, like most other events in its nineteenth-century history, arose out of slavery. On the thirteenth of

May, 1888, the Brazilian Parliament, composed largely of past and present slaveholders, voted for abolition. Over a short period of time, this elite had reached an overwhelming consensus with only the representatives of the province of Rio de Janeiro in the Chamber of Deputies opposing emancipation. The leader of the pro-slavery senators, the baron of Cotegipe, who had been prime minister until a mere two months before, gallantly declared that he would not keep a lady waiting. This lady, the princess regent, wished to sign emancipation into law. Shortly thereafter, amid a shower of flowers, Princess Isabel placed her signature on this historic document.

This image of flowers contrasts rather strongly with that of Abraham Lincoln preparing his Emancipation Proclamation in a Washington filled with the mutilated veterans of Antietam. The English-speaking reader cannot help but be intrigued by the Brazilian experience of abolition without violence. In contrast to the U.S. experience, in Brazil the region that maintained the largest number of slaves subsequently attracted the lion's share of immigrants. This region led the country in terms both of agricultural and of industrial development. Race relations, while far from perfect, lacked and still lack the bitterness found in the United States.

Brazilian slavery has been examined by a number of English-speaking historians (see the works of Leslie Bethell, Robert Conrad, Warren Dean, Mary C. Karasch, Stanley Stein, and Robert B. Toplin, listed in the bibliography). Although the treatment meted out to slaves varied between town and plantation, and from province to province and century to century, in general Brazilian slavery appears to have been as inhumane as that of any other land. If mortality is the measure of brutality, slavery in Brazil proved far more lethal than in the United States, as the latter country imported one sixth the number of slaves as Brazil but had more bondsmen alive at abolition than did Brazil. Brazilian planters worked their slaves literally to death much more commonly than their American counterparts. On the other hand, Brazil experienced far more miscegenation than did the United States. Most slaveholding families had some slave blood in their veins. Manumission occurred more frequently in Brazil, and freedmen enjoyed greater social mobility in Brazil than they did in the antebellum South. Thus, although slaves were brutalized and free blacks were humiliated, the line between black and white proved less rigid in Brazil than in most other slaveholding societies.

Although Brazil's former slaveholders did not have to restore burned mansions, replace confiscated livestock, or rebuild torn railroads, as did their American counterparts after the Civil War, the process of adjustment to free labor proved far from easy. In Rio de Janeiro Province, many planters went out of business. Eighteen months after she received the parade of flowers, Princess Isabel and her family suffered deposition and exile—also without violence, as almost no one saw fit to defend the monarchy. The Republic, attempting to placate the former slaveholders, created inflation, frightened domestic and foreign investors, and broke the wave of optimism that followed in the wake of emancipation. Financial mismanagement, combined with the loss of political legitimacy, produced a decade of coup, countercoup, and civil war. This political and financial instability contrasted with the peaceful decades that preceded the fall of the monarchy and followed the consolidation of civilian rule under the Republic. Abolition in Brazil thus was not just a flower parade.

Preface

The history of abolition in Brazil begins with the termination of the slave trade in 1850. Slave owners realized at this time that the institution could not survive indefinitely, as the captive population did not reproduce itself. More frequently than masters in the United States, Brazilian planters worked their slaves to death. Until abolition itself in 1888, slavery remained both highly lucrative for the masters and, in their eyes, essential to the export economy.

From 1850 to 1888, the reluctant preparation for emancipation dominated politics, economics, and finance. As the slave population diminished, the urgency for a new labor regime became more apparent, a realization driven by several external and internal events. The end of slavery in the United States, in 1865, and Cuba, in 1878, placed a heavy moral pressure on the Brazilian elite. The former event encouraged the passage of Brazil's Free Womb Law of 1871, which liberated all individuals born after its enactment, and the latter coincided with a major Agricultural Congress convened by the government to discuss reforms enabling planters to adjust to the decline of slavery. In 1880, the abolitionist campaign began, and in 1884, the Banco do

Brasil refused to allow slaves to be used as security for loans. Nevertheless, until 1887 the overwhelming majority of planters remained firmly committed to slavery. That year, a combination of expanding demand for labor, the dwindling number of slaves, slave rebellion, military mutiny, and especially the availability of Italian immigrants convinced a significant portion of landholders that they would benefit from abolition.

The coffee harvests of 1887 and 1888 represented the social crisis of abolition. The first of these crops witnessed mass slave flight and the second, following abolition, left planters in doubt as to whether or not freedmen would pick the berries. As it turned out, both harvests proved large and profitable for the planters, and fears of social unrest disappeared as immigrants replaced freedmen on the São Paulo plantations.

The government that achieved abolition, realizing that it needed to institute financial measures to appease the planters, proved to be one of the most active cabinets of the century. In the planters' eyes, however, the magnitude of the change warranted even more energetic responses. The three governments, one monarchist and two republican, that followed the abolitionist ministry tripled the money supply, stimulated stock market speculation, and otherwise tried to buy planter support for their regimes. These irresponsible actions created a bubble known as the *Encilhamento* (literally, "girthing" or "saddling up"). Thus the acute financial crisis ushered in by abolition began in June 1889, under the monarchy, and continued through two cabinets after the proclamation of the Republic. The bubble terminated in November 1891 with the overthrow of President Marshal Deodoro da Fonseca after his failed "stock market coup."

Although Fonseca's successor returned the country to financial conservatism, another decade would pass before Brazil regained stability. The last part of this book covers the unsuccessful as well as the successful stabilization policies in force after 1891. Only with the victory of stabilization in 1901 may we consider the financial crisis of abolition as resolved.

This study follows a chronological sequence after the first chapter that provides a general view of Brazil under the empire. Chapter 2 outlines the development of the international financial system at the time of abolition. The aim of this chapter is to destroy the notion that the finance ministers of the Encilhamento "did not know better," given the comprehension of economics of the period. The experiences of their century, including the inflation caused by the Napoleonic Wars and the successive bank frauds in Europe and the United States, as well as contemporary Brazilian criticism, show that ignorance was not the cause of the bubble. The third chapter narrates and analyzes Brazil's experiences with financial crises up to and including the Mauá failure of 1875, the last crisis prior to abolition. Here we hope to demonstrate the generally efficient way Brazil's nineteenth-century financial leaders defended themselves from domestic and foreign economic shocks. Chapter 4 examines the planters' demands, summarized by the slogan "Capital and Workers," as abolition approached. Chapter 5 considers the financial aspects of the abolition process itself, which culminated in a major bill to restructure the banking system.

Chapter 6 tells the story of the bubble, and covers both the last months of the empire and the first two years of the Republic. Despite their important differences regarding federalism, when it came to finance, the ministry of the monarchist Ouro Preto and the republican Ruy Barbosa and Lucena ministries that succeeded it had more in common with each other than with earlier and later administrations.

The seventh chapter includes the two failed attempts at stabilization following the collapse of the bubble. The first attempt proved to be largely a casualty of civil war. A contraction of the coffee market undid the second stabilization initiative. Of particular interest today is how stabilization finally triumphed, described in chapter 8; a program of increased taxation, reduced spending, and privatization, combined with the elimination of subsidized loans, sustained the currency and initiated a decade of prosperity. The last chapter contains reflections upon Brazil's satisfactory experience with inflation during the age of the gold standard.

The free and articulate Brazilian press of this period was an extremely valuable source for this study. The Brazilian National Library contains full collections of all the important local papers, including the *Gazeta de Notícias,* the *Rio News,* the *Jornal do Commercio,* the *Jornal do Brasil, O Paíz, Cidade do Rio, Correio Paulistano,* and the *Estado de São Paulo,* the first two cited being outstanding. I am particularly indebted to the *Rio News,* published from 1879 to 1901, which gives the views of a sensitive outside observer who was at the same time a spokesman for the commercial community. The editor, Robert Lamoreux, forcefully expressed the views of reformers, both Brazilian and foreign, and I could not resist the temptation to quote liberally from his writings.

The Archives of the Ministry of Finance, also located in Rio de Janeiro, contain complete series of the Council of State opinions, the annual reports of the ministers, and the annual budgets for this period. These archives have a good selection of nineteenth-century publications.

The Instituto Geografico e Histórico Brasileiro holds arguably the country's most valuable collections of correspondence. Three of these collections—those of the viscount of Mauá, Prudente de Morais, and Solon Ribeiro—were particularly interesting. The Casa de Rui Barbosa and the Museu Imperial of Petropolis also have important collections of documents. Outside of Rio, I had the opportunity to utilize the Rothschild Archive in London and Princeton University Library's microfilm copies of the British Foreign Office reports. Beyond these sources, this study made extensive use of contemporary books, many of which have been reprinted over the past thirty years (see the bibliography). Let me take this opportunity to thank the staffs of these research institutions for the kindness they have shown me over the years.

My acknowledgments begin with Stanley Stein, who oriented my dissertation at Princeton, of which this study is an offshoot. Also at Princeton, Lawrence Stone, then chairman of the History Department, and my colleague William Irvine both taught me the power of history. At Princeton and later on, I gained much from exchanging ideas with Frank Colson, Warren Dean, John Gledson, and Robert Levene.

In Brazil, Sergio Buarque de Holanda provided me with valuable insights into the politics of the Brazilian Empire. I would like to thank Mary Karasch for her detailed comments on an earlier version of this manuscript and Pedro Carvalho de Mello and Roberto Ventura for their suggestions on the final draft of the Portuguese edition (University of São Paulo Press, 1996), and to give my special thanks to Steven Topik for his suggestions on the revision of this text in English. Rodrigo Marques talked at length with me regarding nineteenth-century exchange policies. Norman Gall, executive director of the Fernand Braudel Institute of World Economics, in 1992 published an earlier version in English as a working paper. Finally, my wife, Maria da Luz, and my children, Thomas and Katherine, put up with my research for all these years with great patience.

Chapter 1 Interests of the Elite

From 1850 to 1914, Brazil enjoyed both a civilian, legitimate—albeit unrepresentative—political regime and a reasonably stable monetary system, except for one period, from 1889 to 1894. Within these five years, the country suffered two successful coups d'état, military government, and civil war, and the national currency fell from its parity against sterling to one third of this value. World market factors beyond Brazil's control cannot be blamed for these disturbances as coffee prices attained their cyclical highs. Internal problems rather than external shocks caused abrupt alterations in political and financial affairs. The abolition of slavery and its accompanying adjustments provoked this period of disorder and crisis.

The protagonists of this story are the members of the nineteenth-century Brazilian elite: men more than prepared to enslave their fellow humans for profit. The financial policies adopted by successive governments served the interests of this elite with little regard for the needs of the remainder of the society. Of course, this elite was far from monolithic; it included planters, merchants, professionals, and public officials. Planters in expanding areas such as western São Paulo

Province had interests that differed from those in declining zones such as the Paraíba Valley (Rio de Janeiro Province, eastern São Paulo, southern Minas Gerais), not to mention those of the sugar provinces of the Northeast. Thus, financial policy had to accommodate a considerable variety of often conflicting objectives. Given elite values, the needs of the mass of the population were systematically ignored. (Brazil's political divisions were called provinces under the empire and became states with the proclamation of the Republic.)

From independence in 1822 until 1889, when the empire was abolished, Brazil was a monarchy ruled successively by two members of the house of Bragança, Pedro I (reigned 1822 to 1831), and his son Pedro II (1831 to 1889). Both emperors governed under a constitution, and Pedro II, especially, permitted free speech as well as rude attacks upon his person. Both sovereigns chose their ministers without regard to parliamentary majorities. Pedro I faced a determined opposition that in fact finally forced him to abdicate. This emperor, born in Portugal, relied heavily on Portuguese counselors. With the abdication, the Lusitanian influence all but disappeared. Under Pedro II, a two-party system evolved, the parties using the British designations Liberal and Conservative. Socially, both parties had similar constituencies. Neither party espoused abolition and the saying was, "There is nothing that resembles a Conservative more than a Liberal in power." By using the government machine, Pedro II's ministers won every election of his reign, just as the English politicians had done during the previous century. Pedro II's minority, which lasted until 1840, witnessed economic stagnation and civil disorders as well as a number of separatist insurrections. The expansion of the coffee plantations in the decade following the monarch's coming of age helped finance the military campaigns against the separatists. The last major rebellion succumbed in 1849 after which the country enjoyed forty years of domestic peace.

Under pressure from the British fleet, the Brazilian government of 1850 extinguished the slave trade. Brazil at this time had 8 million inhabitants, of whom 2.5 million were slaves. Most slaves worked on coffee and sugar plantations. Contemporaries realized that the slave population would not reproduce itself fast enough to keep pace as the plantation economy entered into a period of rapid growth.[1] The price of slaves rose, causing owners in the less prosperous areas of the Northeast to sell their slaves to planters in Rio de Janeiro, São Paulo, and Minas Gerais. Beginning in 1853, determined slaveholders taxed the interprovincial slave trade in an effort to discourage these sales, maintain slavery's centrality to the Northeast, and thus avoid a sectional conflict like that in the United States. The collapse of the Confederacy in the

United States Civil War left Brazil and Spain (in its colony Cuba) as the last slaveholding states. In 1871, the Brazilian legislature passed the "Law of the Free Womb," whereby all children born to slaves after its enactment were free. This law kept these free-born children under the power of their parents' masters until they reached twenty-one years of age, so the immediate effect of this measure was more psychological than economic. By this time, the census showed that the number of slaves had declined to 1.5 million whereas the total population had increased to 10 million.

The elite that governed Brazil at the passage of the Free Womb Law comprised a few hundred families at most. The political branch of this elite was the product of the two law schools, in São Paulo and Recife, established shortly after independence.[2] The typical successful politician began his career as a police chief and then became a provincial president (governor); both of these positions were political appointments. After serving in the Chamber of Deputies, successful politicians won election to the Senate, a lifetime office. Relations among leaders of the two parties remained amicable, and a number of politicians held investments in partnership with their political opponents.[3] The business elite, though largely foreign and rarely holding political office, maintained close access to the political elite. A considerable element within this political elite owned plantations or came from plantation-owning families. Requests from the large planters and the principal merchants received attention from the members of the political elite.

This small elite acted within the capitalist system with all due rationality. Unfortunately, short-term calculations often led to brutality toward their slaves. Civilized in their dealings with one another in the capital, this elite systematically utilized violence in the interior not only to dominate their slaves but also to prevail against squatters and on occasion in conflict with other planters. The backlands of Brazil resembled the American Wild West, except that no myth of the honest sheriff ever emerged.

Although further studies are necessary to supply quantitative verification, it appears that both upward and downward social mobility were extremely common in nineteenth-century Brazil. Commerce, government office, and plantation agriculture provided three avenues to wealth. Unlike the situation in Europe at that time, one successful generation could raise a family from the bottom to the top of society. Numerous offspring, soil exhaustion, and financial crises pulled many down from the elite just as fast as they had risen. Despite this individual mobility as well as the secular growth of the economy, at any one time power remained in a few hands and served exclusively the bodies attached to these hands. Regional power centers began to shift around the time of the Law of the Free Womb. In the decades before 1871, politicians from the provinces of Rio de Janeiro, Bahia, and Pernambuco (the latter two were northeastern sugar producers) dominated government. Beet-sugar production in Europe undermined the sugar economy of the Northeast during the 1870s and 1880s, while coffee production stagnated in Rio de Janeiro as a result of soil exhaustion and aging bushes. In the twenty years after rail access to the interior of São Paulo Province was established, in 1867, the province grew to become Brazil's major coffee exporter and taxpayer. The central province of Minas Gerais (coffee and cattle) and the far southern province of Rio Grande do Sul (cattle) also came to occupy more important positions during the 1870s and 1880s.

Beginning with Celso Furtado's *Economic Growth of Brazil,* originally written in the 1950s, a consensus exists that the abolition of the slave trade in 1850 marked the start of a period of sustained economic expansion that freed the country from a past characterized by commodity cycles. In 1997 and 1982, respectively, Stephen Haber and Nathaniel Leff, calling attention to the declining product of the Brazilian Northeast, have questioned the validity of Furtado's thesis regarding the second half of the nineteenth century.[4] The value of Brazilian exports multiplied almost six times, as measured in pounds sterling, while the population doubled between 1850 and 1900.[5] This period also witnessed the start of industrialization, and the creation of the railroad network implied accelerated expansion in the domestic economy as well. Thus, Furtado's argument appears to hold. Nevertheless, Haber and Leff have performed an important service in reminding us that cyclical contractions also took place during this half century. Historians have tended to exalt Brazil's impressive growth during this period, but we must not let ourselves forget how São Paulo State and the city of Rio de Janeiro monopolized this development. If there is no "Whig history" of late-nineteenth-century Brazil, there certainly is a triumphant history of São Paulo and Rio in this epoch.

Until the 1980s, it was fashionable to begin consideration of nineteenth-century Brazil by emphasizing the Brazilian Empire's dependence on Europe.[6] Without a doubt, the slaves and free lower classes suffered a cruel form of exploitation at the base of the world economic order. The elite, on the other hand, formed part of the exploiting system. This Brazilian upper class lived better than the middle sector of Victorian England, not to mention English industrial workers. The Brazilian elite not only enjoyed the material and cultural fruits of the nineteenth-century world, but also displayed a reasonable degree of autonomy in dealing with the industrialized countries.

As trade tariffs contributed two thirds of the imperial government's revenues, autonomy in the setting of tariffs was essential to public finance. Pedro I's first treaty with Great Britain, in 1827, sacrificed the empire's freedom regarding tariff policy for fifteen years; it was signed at a low point in Brazil's economic fortunes, and at a moment when the emperor needed British help to maintain his daughter on the Portuguese throne. But by the time this agreement expired, Pedro I had been exiled, and his son's advisers prepared a new tariff that attempted to generate more revenue and to protect the national economy. From the Alves Branco Tariff of 1844 on, the major constraint on customs policy was fiscal; foreign pressure became secondary.[7]

The leaders of the empire took advantage of the opportunities of nineteenth-century "progress." Members of the Brazilian Parliament understood the world capital markets and imposed restraints on both loans and equity investments.[8] They quickly perceived the importance of inventions and sought to attract railroad developers as early as 1830, the year the world's first passenger line opened. Within the legislature, there were well-informed debates concerning the latest foreign ideas—from French literary realism to Victorian parliamentary practices to United States bond-backed banknotes—and ways these might be adapted to Brazil. The Brazilian elite closely followed the product requirements of European markets and responded to market conditions by planting cotton or cocoa and extracting rubber as the demand for these commodities appeared. In 1906, at the end of the period covered by this book, the Brazilian elite devised a scheme to control the world supply of coffee, to the detriment of consumers in the industrialized countries. This Brazilian elite acted in conjunction with the dominant groups of the developed world but can hardly be considered a puppet of these interests.

Nineteenth-century agricultural policy invariably served the interests of the elite. As long as slavery remained economically viable for the principal plantation areas, the state maintained this institution, even in the face of hostile world opinion.[9] The laws relating to land favored the rich, who could obtain "legal" title to extensive tracts previously farmed by squatters, whose rights the authorities systematically ignored.[10] No matter how long the squatters had labored on their plots, the "legal" owners evicted them through frequent and open employment of thugs.[11] Mortgage laws protected planters from their creditors so completely that most potential lenders refused to extend loans for agriculture. The Banco do Brasil directed such credit as did become available for farming exclusively to the largest planters.

The more progressive segment of the Brazilian elite perceived that alternative agricultural policies could have been pursued.[12] These leaders accompanied developments in France and the United States that indicated that small farmers played a significant role in the prosperity of these countries. The northern states of the United States from their inception had encouraged family farms by limiting the size of plots sold from public lands. As the Civil War revealed, the "free soil" economy of the North proved victorious over the plantation economy of the South. Meanwhile, in France, the peasants whose fathers had obtained their own land during the revolution became a prop of the monarchy during the nineteenth century. Toward the end of the century, France and other European countries were already experimenting with agricultural credit unions for small farmers.

Prominent members of the Brazilian court encouraged the immigration of Europeans to establish small farms.[13] Several of these colonies, especially those in Santa Catarina, proved quite successful. However, as the planter elite wanted immigrants to work as laborers on their lands and considered small farmers as a threat, public endeavors in this area suffered severe restrictions. As abolition approached, members of the elite began to consider alternative labor systems such as sharecropping, renting, or even the division of large estates.[14] Many planters could not conceive of life with paid employees. This mentality set limits to all government action, including financial policy.

As the momentum for abolition developed, a group of reformers from within and from just below the elite—military and civil officials, merchants, and professionals—felt that the end of slavery presented the country with an opportunity to modernize. In addition to supporting abolition, these reformers generally favored immigration, industrialization, education, and public works. Many also advocated political changes, including the establishment of a republic, the broadening of the powers of the provinces, and the expansion of the voting franchise, then limited by property qualifications to a minuscule fraction of the population. For some in Brazil, the late eighties became a period of excitement, experimentation, and hope.

Although certain social groups, notably military officers, appreciated that only industrialization could raise Brazil to Europe's material level, the majority of the members of the oligarchy considered industrial growth with mixed feelings.[15] During the decades surrounding abolition, the elite debated the government's role in fostering industry: whether it should be through tariffs, subsidies, or improved transportation. Protectionist tariffs, like Bismarck's celebrated schedule of 1879, received careful attention. Although in fact most

of the governments gave little support, substantial development of light industry took place during the coffee boom of 1885–1895.[16] The development at
this time of a mass market of immigrants and freed slaves provided the fundamental stimulus to industrialization; coffee exports provided the foreign exchange to purchase machinery.[17] During this period, most members of the
elite felt that although industry brought benefits, it also had costs in the form
of higher prices, inferior goods, or increased government spending.[18]

Public finance—the government's revenues, expenses, debts, and inflation—
reveals the essence of a society and its elite values. During the first generation
after independence, the Brazilian state had to devote most of its resources to
the maintenance of order against separatist provincial elites. After 1850, an increasing share of revenues could be dedicated to economic areas of particular
interest to planters and merchants: the development of infrastructure such as
railroads, public utilities, and ports. The imperial state proved to have both
the will and the force to mobilize, through taxes and borrowings, a substantial
share of national income. By the fall of the monarchy, the state had indeed
become an extremely active economic agent, spending a sum equal to half
Brazil's annual exports. (Public finance is discussed in greater detail in the
appendix.)

Changes in government revenues and expenditures evolved gradually under
the empire, but the abolitionist crisis brought about a radical departure in
monetary and credit policies. Prior to abolition, the wealthiest and most powerful elements of the elite held monetary stability as one of their principal
objectives. These men had accumulated fortunes from agriculture and commerce and sought to protect their financial investments—largely government
bonds—from the effects of inflation. The demise of slavery brought this consensus to an end. Indebted planters, both from the declining Paraíba Valley
and the rising western region of São Paulo Province, wanted monetary and
credit measures that increased the volume of currency in circulation.[19] These
men argued that the public debt itself tied up funds that could be used for
"productive purposes." The indebted planters and their merchant suppliers
preferred that the government borrow from abroad, which would induce local
capitalists to invest in or lend funds to agriculture and commerce. The debtor
advocates of "soft money" wished to authorize the issuance of banknotes; they
suggested that more money in circulation would lead to expanded production. It should be emphasized that the conflict between wealthier hard-money
planters and proponents of soft money, who had lower liquidity, was a purely
domestic quarrel. Politicians of both schools made ample reference to foreign

economic thought in their learned debates in Congress, but local constituencies and considerations determined the ultimate decisions. Incidentally, foreign bankers defended themselves from devaluation by denominating their loans in sterling, as did the railroad investors, who enjoyed returns guaranteed by the government.

After abolition, elements of the elite, suffering from both real and imagined hardships as a consequence, demanded vigorous state action. In response, three successive governments—one monarchist and two republican—hazarded an experiment with easy credit. The instrument that they chose was the private banknote. The causes and consequences of this eventful decision are the subjects of this study.

My aim in this book is to demonstrate the following: Abolition of slavery, rather than forces external to Brazil, generated a need for financial reform. The bubble known as the *Encilhamento* took place during a favorable economic conjuncture characterized by high coffee prices and, at least until November 1890, Britain's willingness to make substantial overseas investments. A certain increase in the money supply was indeed necessary at this time in order to facilitate the monetary portion of the wages of immigrants and freedmen. Both the republican and the monarchist finance ministers in power after abolition perceived the need for "easier" money and enacted measures to accommodate the planters. To maintain elite support for their regimes, the monarchist and republican finance ministers also committed serious abuses. These wrongs included allowing private banks to print money to deliver to the owners of these banks, the encouragement of stock market frauds, the give-away of public lands, and the granting of overpriced contracts, notably to transport immigrants. Contemporaries perceived these abuses and removed the perpetrators from power. A major consequence of these dubious acts was inflation that accompanied the great expansion of the money supply. The stock exchange swindles, for their part, damaged the cause of industrialization in Brazil. Although the Encilhamento collapsed in 1891, a full decade proved necessary for the return to financial stability, the delay being caused by a costly civil war, from 1893 to 1895, followed by an unfavorable external situation from 1895 to 1900.

When, at the dawn of the twentieth century, the financial crisis receded, disappointed reformers realized that the opportunity to restructure the Brazilian economy that abolition presented had been lost.[20] Wealth continued to be as unevenly distributed as it had been when one human being could own another.

THE HISTORIOGRAPHY

There are no books on the financial crisis of abolition in English, and only two in Portuguese: Gustavo Franco's *Reforma monetária e instabilidade durante a transição republicana* (1983) and Luiz Tannuri's *O Encilhamento* (1981). Franco's book focuses on the financial reforms that began with abolition, including those of the two last monarchist prime ministers and of the first republican finance minister, Ruy Barbosa. Franco discusses neither the actions of Barbosa's successor, the baron of Lucena, who took the financial scandals to new depths, nor the various attempts at stabilization. My work therefore differs from his in that I try to place the choices of these politicians in their larger historical context, both within Brazil and within the world financial system of the times. My study also covers the subsequent stabilization.

Franco presents his argument clearly. Franco and I agree that Brazil's problems were caused by a domestic situation: the need to pay immigrants and freedmen for their labor after abolition. We further agree that Brazilian leaders were not puppets who conformed to foreign ideas and constraints. Franco does give more importance than I to the Baring crisis of November 1890 as a source of instability (*Reforma monetária,* 127) but does not himself discuss the period after Barbosa's December 1890 reforms. The major point of disagreement relates to Barbosa's motives rather than his actions. Franco admires Barbosa and feels that he had a vision for modernizing Brazil through the use of fiduciary currency. Indeed Barbosa holds a special place in Brazilian history as the defeated "civilian" candidate against a general in the 1910 presidential election as well as a spokesman for abolition and a defender of political prisoners. These contributions notwithstanding, my opinion of Barbosa is that he was a corrupt opportunist. Obviously the burden of proof is on me. The controversy regarding Barbosa began with his contemporaries; it continued with Raimundo Magalhães Junior's *Rui: O homem e o mito* (1965), which was vehemently contested by Americo Jacobina Lacombe's *Á sombra de Rui Barbosa* (1984), and continues to the present day. Nelson Werneck Sodré, an influential Marxist historian of the postwar generation, saw Ruy Barbosa as "the middle class in power," a generalization he however does nothing to substantiate in his *Formacão historica do Brasil* (2004).[21]

Tannuri's account of the Encilhamento also begins with abolition and the accompanying need to pay immigrants and freedmen. Unlike Franco, he continues the story to the crisis of 1900 and Finance Minister Joaquim Murtinho's stabilization. Tannuri takes a rather neutral view of Barbosa, neither praising nor condemning his financial measures. His contribution is to call attention to the different consequences of the bubble years in Rio de Janeiro and São Paulo.

A recent work in English by Anne Hanley, *Native Capital,* focuses on São Paulo during this period. Hanley, like Franco, sees Barbosa as a visionary who tried to introduce contemporaneous universal banking in Brazil (see chapter 5 of her book). One cannot comment on Barbosa without discussing industrialization, the core of his "vision." There are three standard works on Brazilian industrialization: Warren Dean's *The Industrialization of São Paulo, 1880–1945,* Nicia Vilela Luz's *A luta pela industrialização do Brasil,* and Stanley Stein's *The Brazilian Cotton Manufacture.* Luz has negative views on Barbosa, arguing that neither before nor after holding office could he be considered an industrial leader (168–177). In his first chapter, Dean notes the growth of a market in São Paulo for industrial goods to be sold to immigrants and freedmen as well as the need for increased circulation to pay these groups after abolition. He does not discuss the Encilhamento or Barbosa's policies; apparently he did not think these factors had a major impact on the industrialization process. Stein's work has been cited (Hanley, page 86) as a defense of the Encilhamento. My understanding of his seventh chapter is that Stein concedes that a number of genuine industrial corporations began during the bubble, the fraud and excessive speculation notwithstanding. The larger part of chapter 7 covers Minister Serzedello Correia's loan to industry. Correia and his president, Floriano Peixoto, ended the banknote issues of the Encilhamento and battled to stabilize the currency. Accordingly they followed policies diametrically opposed to those of Barbosa. Peixoto and Correia led the most pro-industry government Brazil had prior to 1930. Thus Barbosa does not receive much support from the most widely respected studies on industrialization. Of course, I intend to make the case against the financial policies of the provisional government through my own analysis below.

The Encilhamento forms part of the history of inflation in Brazil. The renowned economist Raymond Goldsmith, writing during a period of prolonged inflation during the late twentieth century (*Brasil 1850–1984: Desenvolvimento financeiro sob um século de inflação,* 1986), uses the bubble to convey the impression that Brazil always suffered from monetary instability. I seek to modify this view, maintaining that the Encilhamento formed one unsatisfactory event within a long period, from 1830 to 1914, of otherwise rather stable financial conditions.

This bubble also figures in the historical evaluation of the Republic. Economic historians of the postwar generation such as Celso Furtado, Caio Prado Junior, and Nelson Werneck Sodré speak of the "Bourgeois Republic." Prado sees the Republic as differing from the empire in that the new order was led by businessmen.[22] The example of Prado's own family, however, contradicts this appraisal, as it owned a banking house and controlled the most important railroad in the province of São Paulo under the empire, and Antonio Prado served as minister of agriculture twice. Prado himself recognizes the respectable economic progress, including in railroads and industry in addition to coffee production, during the two decades prior to the fall of the empire.[23] My view of this period is one of continuous economic expansion under both the empire after 1850 and the Republic. The Republic constituted a major change only in that it transferred power to sectors of the elite representing the most dynamic regions of the country, primarily the Republican Party of São Paulo.

Under Marshal Floriano Peixoto (1891–1894), the second republican president, Brazil had a frankly progressive government with a coherent vision of the future based upon industrialization, education, health (the eradication of yellow fever in the capital), and the populating of the interior, including further railroad construction as well as the transfer of the capital to the current site of Brasilia.[24] Political conflicts were the reason this administration lost its focus and accomplished little. The country enjoyed greater progress under the less avowedly developmental governments of the oligarchy in power after 1894. Most of Peixoto's successors held conservative beliefs similar to those of their monarchist counterparts regarding industrialization and material growth in general.

By the time the Encilhamento was over, in November 1891, the transformation to free labor was essentially completed so that the ex-slaves, no longer a social menace, could be forgotten. The financial consequences of abolition, unlike the social ones, required a further decade to resolve; in the final chapters of this book I analyze the attempts at stabilization following the inflationary outburst that accompanied emancipation. Just as we experienced during the twentieth century, stabilization can be illusive. From the moratorium of 1982 to the Real Plan of 1994, Brazil witnessed a number of failed stabilizations. From this personal experience, many of my contemporaries developed the conviction that stabilization is in and of itself a desirable situation worth certain sacrifices. Although it is clear that coffee and rubber, along with other commodities, brought economic growth to Brazil throughout the turbulent 1890s, development came faster after the stabilization achieved in 1901. I believe that financial stability was vital to growth-oriented statesmen a century ago, just as it is today to leaders seeking both growth and distribution. A government unable to control its fiscal and monetary affairs will ultimately be unable to deliver expansion and equality. The bill for irresponsible policies in all countries and all centuries eventually has to be paid. Under these circumstances, my study looks favorably on Murtinho's stabilization plan, except in regard to his exchange policy. Murtinho erred in failing to disavow the return to parity, an error the British government famously committed a quarter of a century later. Examples well known to Murtinho were the British return to parity in 1821 following the 84 percent inflation of the Napoleonic Wars, and that of the United States in 1879, after its currency had declined to 39 percent of its prewar value during the Civil War. The apparent success of these extreme deflations allows us to understand—even if we do not accept—Murtinho's reasoning. In other respects his stabilization was a success.

Economic historians of the postwar generation labeled Murtinho an imperialist tool. Sodré (335) views the funding loan of 1898 as the consolidation of imperialism in Brazil. The foreign bondholders, who had to wait three years for payment of interest and thirteen years for principal, would certainly have found this renegotiation to be a rather doubtful victory. I shall try to show that Murtinho and his president, Campos Sales, acted with independence in their dealings with the international financial community and inaugurated a period of accelerated growth that lasted until World War One disrupted global markets. The best literature on this minister is Nicia Vilela Luz (*Idéias econômicas de Joaquim Murtinho*, 1980).

My major goal in writing this book was to demonstrate that not only Joaquim Murtinho but also the majority of the finance ministers of this period administered Brazil well in terms of the interests of their social class. Through public finance and the manipulation of the Banco do Brasil they favored large planters, to the detriment of the rest of the population. But these men were neither ignoramuses nor puppets of foreign interests, as writers of the dependence-on-Europe school would suggest.[25] Brazilian statesmen were not fooled by foreign doctrines such as free trade and the gold standard, as they never adhered to the former and only belatedly enacted the latter when it turned out to be in their narrow best interest to do so. The imperial and early republican state actually participated vigorously in the economy. Except during the Encilhamento, Brazil's financial leadership served well the interests of the national elite. I shall demonstrate, in the chapter on the Encilhamento, that this one period of financial recklessness and greater-than-normal corruption lasted but thirty months before reasonably prudent management once again prevailed.

Recently, a consensus seems to have formed against the dependency school among scholars, although many nonacademics in Brazil still almost instinctively blame the central economies for Brazil's backwardness. Two pioneering works on the independence of the state are Nathaniel Leff's *Underdevelopment and Development in Brazil* and Steven Topik's *Political Economy of the Brazilian State, 1889–1930*. Topik takes the "Old Republic," which had the reputation for stagnation as well as decentralization, and demonstrates how active the central government really was. I hope my work joins Leff's and Topik's in helping readers appreciate the creativity and accomplishments of the Brazilian leadership. On the other hand, I also try to show how these politicians ignored the necessities of the vast majority of Brazilian citizens. Institutional defects of this leadership such as, in the financial sphere, the inability to permit foreclosures of mortgages and, in the social sphere, inadequate attention to education still hold back the development of this country.

Chapter 2 The International Financial System

The Brazilian elite, including its members who did not depend directly on agricultural exports, believed that exports provided the only means to wealth, both private and public. The governments of the Brazilian Empire depended upon tariffs for the greater part of their income, and in turn utilized much of this income to foster "improvements" that facilitated international trade. Trade required credit to expand. By the middle of the nineteenth century, foreign credit had become available to finance both overseas commerce itself and projects, especially railroads, necessary to promote exports. For the Brazilian elite, the international system of credit presented major opportunities as well as significant dangers, as contemporaries understood to varying degrees.[1] An understanding of the development of this financial system is essential in order to evaluate Brazil's policies as abolition approached.

International lending began with the medieval "bill of exchange." The bill constituted a promise to pay at a different city, in a different currency (hence the term "exchange"), at a specified time in the future. These instruments proved easier and safer to transfer than gold and circumvented the ecclesiastic ban on charging interest, which was figured into the exchange rate.[2] But the principal purpose of the bill of exchange was for one merchant to extend credit to another while the latter sold his merchandise. Trade required credit to expand. As long as the borrower remained honest and had all probability of disposing of his goods at a profit, he represented an acceptable credit risk. The more substantial merchants discovered that lending could be quite lucrative in its own right in addition to the gains made on the sale of the merchandise itself. Certain mercantile houses, the fourteenth-century Bardi and Peruzzi and fifteenth-century Medici of Florence being perhaps the most famous, began to concentrate their resources on money lending and became bankers, while retaining their wholesale commercial activities. By the sixteenth century, bills of exchange issued by banker-merchants often circulated freely and were endorsed by a series of holders. Thus the bill acted as a forerunner of the banknote and provided a major stimulus to economic development.

In addition to fellow merchants, these early bankers encountered another class of borrowers: princes. Wars always cost a good deal, and most monarchs had to borrow to finance their campaigns. As governments could not be liquidated like commercial ventures, financiers considered them to be excellent risks. Moreover monarchs granted valuable privileges to their bankers, such as major wool export allotments. Unfortunately, however, it happened that princes met their obligations for years but then suddenly became unwilling or unable to pay. During the fourteenth century, King Edward III of England suspended the service of the royal debt during the Hundred Years' War, contributing to the overthrow of the Bardi and the Peruzzi. Two centuries later, the Spanish monarchy defaulted and broke the Fuggers of Augsburg, Europe's foremost bankers of the time. Nonetheless, lending to the state continued and expanded.

In the seventeenth century, various states chartered privileged joint-stock banks as a vehicle for obtaining credit. The Bank of England, which came to be the most important of these institutions, incorporated in 1694. For the first hundred years of its existence, the bank placed most of its resources with the government; commercial lending remained a peripheral activity. Beginning in the second half of the seventeenth century, a number of English goldsmiths and other merchants dedicated themselves to money lending and established private banks. These banks accepted deposits and issued banknotes that substituted "inland bills"—bills drawn by merchants in sterling payable in England—as the circulating medium.[3] In this manner, Britain began to have a circulating medium based on instruments other than metal coins.[4] Banks created loans by delivering notes to their clients, who utilized these papers to pay for goods. As long as the successive holders of the notes did not present them for redemption in money—that is, gold or silver—banknotes generated interest-free funds for the banks to lend.

Banknotes constituted an important source of earnings for banks as long as they circulated. In London, by the 1770s the notes of private bankers were being presented for payment in ever shorter periods of time and gradually came to be replaced by notes issued by the Bank of England, which represented a lesser risk for note holders.[5] In the countryside, on the other hand, private banknotes circulated through the end of the nineteenth century. In London, deposits, made with gold, silver, or Bank of England notes, replaced banknotes as the bankers' principal source of funds.[6] Deposits could be either interest-bearing, in which case there was usually an understanding that they would remain in the account for some period of time, or non-interest-bearing. Funds could be transferred by written instructions, that is, by check. The first checks began to circulate during the 1650s, and checking became common during the eighteenth century. In compensation for non-interest-bearing accounts, banks offered the service of checking as well as relative security.

The use of Bank of England banknotes expanded significantly during the Napoleonic Wars. With gold flowing out of Britain to pay for its overseas commitments, the government declared Bank of England banknotes to be inconvertible in 1797. The bank did not have to redeem its banknotes in gold, and its notes circulated as money. To accommodate the needs of war, the bank found itself issuing large numbers of notes, which expanded the money supply and created inflation; prices rose 84 percent between 1790 and 1810.[7] When the wars ended, a few thinkers considered reestablishing convertibility at the prevailing lower value of sterling, but those who wished to return to the much higher prewar parity carried the day.[8] As the bank reduced lending and its banknotes outstanding, the economy entered into a severe recession. By 1821, normalcy returned, and the payment of specie (gold in exchange for banknotes) could be resumed. Prices fell to below their 1790 levels.[9] Bank of England notes remained freely convertible into gold without interruption until World War I. The fear of inflation caused by excessive issue of banknotes also remained.

When Britain resumed convertibility, it became the first country to go on the gold standard. All other trading nations, including France and the United States, continued on a bimetallic, or gold and silver, standard. England itself had remained absolutely bimetallic until 1774, when it made silver legal tender for commitments only up to £50. In 1783, this ceiling was lowered to £25 and remained unchanged until the suspension of convertibility in 1797.[10]

Bimetallism had existed since Greek antiquity, and few thinkers of the early nineteenth century questioned the intrinsic worth of gold and silver. On the contrary, silver served as the natural means of payment for small and medium-sized transactions, and gold filled this need for larger purchases. The two metals appeared to be complementary. The disadvantage of bimetallism, however, was that the ratio of the value of gold to that of silver changed with the relative supply of both metals. From the Middle Ages to the early nineteenth century, the ratio of gold's value to silver's hovered between 10 and 15 to 1. A major fluctuation in the ratio gave a debtor a chance to discharge his obligations in the depreciated metal. The use of one metal eliminated this danger.

Under the gold standard, the volume of gold held in an economy directly affected the circulating medium—at the time, coins and banknotes. After 1844 the Bank of England could issue new banknotes only up to the value of the gold in its vault. These notes stimulated all segments of the economy. The gold standard connected the individual national economies to a world financial system with its hub in London. A country with a deficit in its balance of payments would see its gold migrating to banks in the surplus economies. The deficit country would therefore suffer a decline both in the number of banknotes circulating and in economic activity. With less money, both banknotes and coins, in circulation, prices tended to decline, making exports more competitive. Increased exports by the deficit country would bring the balance of payments back into equilibrium by attracting gold to its economy. Many contemporaries thought that the gold standard in fact automatically stabilized the international financial system.

During the decades following the resumption of specie payments, merchants, bankers, and politicians engaged in a heated debate concerning the nature of banknotes. One group, the "banking school," recalling that banknotes originated in specific underlying trade transactions, felt banks should be allowed to create sufficient notes to finance all "legitimate" trade transactions.[11] Their opponents, the "currency school," replied that banknotes had in fact become money. By expanding the volume of such paper, the money supply increased, provoking a rise in prices. That banks stood willing to redeem their notes in gold tempered but did not eliminate the inflationary effect produced by more money chasing the same volume of goods. With peace, after the Napoleonic Wars, and the ongoing Industrial Revolution, the quantity of Bank of England notes in London and private banknotes in the country-side, all fully convertible, increased significantly after the resumption of specie payments in 1821. Partially as a consequence of this expansion of money and credit, Britain experienced two major financial crises, in 1825 and 1839, and the Bank of England almost had to suspend convertibility of its notes.[12] In 1833, the notes issued by the Bank of England became legal tender.

As a response to these crises, the conservative "currency school" had its way securing passage of the Bank Charter Act of 1844. This famous legislation pro-hibited all institutions other than the Bank of England from issuing bank-notes in excess of the value of notes then outstanding that they had already is-sued. The act called for dividing the Bank of England into a banking department and an issue department, and marks the beginning of the bank's explicit central banking functions. The issue department received a capital of £14 million in government bonds as backing for issuing an equal value of bank-notes. Beyond this £14 million, the bank could issue notes to the extent of the gold in its vaults.[13] Conservatives assumed that they had tied the money sup-ply to gold, and that in consequence, financial crises could be avoided or at least attenuated. But the conservatives were in for future surprises, as the ex-ponential growth in bank deposits during the second half of the nineteenth century was what determined the size of the money supply in Britain.

Before reviewing other aspects of credit in Victorian Britain, let us examine the career of banknotes in the United States. For the contemporary Brazilian legislator, that country, also a former colony, served as a more useful model. Like Brazil, the United States imported substantial amounts of capital from Britain; in fact, throughout the nineteenth century, the former British colony received more British debt and equity funds than did any other area. By bor-rowing heavily and, at times, excessively, from England, the United States helped provoke a number of Europe's major financial crises. The United States was also by far Brazil's largest market for coffee.

Immediately after American independence from England, several states of the United States approved charters for incorporated banks and a number of unincorporated, or private, banks also established themselves. Only the incor-porated banks could issue banknotes, their value generally restricted to that of the bank's capital. Within the eastern states, deposits had already become a more important source of funding than banknotes, though this was not yet per-ceived by contemporaries.[14] From 1791 to 1836, except for one five-year period, America had a federally chartered Bank of the United States that limited the is-sue of banknotes by state banks by presenting these instruments for payment.

During this period, the number of banks expanded significantly, and the Bank of the United States maintained an orderly circulating medium. Other than during the Civil War, the American banks only departed from the bullion standard from 1814 to 1816 (when the country had no federal bank), from 1837 to 1838 (after the expiration of the second federal bank's charter), and for a few months during the financial crisis of 1857.[15]

Until 1837, each new incorporated bank required a specific act of its state legislature in order to organize. That year, New York, which had already become the financial center of the country, allowed banking corporations to form if they met minimal conditions. The 1837 New York law, subsequently copied in a number of other states, authorized banks to issue banknotes equal to their capital, the notes guaranteed by bonds rather than gold.[16] The note holder could present his note for redemption in specie. If the bank lacked metal to pay, the state could sell the bond that served as the guarantee of the banknote. In practice, the notes tended to circulate for long periods before presentation so that relatively little specie moved about physically. By mid-century, the United States had the greatest number of banks and the highest circulation of banknotes in the world, except for Britain.

The aggregate of banknotes issued in the United States often reached inflationary levels, as demand for credit remained high. By the middle of the century, deposits surpassed banknotes as the major source of funding for banks throughout most of the country, as had already occurred in Britain.[17] As a consequence of insufficient regulation, especially after the expiration of the Bank of the United States, abuses abounded. Banks, especially in the West, repeatedly defaulted as a result of issuing banknotes backed by fraudulent securities.[18] Contemporary bankers had a rule of thumb that issuing banks should retain cash on hand equal to at least one third of their outstanding banknotes.[19] All too frequently failed banks maintained the necessary cash at inspection time, borrowing from shareholders or others to cover their needs for these occasions.[20] As late as 1860, the circulating medium of the United States was equally divided between coins and banknotes; bank deposits approximated banknotes in the aggregate as well.[21] In 1863, during the Civil War, in order to better control the circulating medium, Congress imposed a prohibitive tax on banknotes of institutions other than nationally chartered banks that were federally inspected. These national banks could issue banknotes for a value of up to 90 percent of their capital, secured by federal bonds and redeemable in paper money, as the war had forced the government to suspend convertibility. Over the following generation, banknotes declined in importance from one third to one eighth of the circulating medium as silver coinage and government silver certificates expanded.[22] A limited number of banknotes issued by privately owned banks circulated as late as the 1920s.

The United States had been bimetallic until the Civil War. To finance the war, the government suspended convertibility and issued vast numbers of greenbacks without bullion backing. The inevitable inflation occurred: prices doubled and the dollar lost over half its value relative to sterling. After the war, the treasury retired the greenbacks, prices fell, and the exchange rose. Major groups, notably farmers, opposed the establishment of convertibility to gold alone, especially in the years following the crisis of 1873.[23] That year the United States demonetized silver, so when the country resumed convertibility in 1879, it adopted the gold standard and remained on it until 1933. Accordingly, after 1879 banknotes could be redeemed in gold or paper money, which had exactly the same value. During the 1870s, France, Germany, Switzerland, and virtually all of the other hard-currency nations also adhered to the gold standard. Weaker economies followed suit, borrowing from abroad to place their monies on the gold standard. Italy did this in 1881 and Austria-Hungary, in 1892.[24]

Another major financial development in the nineteenth century was the extension of limited liability. Due to the collapse of a number of fraudulent joint-stock companies as the end of the South Sea Bubble in 1720, British lawmakers made it difficult for new corporations to establish themselves,[25] and until 1826 the establishment of a joint-stock bank required a specific act of Parliament. Legislation passed in 1826 allowed these banks to have more than six partners, the limit for private banks. Partners in the joint-stock banks did not enjoy explicit limited liability. The Bank Charter Act of 1844 went backward in that it reaffirmed the liability of partners under the 1826 law. Finally, through a series of laws passed between 1857 and 1862, the establishment of corporations in general was permitted and simplified. By means of an act passed in 1858, Parliament expressly recognized limited liability.[26] In Brazil, by way of comparison, the baron of Mauá founded his bank in 1854 and shortly thereafter converted it into a limited partnership that provided for limited liability of all shareholders, save the baron himself. In France and Germany, limited liability became common only in the 1870s. For instance, the Rothschilds had to organize their Berlin bank as a limited partnership in 1856, as the Prussian government would not authorize limited liability in spite of its relationship with this illustrious house. In 1882, most nonfinancial companies in Brazil received the right to be organized with limited liability.

In practice, British bank stockholders did not really enjoy limited liability immediately following the legislation of the 1850s. The earlier joint-stock bank charters stipulated that only a small fraction, typically a quarter or a fifth, of subscribed capital be paid in. The remainder, denominated "reserved liability," fell due if the bank encountered difficulties.[27] After the spectacular failure in 1878 of the City of Glasgow Bank—in which shareholders were forced to pay five times their original investments or see their possessions sold at public auction—shares could only be marketed with true limited liability.[28] At this time a number of private banks still survived as proprietorships or partnerships with unlimited liability.

The British commercial banks satisfied the needs of merchants for working capital. Typically loans were extended for periods of only three or four months. In 1800, for instance, the Bank of England granted credit for short tenors and only to merchants resident in London known to a director of the bank.[29] Customarily the signatures of two substantial merchants were required, ideally the buyer and the seller of the goods financed. Private banks had similar credit standards.

The Bank of England resolved the borrowing requirements of the state through direct lending and primarily through the sale of government bonds. The several wars of the eighteenth century had left the country with an astronomic public debt. As English subjects held most of this debt, it did not appear to most observers to have a negative impact on the economy.

In addition to merchants and the state, two other important groups of borrowers had arisen by the nineteenth century: landholders and railroads. Loans to landowners on the security of their estates—mortgages—had existed since the Middle Ages. But before 1700, the mortgage generally was a sign of unsuccessful husbandry and a prelude to sale. Heavy investments in agricultural improvements during the eighteenth century obliged even the more prosperous estate managers sometimes to resort to mortgages that could be discharged over several years. Specialized mortgage bankers handled these advances, which were obtained with relative ease at reasonable costs, usually 5 percent, throughout the eighteenth and nineteenth centuries.[30] More commonly, however, agriculture acted as a generator of resources to deposit with banks or purchase bonds rather than as a reason for borrowing.

Railroads and other means of transportation such as canals became great users of the funds provided by agriculture. Like the government, railroads issued bonds that matured over a number of years and could be sold to landholders, merchants, and professionals. These bonds were placed through institutions known as merchant banks that by the first half of the nineteenth century had already differentiated themselves from the commercial banks. Perhaps the most famous merchant bankers were the British branch of the Rothschild family, whose bank underwrote all of Brazil's bond issues from 1855 through the Funding Loan of 1898.

During the eighteenth century a good deal of individual wealth appears to have been accumulated by landholders and merchants, especially in the Low Countries, England, and France. The English public funded debt paid 6 percent per annum until 1717 when it declined to 5 percent reducing to 4 percent in 1727 and 3 percent in 1742.[31] This fall in local rates set the stage for Britain's lending abroad. After 1742, a succession of foreign wars delayed potential overseas lending, which also suffered from a lack of creditworthy government borrowers; many states appear to have been poor risks, and before railroads, there were no other wholesale takers of international funds.

Until the French revolutionary armies invaded the Netherlands, the Dutch led the world in international lending with the British a distant second place. In fact, earlier in the eighteenth century, the English state constituted the Dutch bankers' major customer. Dutch international lending had become significant as early as the seventeenth century. Until the Treaty of Utrecht in 1713, the Netherlands authorities guaranteed overseas loans, which generally went to Holland's wartime allies. After Utrecht, Dutch investors had to rely exclusively on their foreign, especially British, government borrowers for repayment. From the 1760s on, several German and Scandinavian monarchies became important borrowers, issuing their bonds on the Amsterdam exchange through the Dutch merchant bankers.[32]

A secondary market for trading in bonds and shares developed in Amsterdam in the early seventeenth century. A similar market appeared in London during the last two decades of that century. Before the construction of a physical exchange, both bonds and shares were traded in coffee houses. Originally only three chartered corporations enjoyed liquidity: the Bank of England, the East India Company, and the South Sea Company. Later, during the eighteenth century, shares of canal companies became prominent. A stock market emerged in New York in 1792 and in Rio de Janeiro in 1848. Throughout the nineteenth century, railroad shares dominated all of these stock exchanges. Industrials became conspicuous only at the very end of the century in the most advanced markets.

When railroad construction began in England in the 1820s, local merchant bankers already had experience underwriting international bonds. British banks sold railroad bonds to their existing individual investors. By the 1830s, France and the Netherlands started to build rail lines as well. Continental businessmen soon discovered that not only technology but also capital could be found north of the Channel. Thus railroads and British merchant bankers blossomed forth together during the first three decades of the nineteenth century.

Significantly, merchant bankers did not retain the long-term obligations of either railroads or foreign states. The merchant banks underwrote these issues assuming risks during the placement period that took a few weeks. Individual investors accepted the hazards for the duration of the bonds, which could be as long as thirty years. British commercial banks avoided loans of over ninety days and did not participate in the bond business. On the Continent, notably post-unification Germany, the "great banks" undertook both merchant and commercial banking activities assuming in addition long-term loans and equity positions in railroads and industries.[33] After Germany became a global power in 1870, its banks became examples for the rest of the world and provided an alternative to the Anglo-American model. Banks everywhere avoided retaining long-term exposure to foreign governments.

In the decade following Waterloo, non-British businessmen and governments, including those of the newly independent Latin American states, discovered the London stock and bond markets. British merchant banks sold to their fellow countrymen shares and bonds of South American mining ventures, many of which later turned out to be entirely fraudulent. With the financial crisis of 1825, the first wave of Latin American bond defaults hit the London market.[34] At this time, the Brazilian Empire first became a foreign borrower. In return for the recognition of Brazilian independence and British assistance in the struggle to place his daughter on the Portuguese throne, Emperor Pedro I accepted responsibility for £3 million of Portugal's war debt to England.

The uses to which foreign loans are placed determine whether these advances are beneficial. If capital is employed in increasing productive capacity, railroads for instance, the borrowing country should have a sufficient rate of return so as to service its debt and expand its economy at the same time. On the other hand, when loans are utilized to sustain consumption beyond an economy's production, foreign borrowing is often quite negative. Both types of lending occur simultaneously. Pedro I's assumption of the Portuguese debt did not add to Brazil's economic capacity, but the credits taken to finance railroads and utilities did.

In spite of periodic reverses, including the repudiation of the external debt of several states of the United States in 1837, international lending grew continuously during the nineteenth century.[35] Low rates of interest, reflecting relatively limited opportunities in the industrialized countries, induced investors to venture their money abroad, in the form of bonds. In addition, the desire to sell goods for which the foreign buyer could not pay immediately caused merchants to extend credit to their overseas correspondents. Demand for loans from capital-poor states and their merchants continued high because local funds were difficult to find and thus expensive by definition.[36] International lending came to be divided in three parts: the public debt, the private long-term debt, and trade debt.

The public debt generally was the largest component of the three, consisting of loans taken for rails and other infrastructure as well as obligations relating to defense and wars. In the case of Brazil, at the end of the empire in 1889, the public foreign debt reached £30 million. At this time, the private long-term debt probably stood between half and three quarters of this figure.[37] The rail lines were the major users of private long-term foreign debt; fewer resources went to central sugar mills, mines, and utilities. We can hazard an estimate for trade debt, although we lack precise figures. In 1889, Brazil imported commodities worth £21 million. Overseas exporting houses financed many of these goods for terms up to one year.[38] If the average credit had a tenor of four months, this quantity of imports implied a commercial debt of £7 million, which is probably the minimum. Short-term financing could maintain the level of imports while exports declined. On the other hand, when crises hit Europe, especially England, this credit could be abruptly reduced, regardless of the situation in Brazil.

Like other debtor countries, Brazil proved vulnerable to the interruption of international credit; the empire had a continuous deficit on its balance-of-payments current account.[39] Although, after the abolition of the slave trade in 1850, Brazil invariably enjoyed a surplus on its commercial account, the payment of interest, insurance and freight, immigrants' remittances, travel, and dividends provoked a deficit on the current account while the state went increasingly into debt. Contemporaries perceived this problem.[40] In 1889, the principal balance-of-payments items stood as follows: exports £25 million, imports £21 million, interest and amortization of the public foreign debt £1.9 million, interest on private railroad debt guaranteed by the government £0.8 million, remittances a minimum of £3 million.[41] This same year coffee prices attained excellent levels, but the current account ended in deficit, even before travel, insurance, and freight, all of which were negative, were considered. Although the public debt service ratio was only 11 percent, a modest number by present standards, the more prudent financial leaders understood the fragility of their external situation.[42] ("Debt service ratio" expresses interest and amortization, the service of the debt, as a percentage of a country's exports. Thus, an 11 percent debt service ratio means that the debt service costs were 11 percent of exports.)

Late-nineteenth-century Brazil made ample use of the world financial system, taking long-term loans from merchant bankers, trade credit from merchants, and equity investments from interested parties. The imperial elite appreciated the advantages they obtained from access to world markets and generally discharged their obligations in a satisfactory manner. Without foreign loans, there would have been fewer railroads, if any at all; agricultural production would have been lower; and the elite's standard of living would have been less generous.

Although Brazil's financial leaders understood the benefits to England of free trade, the gold standard, and the conservative banking practices that had evolved there, Brazil's elite groups adapted these institutions to their own realities.

Chapter 3 Credit and Crises,
1850 to 1875

The world economy suffered a number of crises during the nineteenth century. All these crises originated in a cyclical overextension of credit. In addition to banknotes, credit could be generated by banks lending their deposits and by merchants selling goods on terms. In the case of Brazil, a good deal of credit came from foreign companies that allowed payment on terms of up to one year on imports. As optimism increased, bankers and merchants extended ever more credit for ever longer periods to ever less creditworthy borrowers and customers. Success in boom years made, and still makes, bankers and merchants progressively less cautious.[1]

In each instance, a deflationary event took place that brought the boom to a close. Twice early in the century, the major factor in the onset of the crisis was a failed harvest in England, which caused a sudden need for gold to import basic foodstuffs, notably wheat. The price of wheat would increase and specie would flow out of the importing country. Suddenly money went to a premium, and everyone struggled to collect from his debtors. Merchants and speculators who borrowed to purchase goods other than wheat could not renew their loans and found themselves compelled to liquidate their positions hastily. Merchandise lost value as more and more came on the market. This type of crisis resembles somewhat the oil crisis of 1973, when immense amounts of money flowed out to pay for a commodity as basic to our era as wheat was to the nineteenth century.[2]

As the nineteenth century progressed, this type of financial crisis gave way to a panic of overproduction. In this case, a boom collapsed when businessmen borrowed to manufacture more goods, including fixed capital goods such as railroads, than consumers wished to purchase. As debts came due, borrowers lacked the funds to pay. Once again there arose a general scramble to obtain liquidity. Merchandise and shares fell in value. The worst of these crises came in 1929, but the crash of 1873 also left the world economy in a prolonged, if less severe, depression.

Countries such as Brazil suffered in both varieties of panics. As credit tightened in Britain, the volume of import finance offered her trading partners declined sharply, while British merchants demanded repayments from Brazilian customers in order to fulfill their obligations at home. The volume and price of Brazilian exports usually decreased together. Meanwhile the bond market for long-term borrowings closed while interest on past loans had of course to be paid in gold. In this manner, Brazilian merchants and planters experienced severe liquidity problems as a result of the general crisis of world trade. At each of the major crashes, many Brazilian firms as well as British ones went bankrupt.

The illiquid structure of Brazilian finance tended to exacerbate these crises. Both the incorporated banks and the unincorporated banking houses had merchants and planters' factors as their principal clients. These two types of borrowers lacked liquidity as they found themselves forced to continuously renegotiate credit to the planters. Prudent banking practice as known in England taught that funds should be lent for terms up to ninety days on accepted drafts.[3] Accepted drafts bore the guarantees of both the buyer and the seller of a good such as coffee or cloth. When they financed unsold commodities, British banks lent no more than two thirds of the value of the goods pledged as collateral, also for periods no longer than ninety days. British banks avoided financing unharvested crops, and in fact lent to commerce and industry rather than agriculture. British farmers, unlike their counterparts in Brazil, had relatively easy access to long-term mortgage loans. The British banks, when they established Brazilian operations in 1863, discovered that they could not follow London practices in Rio de Janeiro.[4] The British bankers found themselves extending indefinite credits that rarely could be dis-charged. Many loans, though made to merchants, depended ultimately upon the performance of planters. Banks had difficulties in realizing or even attach-ing the planters' assets. As we shall discuss, Brazilian mortgage law made it impossible to foreclose on rural property; the planters' other major asset, slaves, also did not prove an entirely satisfactory security. In general the Brazil-ian economy at that time suffered from a chronic lack of liquidity.

On their liability side, the British banks discovered that in Brazil, bankers paid interest even for funds at call. In Britain, deposits at call received no inter-est as compensation for the banker's providing safekeeping and the service of paying checks. Brazilian bankers, short of capital, agreed to pay interest, often up to 4 percent per year, on call money.[5] Brazilian banks also paid higher inter-est on their time deposits than did British banks.[6] Prudent banking dictated that a bank maintain in its vaults cash equal to one third of its call liabilities so as to survive a period of heavy withdrawals.[7] Consequently an institution that paid 4 percent on its call deposits had to charge 6 percent on loans to break even—as one third of its funds remained idle, earning no interest. A much higher lending rate would be necessary to provide a reserve for bad loans as well as a reasonable profit.

Let us now turn our attention to the history of local banks in Brazil. The country's first experience with an incorporated bank proved to be unhappy. The Banco do Brasil, established by the Portuguese government in 1809, had to be liquidated twenty years later. It served a bankrupt state that forced it to issue banknotes out of all proportion to the gold in its vaults. As a conse-quence of this inflation in banknotes, the exchange rate of the milreis, the Brazilian currency unit, fell from 67 pence at independence in 1822 to below 30 pence by the fall of Pedro I in 1831. The government took over responsibil-ity for the Banco do Brasil's banknotes after its liquidation, turning these notes into paper money.

From 1829 to 1838, a period of economic depression and civil war, Brazil had no incorporated bank at all. Larger merchants operated banking houses that discounted drafts and made advances. A worldwide crisis in 1837, provoked by Andrew Jackson's irresponsible financial policies allied to a bubble in cotton land in the United States, convinced the commercial community of Rio de Janeiro that it needed an institution more substantial than the banking houses. The privately owned Banco Comercial do Rio de Janeiro opened in 1838. Four other private chartered banks conducted business by 1852, one each in Salvador, Recife, São Luis, and Belem. None of these institutions had authorization to issue banknotes although they did issue short-term vouchers.[8] The script of these banks never became a significant part of the circulating medium.

The years after the establishment of the Banco Comercial do Rio de Janeiro, Brazil witnessed a dramatic expansion of coffee production. During the 1840s, revenues from coffee permitted the government to reorganize the army, which had all but disintegrated after the overthrow of Emperor Pedro I in 1831. This new army was used to put down provincial rebellions, which became endemic after the emperor's departure. The last revolt terminated in 1849; domestic peace continued without interruption until the end of the monarchy in 1889.

Also during the 1840s, 1846 to be precise, recognizing the de facto exchange situation that had existed since 1827, the government reduced the parity of the milreis to 27 pence. To defend this parity, successive ministries maintained the volume of paper money constant for two decades. Countries on the gold standard maintained fixed parities against gold and therefore against each other. As we shall see, Brazil's exchange rate fluctuated within a much broader band around its parity than did gold-standard currencies. This nonadherence to the gold standard probably worked to Brazil's benefit.

In 1850, four decades after the United States, the Brazilian elite, pressured by the Royal Navy, reluctantly abolished the importation of slaves. During the five years previous to this event, slaves constituted one third of total imports. By removing this currency drain, Brazil achieved a surplus on its balance of trade that continued for almost all of the remaining years of the empire. The abolition of the slave trade also released capital that could be used for railroads, commerce, agriculture, and banking. The fifties became years of euphoria with heavy speculation on the Rio stock exchange, organized in 1848, and on foreign exchange and debt securities markets. Also in 1850, the Brazilian authorities promulgated the country's first commercial code. Significantly, Irineu Evangelista de Sousa, the future viscount of Mauá, and already Brazil's foremost entrepreneur, drafted this measure in cooperation with three prominent politicians.[9]

The year after the abolition of the slave trade, Mauá established the second Banco do Brasil, a private institution with the right to issue banknotes. At the bank's inauguration, Mauá expressed his desire to emulate the spirit of association prevalent in England and the United States.[10] Following best international practices, he managed to have 80 percent of the subscribed capital paid in within the two years that he directed this bank.[11] Furthermore, under his conservative administration, banknotes issued remained within 25 percent of paid-in capital.[12] Two years later, the government obliged the two private banks in the capital, the Banco do Brasil and the Banco Commercial do Rio de Janeiro, to merge and form the so-called "third" Banco do Brasil. Within another two years, the authorities forced the four commercial banks in the north of Brazil to surrender their charters and become branches of the Banco do Brasil. By reserving the right to nominate the president and vice president of this institution, the finance minister, the viscount of Itaborahy, assumed control of the country's largest source of credit. This bank proved to be an indispensable grantor of favors to the friends of the successive ministries. Itaborahy left office shortly after the merger decree and was later appointed president of the new institution by his successor.

In opposition to this arbitrary act, Mauá and his associates founded the Banco Mauá MacGregor the following year, 1854, as a banking house or private bank. Mauá and his partners did not enjoy limited liability. At this time, the United States remained the only country that automatically granted limited liability to its banks. In the United Kingdom, limited liability became generalized later in the decade, in 1858, and France and Germany only made this type of organization freely available after 1870. The Brazilian elite closely monitored developments in all four countries, and in 1857, Mauá's friend, Finance Minister Souza Franco, obtained a charter of limited partnership (*sociedade em comandita*) for Mauá's bank, in line with the French law of July, 23, 1856.[13] As the general partner (*socio ostensivo*) of a limited partnership, only Mauá had unlimited liability. His limited partners (*socios comanditarios*) had limited liability, just like shareholders of corporations, although they did not enjoy voting rights. The limited partnership allowed Mauá to raise capital from nonexecutive partners and thus represented a major improvement over the private bank structure. One must remember that even in England and the United States, leading merchant banks such as the Rothschild and Morgan banks continued as partnerships without limited liability until well into the twentieth century. Mauá's bank established a branch network that included São Paulo, Rio Grande do Sul, the Plate, and after 1864, Recife and Belem. The Banco Mauá MacGregor in time rivaled the Banco do Brasil in stature, if not in size.

The 1853 act establishing the "third" Banco do Brasil authorized it to issue banknotes up to twice its net paid-in capital.[14] These notes had to be convertible into gold at a par of 27 pence or into government paper money. Although the milreis continued to be worth around 27 pence, frequently rising above this level, it would be less than accurate to claim that Brazil adhered to the gold standard. Under the gold standard, the value of a currency generally fluctuated within the "gold point," or rate, where it became profitable to transport bullion from one market to another. Writing in 1896, J. P. Wileman observed that gold would move between Paris and London for as little as a quarter of a percent and from those cities to Lisbon for 1.2 percent.[15] He estimated Brazil's gold point to be somewhere between 2 and 4 percent, given the high freight and insurance charges there. In the 1850s, Brazil's gold points must have been wider yet, although the Council of State estimated the gold point at 1 ⅛ percent in 1858.[16] In fact, during the four years following the 1853 act, the milreis traded at between 22 and 30 pence.[17] This broad band, reaching 25 percent below parity, indicates that mid-century Brazil did not quite achieve membership in the club of gold-standard nations. During the fifties, the early sixties, and again in 1889, at those times when the milreis traded above par, banks sought to convert their banknotes into gold coins at par. To show the government's interest in attaining a fully convertible currency, the 1853 act directed the Banco do Brasil to gradually retire the paper money in circulation, commencing in two years. The bank was to replace 10,000 contos (a conto is one thousand milreis), equivalent to one third of its capital, of paper money with its banknotes and deliver this paper money to the treasury as an interest-free loan. As the government allowed the bank to issue notes valued at up to twice its capital, this obligation seemed rather minimal in its impact. At the completion of this replacement process, Brazil would in theory have only convertible banknotes in circulation.

In spite of the government's gestures in the path of the gold standard, the act of 1853 proved in fact to be inflationary. The Banco do Brasil could issue banknotes up to twice the value of its net paid-in capital. The act defined this term as paid-in capital less fixed assets such as bank premises and less amounts used to retire government paper money—an obligation to start only in two years' time. As stockholders could pay in their capital with paper money or the notes of the Banco do Brasil, the law set rather loose limits on the growth of banknote issues and thus did not mandate the adoption of conservative banking practices in effect elsewhere. In contemporary Britain, the Bank Charter Act of 1844 had restricted the Bank of England to issuing notes backed 100 percent by gold in its vaults. The banks in the United States after 1837 generally had to provide 100 percent backing in government bonds. In fact, within two years the Banco do Brasil increased the circulating medium by half. In 1855, only one year after the merged institution began conducting business, the authorities permitted Itaborahy to raise its issue from twice to three times its net paid-in capital.[18]

This increase in the circulating medium, allied with buoyant coffee exports and the release of capital for investments following the termination of the slave trade, resulted in seven years of boom on the Rio securities and exchange markets. During this period, the Banco do Brasil and the solid Dom Pedro II Railway launched their shares, as did a number of fraudulent ventures. Most of the credit institutions engaged in foreign exchange and stock speculation and financed other speculators of merchandise and shares. Although the financial system was consequently quite vulnerable in 1857, Finance Minister Bernardo de Souza Franco managed to defend Brazil from most of the effects of the international crisis of that year. The crisis of 1857 began with the suspension of banks in the United States and spread rapidly to England and the Continent. Many banks and commercial houses failed, especially in the States. When Souza Franco heard of the crisis, he immediately allowed the Banco do Brasil to expand its note issue to over three times its capital and suspended convertibility, making these notes legal tender.[19]

As always occurred in times of panic, foreign merchants, requiring specie to settle their obligations at home, ceased to extend credit in Brazil and repatriated whatever gold they could obtain. Without the banknotes, many Brazilian houses would have gone bankrupt. These instruments provided the necessary means for business to continue, replacing the gold that the foreigners removed from circulation. The decree of inconvertibility made the Banco do Brasil invulnerable and headed off a run on that institution. Although at first it may appear that inconvertibility should have provoked inflation and furthered the devaluation of the milreis, in fact the reverse happened. After the new issues, the milreis rose in value because of the restoration of confidence. During the crises, foreigners as well as Brazilians sent their gold abroad not only to discharge obligations but also to defend themselves against commercial failures in Brazil. After the decree of inconvertibility, the second reason for capital flight diminished, and funds flowed back into the country. Contemporaries appreciated this phenomenon.[20]

Bernardo de Souza Franco enjoyed a distinguished political career governing Pará, his home province, as well as representing it in the Chamber of Deputies and the Senate before becoming finance minister. Shortly after he left the government, the emperor made him a viscount and appointed him to the Council of State. As the Senate and the Council of State were lifetime appointments, he remained active in politics until his death in 1875. Viscount Souza Franco numbered among the statesmen most knowledgeable concerning finance, having published a study on Brazilian banks in 1848. A close friend of Mauá's, Souza Franco supported the banker by allowing the Banco Mauá MacGregor to function as a limited partnership. The banker for his part helped Souza Franco maintain the exchange rate during the 1857 crisis by aggressively selling drafts on London when the Banco do Brasil refused to do so.

In his study of banks, Souza Franco praised the New York Free Banking Act of 1837. By the time he became finance minister, this measure had two decades of success to its credit, a success shortly to be confirmed by the rapid return to convertibility of the New York banks after the 1857 panic. The New York institutions suspended convertibility for only two months while banks in other states remained off convertibility for a longer period. Souza Franco adapted the New York act to the Brazilian situation. He understood that institutions that backed their banknote issues with bonds could be protected from the risks of exchange devaluation if these bonds could be sold for paper money and the paper money could be used to discharge obligations to the note holders. Brazil had paper money.

Starting in August of 1857, before the crisis, Souza Franco promulgated a series of decrees permitting incorporated banks to issue banknotes up to the value of their capital, as in New York, with 100 percent bond backing, and convertible into paper money.[21] The finance minister also provided the alternative of issuing notes in a sum up to three times capital, convertible only into gold. As the wide fluctuations of the exchange rate made convertibility into gold impractical, all the institutions established during Souza Franco's tenure adopted bond backing. The business community applauded his measures, and six new banks incorporated, purchased bonds for backing, and issued banknotes. Contemporaries felt that funds that had been "tied up" in the public debt would now be released to finance productive enterprise. In fact, though Souza Franco's system was more restrictive than the Banco do Brasil Act of 1853, it also led to an expansion of the circulating medium. By 1860, the new banks had 14,000 contos in banknotes outstanding (£1.4 million) as compared to approximately 40,000 contos each of paper money and Banco do Brasil banknotes.[22]

Souza Franco proved to be the most "developmental," to use an anachronism, finance minister of the empire. In addition to his banking initiatives, shortly after taking office, he passed measures providing government guarantees for four key railroads: the Dom Pedro II, from Rio de Janeiro to São Paulo through the Paraíba Valley coffee zone; the Santos-Jundiai Railway, destined to open the interior of São Paulo Province to coffee; and a line each from the sugar ports of Salvador and Recife to their hinterlands. He envisioned the imperial government's purchasing up to one third of the capital of each of these railroads.[23] He also contracted Brazil's first external railroad loan, for the Dom Pedro II.[24] In spite of the great advantages of railroads, a considerable portion of the elite opposed these guarantees, positive French precedents notwithstanding.

The decade of the fifties witnessed the establishment of banks, railroads, and other public utilities. Without the drain of slave imports, the coffee economy grew and prospered. As in contemporary Europe and the United States, regulation of financial markets proved lax to nonexistent, so fraud thrived. Souza Franco and his allies were not insensitive to the special opportunities that banks of issue enjoyed in this regard. On October 8, 1857, the finance section of the Council of State, presided over by the finance minister, made the following recommendations for banks of issue.

1. Banks of issue may commence business and transfer shares only after 25 percent of capital is paid in.
2. Banknotes must be backed by two-name commercial paper with tenors to four months and one-third reserve in metal.
3. Two thirds of capital must be used to finance paper up to 180 days, the remaining third on security of shares or long-term government bonds.
4. Dividends to be paid only out of profits.
5. A bank that fails to honor its note is to be liquidated.
6. Subscribers of shares are responsible for the full amount subscribed, even if they transfer their shares.
7. Balance sheets must be published within eight days of the end of the month.
8. Corporations are authorized to exist for up to ten years.
9. No loans can be secured by shares of the lending bank.
10. Authorized corporations must raise initial capital within a stipulated period.
11. The Government is authorized to appoint an inspector for each bank.

The combination of items 1 and 6 provided for reserved liability, a feature that continued in subsequent Brazilian legislation, including the important corporation laws of 1882 and 1890. Reserved liability, a contemporary British commercial practice, held a subscriber of shares in a limited-liability corporation liable to the full extent of his subscription. If he paid in one quarter of subscribed capital and the company failed, he would have to pay the remaining three fourths or see his assets seized and auctioned. Item 2 marks a departure from the 1837 New York banking act, which utilized government bonds as backing for banknote issues. In this case, the Council of State appeared to prefer short-term commercial paper to long-term government bonds. In fact, Souza Franco's decree authorizing the establishment of the Banco da Bahia, the only one of his banks still in existence, foresaw an issue backed half by government bonds and half by commercial paper (article 10 of Decree 2140 of April 3, 1858). The aim of items 4, 5, 6, 7, 9, and 11 is to limit common abuses the Councilors of State detected in the market.

On October 8, 1857, the Council of State also opined specifically on a charter application of the Banco Industrial e Hypothecario. The Council conceded issue rights but denied the bank's request to engage in colonization, commerce, and mortgages, as well as railroad and tram line development.[25] Souza Franco and his associates wished banks to limit their activities to commercial banking, French and German examples to the contrary notwithstanding.

Souza Franco served as finance minister for just eighteen months. Though accused of provoking inflation through his six banks of issue, in fact these institutions expanded the circulating medium much less than the Banco do Brasil did. Victor Viana, the historian of the Banco do Brasil, places Souza Franco in the group of men whose policies were inflationary, together with Ruy Barbosa and the baron of Lucena of the Encilhamento.[26] In fact, however, the available sources reveal Souza Franco to have been a far more responsible official. He carefully studied banking in the United States and sought to adapt the most applicable foreign practices to Brazil. He also took precautions to make local financial institutions follow prudent banking practices and limit themselves to safe commercial transactions. In these aspects he differed fundamentally from Barbosa and Lucena, as we shall discuss in chapter 6.

Conservatives in Congress felt that severe problems had been only narrowly avoided in 1857. Even though they admitted that the government-dominated Banco do Brasil had been the major contributor to the increase of the circulating medium, they feared the inflationary potential of Souza Franco's institutions and particularly disliked the idea of banks that they could not control issuing notes.[27] They also still aspired to a gold standard. In 1860, after Souza Franco left office, these conservatives passed the "Law of Obstacles" (Law 1083 of August 22, 1860), requiring banks to redeem their banknotes in gold or go into liquidation. Whenever the milreis went below par, such redemptions would result in a loss. For this reason, the banks established under Souza Franco all had chosen to issue bond-backed notes convertible into paper money. Over the next three years, because of the Law of Obstacles, three new banks relinquished their issuing privileges and the other three merged with the Banco do Brasil.[28] Echoing the Bank Charter Act of 1844, the Law of Obstacles prohibited banks other than the Banco do Brasil from issuing notes beyond the sums outstanding during the first half of the year. Unlike the British law, the Law of Obstacles allowed the Banco do Brasil to issue banknotes twice the value of the metal in its possession. The 1860 act gave banks one year to begin redeeming notes in gold or silver as well as an escape clause for those institutions unable to redeem but willing to surrender their issuing privileges. Whenever the milreis traded above par, as it did in October of 1860, two months after the Law of Obstacles but one month before the enabling decrees, the Banco do Brasil could redeem its notes in metal. The only other institution to issue convertible notes, Mauá's bank, did so infrequently and in small volumes.[29] The outbreak of the Civil War in the United States at the beginning of 1861 caused capital flight and pessimism in Brazil, as the States was Brazil's major market. Quietly the Banco do Brasil abandoned the convertibility of its notes.[30]

Contemporaries saw the expansion of banknote issue up to 1857 as a cause of that crisis, but the crisis of 1864 came during a contraction of the money supply. Although exports and the economy as a whole grew significantly from 1860 to 1864, the circulating medium contracted from 96,000 contos to 84,000.[31] Exports are a close proxy for the monetary economy, and a comparison of the growth of exports to the growth of the money supply helps explain the crisis of 1864. The numbers given in table 1 are imprecise because they do not take into account all elements of the money supply, including deposits at banks and banking houses as well as script and metal in circulation. When the milreis achieved par, metal did constitute an important part of the circulating medium. Table 1 is meant to be merely suggestive. The sum of deposits at incorporated banks appears to have been about half the sum of banknotes plus paper money in 1864, but rose to something in excess of these aggregates by the end of the empire.[32] Total liabilities, including deposits and other borrowings, of the four unincorporated banking houses that failed in 1864 surpassed 70,000 contos, a sum almost equal to the whole circulating medium.[33]

In conjunction with the contraction of the circulating medium, the situation of the Rio de Janeiro financial market became tight each year during the harvest season in the northern provinces of Brazil. A dress rehearsal of the 1864 crisis occurred in September of 1862, exactly twenty-four months before the major upheaval. From 1850 on there had been a continuous drain of capital from Rio to Recife and Salvador for the purchase of slaves. During the

Table 1   Exports and the Circulating Medium, 1835 to 1894 (in Thousands of Contos)

Fiscal Year	Exports	Paper Money	Banco do Brasil Notes	Other Banknotes	Metal
1835–36	41	31	—	—	NA
1840–41	42	40	—	—	NA
1845–46	54	50	—	—	NA
1850–51	68	47	—	—	NA
1855–56	94	47	—	—	NA
1856–57	115	46	25	2	NA
1857–58	96	44	50	—	20
1858–59	107	42	39	14	NA
1859–60	113	41	41	14	36
1860–61	123	39	38	14	NA
1863–64	131	30	50	4	NA
1865–66	157	28	85	2	NA
1870–71	168	150	41	2	NA
1872–73	215	151	32	2	NA
1875–76	184	150	28	2	NA
1880–81	231	189	24	2	NA
1885–86	195	187	19	2	NA
1889	256	179	12	19	85
1890[a]	326	168		303[b]	NA
1891	574	168		346	NA
1892	784	215		341	NA
1893	708	286		341	NA
1894	767	367		341	NA

[a] From 1890 to 1894, figures are notes outstanding at year-end. After November 23, 1891, no new notes were issued.[34] [b] Lucena's finance ministry report of 1891 may have exaggerated this number to shift more of the onus for inflation onto his predecessor, Ruy Barbosa.

sugar, cotton, and tobacco harvest, strong seasonal flows to these centers took place. With the American Civil War, cotton production boomed in Maranhão and neighboring provinces, requiring a particularly large transfer of resources. Only the Banco do Brasil and, after 1864, the Banco Mauá MacGregor and the British banks had branches in this part of the country; for the other banks and banking houses, these seasonal outflows to the North represented considerable loss in liquidity. The American Civil War brought prosperity to the cotton producers, but it caused distress among the coffee planters as their most important market decreased its consumption sharply during the years 1862 to 1864. A number of firms failed in September of 1862, precipitating a flight of deposits from the banking houses. At this time, the baron of Mauá noted to his branch manager in Rio Grande that his house had benefited by this panic but that the concerns of Antonio Souto, the owner of the largest private banking house, and Antonio Gomes appeared to be in a perilous situation.[35] On this occasion, the bankers of Rio, led by the Banco do Brasil, extended credit to the troubled houses and avoided the collapse of major financial institutions.[36] With the flow of coffee export earnings into the capital and its hinterland, even at reduced levels, the market rebounded quickly so that by the end of the year, the exchange had returned to parity and the Banco do Brasil could once again, briefly, redeem its notes in gold.[37]

As it turned out, Souto never truly recovered from the events of 1862. In March of 1864, Mauá wrote that if the government did not find in favor of Souto regarding a contract for the União e Industria Road, Souto would go into bankruptcy and would take down fifty commercial firms with him.[38]

The year 1864 proved to be an excellent one for cotton, in terms of volume and price, but a poor year in both regards for coffee. Following several decades in which coffee production increased in volume while maintaining good prices, output from the Paraíba Valley stagnated. The planters of this region had not taken care of their land and did not replace old trees when their fertility declined. A coffee disease afflicted the valley in 1864, causing an actual drop in production that year. Meanwhile the price of coffee on the international markets continued to suffer the effects of the American Civil War. Since Rio's hinterland depended upon coffee sales, money became scarcer in the capital.

Although scholars traditionally do not consider 1864 a year of financial crisis in English history, extreme tightness prevailed on the London money markets that year. The problems began in November 1863, when precious metals flowed out to India, as well as Brazil and Egypt, to purchase cotton. The Bank of England's discount rate rose from a normal level of 4 percent to 8 percent, a level of interest attained only during severe crises. In May of 1864, with the war between Denmark and Prussia, the discount rate went even higher, reaching 9 percent. With this short conflict resolved, conditions loosened somewhat, but the need for cotton imports forced the rate back up to 9 percent from September to November.[39] In December, General William Tucumseh Sherman's march through Georgia in the U.S. Civil War reassured the markets that this conflict would soon terminate, allowing cotton supplies to return to normal. Gradually the discount rate declined, reaching 3 percent in June 1865, two months after the Confederate surrender. We may therefore consider at least the period from May to November 1864 as a time of world financial crisis.

Meanwhile in Brazil the country had become involved in conflict in the Plate Basin. On August 31, 1864, the empire delivered an ultimatum to the government of Uruguay, to be followed shortly by the invasion of that country.[40]

The speculation that took place in Rio de Janeiro's financial center prior to the 1857 crisis had resumed shortly thereafter. Financiers played the currency market, buying sovereigns or drafts on London in the expectation of the milreis's decline and selling these assets on the hope that the local currency would appreciate. Banks lent money on the security of shares in doubtful ventures. Banks and banking houses also made various types of bad loans that they kept renewing so as to delay acknowledging losses. Fraud perpetrated by clients against financial institutions as well as by the banks themselves was rampant.[41] The most common form of fraud consisted of merchants discounting drafts for goods they had not yet sold or that in fact did not exist. Banking houses borrowed from the Banco do Brasil and the public in a continuous battle to stay open. All of these factors—the contraction of the circulating medium, the transfer of funds to the North, the low earnings from coffee, the crisis in England, and the fear of war in the Plate—resulted in borrowing becoming increasingly difficult during the course of the year.

On September 10, 1864, Souto suspended payments. A panic followed in which a number of major banking and commercial establishments failed. In spite of all of the negative factors affecting the financial markets, both the financiers and the politicians were surprised when the crash finally came. After three days, the government suspended the convertibility of the Banco do Brasil banknotes, once again making them legal tender. The bank then raised its outstanding notes to 87,000 contos, an immense sum that represented an almost 40 percent increase in the circulating medium over a few months. The government's actions saved a number of firms from failure, but unlike in 1857, a good deal of wealth disappeared as several important banking houses had to be liquidated. Souto's creditors received only 25 percent of their deposits, and the creditors of some other concerns were even less fortunate.[42] The Rio business community experienced a depression for a number of months until war procurement brought prosperity back.

Early in 1865, the empire concluded its short war with Uruguay but became engaged in a long, expensive struggle with Paraguay. With the need to finance this war, the government abandoned its idea of adhering to the gold standard and decided to abolish banknotes once and for all. While the ministry was negotiating an amended Banco do Brasil charter to reflect these changes, events in Europe provoked another crisis. In May of 1866 Bismarck declared war on Austria. The Bank of England raised its discount rate to 10 percent.[43] England's largest bill broker, Overend, Gurney, guilty of the same abuses as the Brazilian banking houses, found it impossible to continue borrowing and succumbed on May 10. Also that month, the Kingdom of Italy suspended convertibility. The brunt of this crisis in Brazil fell on the British banks. Mauá, who had been discussing a merger with the London and Brazilian Bank, called off the talks.[44] With the money supply expanding because of the Paraguayan War and Banco do Brasil notes already legal tender, Brazilian firms had a relatively easy time of this crisis. After Austria and Prussia made peace in August, the Bank of England lowered its rate, which reached 3 percent early the next year.

Ultimately, the Great Emancipator, Abraham Lincoln, assassinated in 1865, cast an even longer shadow on Brazil than did the very live Bismarck. The end of slavery in the United States encouraged the members of the Brazilian elite who favored gradual emancipation, a group that included Souza Franco, Mauá, and the emperor himself. Save for military officers, few individuals at or close to the elite advocated immediate abolition, but in 1866, the emperor appointed the first emancipationist prime minister, Zacarias de Góes e Vasconcelos. This statesman wished to follow the examples of other former slave societies, including continental Portugal and the state of New York, which freed slaves' children born after the promulgation of the Free Womb Law. Souza Franco, in the Senate and the Council of State, supported this ministry's suggestion that within ten years of the law's approval Parliament should set a date for the final extinction of slavery.[45] The Paraguayan War provided an excuse for Zacarias's opponents to delay this measure. In 1868, as the consequence of a dispute between the government and the duke of Caxias, a slaveocratic general whose services on the front everyone, including the prime minister, thought necessary, the emancipationist government fell. The Conservatives who came to power ignored emancipation for the remainder of the conflict. Once the war ended in 1870, the Conservatives proposed the Law of the Free Womb, which finally passed, after a bitter internal dispute, on September 28, 1871. As the final wording of this law gave control over the "free born" children of slaves to their parents' masters for twenty-one years, many contemporaries saw this measure as a means of extending slavery.[46] Slave owners, however, considered the Free Womb Law a major defeat.

Following the overthrow in France of Napoleon III and the establishment of the Third Republic in September 1870, a Republican Party formed in Brazil in December of that year. The passage of the Free Womb Law in 1871 contributed to the expansion of the party, as disgruntled masters held the emperor responsible for this legislation.[47]

The year emancipation became an issue, 1866, Prime Minister Zacarias attempted to give slaveholders financial compensation in the form of mortgage lending. Two thirds of the Banco do Brasil's loan portfolio, nominally short-term advances, was considered uncollectable, as these credits ultimately depended upon the performance of illiquid planters.[48] Many facilities had been granted for political rather than financial reasons. In September of 1866, Law 1349, which was supported by the archrivals Souza Franco and Itaborahy, established the Banco do Brasil's mortgage portfolio, thus transforming existing overdue advances into mortgages.[49] This law also made the bank more independent of the government as the latter relinquished the right to appoint the bank's president and vice president and prohibited the bank from issuing new banknotes. Without the privilege of issue, the directors promptly closed all of the bank's branches other than the reliably profitable office in São Paulo. Between the crisis of 1864 and that of 1875, the bank's outstanding notes fell gradually from 87,000 to 28,000 contos.[50]

The Paraguayan War, which lasted from 1864 until 1870, caused the government to appropriate all the Banco do Brasil's gold, an action that profoundly affected contemporaries, to the point where even novelists decried it.[51] The war retarded the development of railroads, several of which were under construction, and placed great pressure on public finances. Brazil's gold flowed to the Plate, enriching Argentine contractors, and to Europe to purchase armaments. To meet its internal obligations, the government placed large amounts of paper money in circulation. Although the Banco do Brasil redeemed its notes in compliance with its 1866 agreement, in the four years prior to 1870 the government expanded the circulating medium by over 50 percent, forcing the exchange rate down to 17 pence, the lowest value during the entire history of the empire.

The war came to an end at a favorable moment in the world economy. All the major Western countries enjoyed periods of rapid growth, resulting in increased demand for coffee. Coffee earnings permitted the milreis to recover its parity of 27 pence.[52] Although the interest on the war debt placed a strain on the imperial budget, the positive trade situation allowed the government to avoid a further increase in the supply of paper money while the Banco do

Brasil redeemed a further third of its outstanding banknotes. Thus, from 1870 to 1875 Brazil had high export revenues, a rising exchange rate, and a reduction of its circulating medium. The completion of the Santos-Jundiaí Railway in 1867 had opened the west of São Paulo Province to coffee cultivation. Output increased significantly in this region, one that proved to be extremely fertile and ideal for coffee. In the meantime, production in the Paraíba Valley declined, so the volume of Brazilian exports during these years grew relatively little.

Like the panics of the 1860s, the empire's last crisis, that of 1875, had its origins in Central Europe, England, and the United States. Germany's victory over France in 1870 in the Franco-German War was accompanied by a change in corporate law in both countries as well as in Austria-Hungary, one that permitted the founding of limited-liability corporations. A number of legitimate entities, such as the Deutsche Bank, were founded, but in the rush of enthusiasm, so were a number of sham financial institutions. The euphoria continued until May of 1873, when the Vienna Stock Market suffered a *Krach* (crash), which spread quickly to Berlin. In response, the Bank of England raised its discount rate to 9 percent.[53] Four months later, Jay Cooke & Company, the foremost banking house in the United States, failed, largely owing to excessive investments in railroads. Coffee prices remained high, and the Brazilian economy continued moving ahead without any visible signs that a worldwide "Great Depression" had begun.[54] Germany tightened up its regulations with the government-controlled Reichsbank assuming a quasi monopoly of banknote issues in 1875, in line with the practice of the Banque de France since 1848. With private banknotes already in decline in Britain and the United States, Germany's action signified the impending demise of the private banknote worldwide. In May of 1875, fully twenty-four months after the *Krach,* the depression arrived in Brazil. Coffee prices began to weaken. The Banco Mauá MacGregor suspended payments, which was followed by the bankruptcies of the Banco Nacional and the first German bank in Brazil.

Although the imperial government had often failed to support Mauá's industrial efforts, it had propped up his bank as long as it could. With the bank's collapse came the fall of his close personal friend, Prime Minister Rio Branco (José Maria da Silva Paranhos, viscount of Rio Branco), who had used his influence with the Banco do Brasil to obtain large advances for the Mauá Bank.[55] Like other bankers in Brazil, and in spite of his hardest efforts, Mauá had allowed himself to make a number of illiquid loans.[56] Furthermore, he had immobilized a large sum of capital in the construction of the

Santos-Jundiaí Railway that he proved unable to recover because of bad faith on the part of this British concern. His banking activities in Uruguay, where he suffered the effects of hostile governments and dishonest employees, also turned out to be a burden.[57] In fact, his Montevideo bank came close to failing as early as 1864, as a consequence of the Brazilian invasion of Uruguay. But Mauá could not extricate himself from Uruguay as his banknotes constituted a major part of the circulating medium of the country, and Mauá's ability to transact exchange among the markets of the Plate, Rio Grande do Sul, Rio, and London formed the base for his banking empire.[58] By liquidating his other ventures, Mauá made good all of his debts, an unusual accomplishment.[59]

When Mauá suspended, the 1866 act prevented the Banco do Brasil from issuing new notes. To serve the same purpose of assuring liquidity to the system, the government printed paper money that it lent to the Banco do Brasil on the security of that institution's bond portfolio. Consequently, in this crisis, as well as in the three previous ones, the worst contractionary effects of the gold standard were avoided by decreeing inconvertibility and placing large amounts of paper money or banknotes in circulation.

By the time of the Mauá crisis, a fairly sophisticated financial community had evolved centered on Rio de Janeiro's Rua do Ouvidor and Rua Direita. Rio dominated the empire's commerce, finance, and government while its hinterland, the Paraíba Valley, still provided most of Brazil's coffee and over half of its total exports. The imperial treasury collected 50 percent of its revenues and disbursed 60 percent of its expenditures in the capital and the Rio financial institutions held well over half the deposits of the entire country.[60] Rio had five local, two British, one French, and one German limited-liability banks plus a number of unincorporated banking houses.[61] The Banco do Brasil led the credit system, with half of the deposits of all the joint-stock banks. Although privately owned and managed, it acted as the fiscal agent of the state, receiving substantial government deposits and making frequent advances to the imperial administration. It could no longer issue banknotes, but its existing notes circulated like paper money in Rio de Janeiro and in São Paulo, where it maintained a branch. The English banks had branches, whereas the Banco Mauá MacGregor had been the only other domestic institution with more than one location. The Banco do Brasil concentrated its lending activities in the province of Rio de Janeiro and in the imperial capital, while a small part of its portfolio went to São Paulo and Minas Gerais. The financial elite had continuous and close contact with the political elite through

the Banco do Brasil and other institutions. No fewer than seven prime ministers of the late empire—Itaborahy, Rio Branco, Sinimbú, Dantas, Cotegipe,
João Alfredo, and Ouro Preto—served as bank presidents or directors at one
stage of their lives and could be considered closely linked with the financial
community.[62]

The elite had experienced four crises from 1857 to 1875. They had witnessed
how credit expansion in the 1850s led to speculation and volatility in the exchange rate. The leaders of this generation saw how investors, themselves included, paid for the bankers' and merchants' wholesale fraud through losses
during the panic of 1864. The crisis of 1866 had left the country unscathed,
but that of 1875 reminded the elite of Brazil's vulnerability to events outside its
control. During these years, the elite had experimented with having one bank
of issue on a modified gold backing, and this had led to monetary expansion.
This system had been replaced by one that permitted several banks of issue
with bond backing. A few years later the elite returned to one bank of issue,
this time with a deflationary monetary policy. Finally, after 1866, the financial
leaders tried to do without any bank of issue at all, printing government paper
money instead.

Through all of these changes, the financial elite learned that inconvertibility had spared Brazil from the worst of the crises, especially effectively in 1857
and 1866. Brazil's inconvertible currency worked. Without imposing the
rigidities of a true gold standard, Brazil's leadership reached 1875 with a rapidly growing economy and with the milreis trading freely at 27 pence, its official exchange rate parity since 1846.

Chapter 4 Coffee Planters

Planters, especially coffee planters, dominated the Brazilian Empire, but this hegemony did not make for uniform financial policies. Within the planter class, different groups had conflicting views regarding which measures best served their interests. Moreover, the planters shared power with various other elements of the elite, including politicians, public officials, merchants, and financiers, whose objectives did not always coincide with those of the agrarian sector. The wealthier planters, many of whom sustained losses from the bankruptcies of 1864 and 1875, worried about the security of their financial assets. Less prosperous farmers perceived the financial system primarily as a club from which they were excluded. By the time of the collapse of the Mauá MacGregor Bank in 1875, the planters as a whole saw the approach of the abolition of slavery as their paramount concern and realized that financial reforms would accompany this social transformation.

Planters' agents called commission merchants or factors provided the link between the planters and the financial system.[1] These businessmen sent slaves, farm implements, clothing, and foodstuffs to the planters on account, the bill to be settled when the coffee was sold. Ostensibly the factor obtained his income through commissions on the planters' purchases and sales. In fact, given that the price of coffee fluctuated and the planter had no way of knowing the exact price it would be sold at, factors could become wealthy in a short period of time by underreporting their sales prices.[2] These agents had considerable leverage over the planter through the control of credit. Banks and banking houses generally did not lend to planters because these loans could not be foreclosed. But financial institutions did lend to factors, who were members of the Rio merchant community and were known to the bankers. Each factor supplied a number of planters, so each represented a more diversified credit risk than any individual plantation owner. The factors charged planters a commission, customarily 2 percent per annum, for funds borrowed from the financial system.[3] Through the mechanism of the factor, the need for money in the interior of Brazil could be greatly diminished. The planters' purchases of goods acquired in Rio became debits on their agents' books while coffee sales provided credits. Similarly, the planters' payments to free laborers could be made through a credit on the plantations' books, while goods advanced by the planters became debits. Abuses on both sets of books abounded.

By way of comparison, United States slaveholders also depended upon factors for short-term financing. In the United States, many of the largest plantation owners were also factors and even became bankers.[4] Accordingly there was less conflict between planters and merchants than allegedly occurred in Brazil. Many factors and most wholesale merchants in Brazil were in fact foreigners, a circumstance that tended to accentuate differences in that country. Other coffee factors, though, were Brazilian, and several large planters, for example, the Teixeira Leites in Rio de Janeiro and the Prados in São Paulo, even became partners in banking houses.[5] The Prados also owned shares in and dominated the São Paulo branch of the Banco do Brasil, and prominent American planters held analogous positions in the Mississippi branch of the Bank of the United States.[6] In the United States as in Brazil, banks extended credit on the security of slaves, but in the States, planters also had access to long-term mortgages on land because the legal system provided for foreclosures.[7]

In the United States as in Brazil, slaveholders occasionally tended to lack liquidity. During the American Revolution, tobacco planters notoriously defaulted against their Scots creditors, and the slave states proved to be the worst debtors during the 1837 crisis. This observation notwithstanding, in the United States, slavery coexisted with the institution of the foreclosable mortgage.

Brazil's institutional obstacles to foreclosure must therefore be attributable to variables other than slavery.

Although the factors resolved the planters' short-term financial needs, long-term financing in Brazil proved to be more difficult.[8] Mortgages on land appeared impracticable for a number of reasons. In the frontier areas, there was no market for the land, and it represented little cost to the planter. His principal expenses for acquiring his plantation were the payments to the thugs he hired to expel the squatters who had engaged in subsistence agriculture.[9] Even in long-settled regions, title to the land often remained vague, making the execution of mortgages problematical.[10] There also was a law that mortgages not exceed half the value of the land. In order to foreclose, the creditor would have to pay the planter a sum equal to his original loan, in theory the other half of the value of the land.[11] This measure, designed to protect the planters, made mortgages on land impossible.

Slaves had served as security for long- and short-term loans since the colonial period. Obviously, the slave also had severe drawbacks as a form of collateral. He could die, run away, or be sold without the creditor's permission. Accordingly banks displayed little enthusiasm for making long-term loans directly to planters that were secured by slaves. For lack of a better alternative, the Banco do Brasil used slaves as collateral when it established the country's first mortgage portfolio as part of the 1866 agreement with the government.[12] The bank took 25,000 contos' worth of existing loans—the equivalent of £2.5 million—and converted these into chattel mortgages on slaves. Contemporaries assumed that these mortgages went exclusively to those in political favor who already owed short-term loans to the bank through the factors, and who could not meet these obligations.[13] Thus the early mortgages represented a mere accounting change, from short-term to long-term, on the bank's books. No additional funds reached the planters.

The value of slaves as collateral became less dependable as a consequence of the Law of the Free Womb, passed on September 28, 1871, whereby all children of slaves born after this date were declared free. To compensate the planters for their loss, the Banco do Brasil in 1872 lowered interest and amortization charges on mortgages from the original 9 percent to 6 percent per year. Since the bank's cost of funds exceeded this level, the reduction clearly was dictated by politics. Virtually all the funds lent went to the planters of the Paraíba Valley.[14] As abolition approached, the bank became progressively less willing to make long-term advances secured by slaves. In 1884 it raised its interest rate and ceased lending on slaves altogether. Thereafter, the bank approved few mortgages, accepting as collateral for these loans coffee trees, machinery, or urban real estate.

Both the planters and the government realized that abolition would require a number of changes in official policies, including those related to the financial system. As of 1878, when Spain freed the slaves in its colony of Cuba, Brazil became the only slaveholding society in the "civilized world." In the same year of 1878, three years after the Mauá crisis and ten years before abolition, the Liberal Party returned to power, after a decade in opposition, with an ambitious reform program.[15] Shortly thereafter, Prime Minister Sinimbú invited planters from the coffee-producing provinces—São Paulo, Rio de Janeiro, Minas Gerais, and Espirito Santo—to send delegates to an Agricultural Congress to discuss measures for easing the impact of emancipation. The minutes of this congress offer a broad view of the plantation owners' thinking. No fewer than 279 planters, along with Sinimbú's whole cabinet, attended this congress, which received widespread coverage in the press.[16]

On the first day of the congress, the planters selected two committees to draft specific proposals to the government. One of these committees, the "Paulista" committee, represented São Paulo only, and the other represented the remaining three provinces. Although the Paraíba Valley (Rio de Janeiro, southern Minas Gerais, and eastern São Paulo) was still the richest and most powerful region of Brazil, its planters already understood that the valley had entered into an irreversible decline.[17] A planter from the county of Paraíba do Sul told the congress that the difficulties facing the region transcended the acts of government. "The fertile province of Rio de Janeiro, the principal source of our wealth . . . will soon be abandoned to sweet grass. . . . For example, I cite Vassouras which, having been the richest coffee-producing county, is now decaying, due solely to the exhaustion of the land and not to the lack of labor and capital."[18] In addition to the exhaustion of the soil, the same speaker correctly observed that the problem of the Paraíba Valley was the basic inferiority of the land.[19] As a planter from Minas declared, European immigrants could earn a living wage on the flatter "Paulista" (located in the São Paulo region) coffee plantations but not on the hilly Mineiro ones.[20] This insight came almost a decade before the movement of immigrants to São Paulo became significant. In spite of its fundamental inferiority to the western region of São Paulo Province, the Paraíba Valley had developed earlier because of its proximity to and the relative ease of its penetration from the imperial capital of Rio de Janeiro.

The participants of the congress acknowledged that the future belonged to the lands of western São Paulo Province, and financiers also recognized its importance. The Banco do Brasil issued banknotes only in Rio de Janeiro and in São Paulo, while the two principal bankers of the empire, Mauá and Francisco Mayrink, although residents of Rio, made heavy investments in São Paulo.[21] At the most recent census, 1872, the city of São Paulo had but 23,000 inhabitants, less than a tenth of the imperial capital, and its development as a commercial center was hindered by its isolation from the ocean by the coastal escarpment. But with the completion of the Santos-Jundiaí Railway in 1867, which crossed the coastal escarpment, this obstacle had been overcome, and coffee plantations had begun to spread westward. By the time of the congress, railroad lines financed with local capital had expanded into the province. Of the Brazilian provinces, only São Paulo could build lines without official guarantees, a practice that several Paulista planters at the congress actually condemned. Within a decade of the congress, coffee plantations and railroads both extended deep into the province. It was significant that the leaders of São Paulo's committee came from the county of Campinas, at that time considered the center of western São Paulo.

The Paulista committee summarized its request to the government in two words: capital and workers.[22] The Paulistas wanted to encourage European immigration by means of subsidies, and by granting easy naturalization, civil marriage, and freedom of religion to the new arrivals. Until the time of the congress, the flow of immigrants had remained slight and a considerable fraction of the few who did come were from the Protestant areas of Germany and Switzerland, so that these measures appeared to be highly important.[23] The Paulistas declared that they wanted the rights of the immigrants to be safeguarded. On the other hand, they insisted upon strict work contracts and wished to jail colonists who did not toil with sufficient vigor. In practice, the planters wanted to force immigrants to work, a sign that the slave-owner mentality continued and that planters either could not or, more probably, would not pay an attractive wage. The planters urged the government to cease establishing colonies of small farmers; all immigrants should be sent to work on the large plantations. And the Paulistas registered their willingness to recruit Chinese laborers if sufficient numbers of Europeans did not come forth.[24]

The planters from Rio and Minas agreed with their colleagues from São Paulo regarding the necessity for capital and workers. They too believed in the use of force to compel immigrants, as well as native Brazilians, to meet work contracts. The work contract created a highly unfavorable situation for rural laborers, particularly in combination with the institution of the plantation store. Colonists had to purchase necessities from the planters' stores, but they often found it difficult to break even; since planters controlled the records of debits and credits, a type of debt peonage developed.[25] Frustrated at this debt trap, many colonists "broke their contracts," fleeing the plantations to avoid their debts. The planters attempted, often with success, to maintain their colonists through recourse to violence.

Several of the delegates to the congress presented more positive solutions for the labor problem. A planter from Queluz in the Paraíba Valley reported that he had five hundred free Brazilians tilling his lands, with excellent results, suggesting that native labor could be hard-working and efficient.[26] A planter from another part of the valley requested the government to encourage migration from the Northeast, which was then suffering from the Great Drought.[27] Sharecropping had its partisans and its opponents, and some individuals advocated a form of land reform.[28] Unused land, according to the reformers, should be taxed to oblige owners to sell. The government should, if necessary, purchase uncultivated land at a stipulated price and distribute it to European or Brazilian colonists.[29] Another reformer, prophesying abolition within ten years, recommended converting slaves into rent-paying tenants.[30] It is significant, however, that the only legislation directly resulting from this congress, a law passed on March 15, 1879, dealt with the enforcement of work contracts. On the whole, the planters could not conceive of agricultural labor without some form of coercion.

Regarding public finance, the planters all deplored the government deficits, suggesting that money could be saved by not guaranteeing funds invested in railroads and by reducing further the military's share of the budget.[31] Criticism of railroad spending appears short-sighted, as railroads had contributed decisively to the development of agriculture. Several delegates made recommendations that would in fact have increased the deficit. They wished to reduce the export tax without substituting another source of revenue.[32] Cesario Alvim, a future governor of Minas, asked the authorities to pay a bounty to those who worked on the land for five years,[33] a request that demonstrates a desire to pass the planters' direct expenses on to the society as a whole. As has been so often the case, the rural elite wished to eliminate the public deficit . . . as long as their interests did not suffer.

Both the Paulista committee and the representatives of the other provinces wanted the government to encourage the creation of rural credit banks, private institutions that would specialize in mortgage lending. Specifically, the planters requested the authorities to guarantee principal and 5 percent interest to foreign investors who purchased bonds issued by the rural credit banks.[34] The concession of government guarantees for international investments had been decisive in raising funds for railroad construction. These guarantees had encouraged the construction of useful lines as well as of railroads that had little economic rationale and proved a burden on the public treasury. Just as the government had to pay the holders of the railroad securities, it would have to remunerate the lenders to the rural credit banks in the event that the planters did not honor their commitments. As the planters usually discharged their mortgages from the Banco do Brasil late, if ever, contemporaries imagined that guarantees for rural credit banks would become a heavy drain on the treasury.

Three years before the Agricultural Congress, in 1875, the Brazilian Parliament had passed a law enabling the organization of rural credit banks and guaranteeing foreign long-term loans to these institutions. This law also provided for guarantees of capital employed in central sugar mills, a measure that was of interest to planters of several counties in Rio de Janeiro and São Paulo. But at the time of the congress, this law was still inoperative. Before it could go into effect, complementary regulations had to be enacted. Prime Minister Sinimbú's successor did in fact issue the enabling decrees in 1881 that established strict requirements for obtaining guarantees.[35] Whereas the Paulistas wanted freedom to organize rural credit banks in each province, the other committee favored establishing one bank in the capital, with provincial branches.[36] The political influence of the Paraíba Valley planters made this alternative more attractive to them. To make mortgages more interesting for lenders, planters from both São Paulo and the other provinces proposed to modify the land law that made it practically impossible to foreclose.[37]

Of great significance for the course of our story, many of the planters at the congress hoped for a radical departure from the conservative monetary and credit policies then in force. They advocated a rapid increase in the money supply through the issue of banknotes. Following the "Banking School," which had lost its case in Britain thirty years before, a group of planters argued that banknotes issued to finance trade transactions represent the goods involved and therefore are not inflationary.[38] This same group noted that the money supply depended more on deposits than on banknotes, an accurate description of the English situation but perhaps not yet applicable to Brazil. This group blamed the crises, especially that of 1864, on imprudent lending to illiquid or fraudulent borrowers. The latter class of debtors included those who financed the sale of nonexistent merchandise. If banks managed to lend only for genuine trade transactions, they would not suffer the worst consequences of these crises. Furthermore, the argument continued, in 1864 the banking houses that collapsed were those that could not issue banknotes, whereas the issuing of notes by the Banco do Brasil had prevented the crisis from becoming much more severe.[39] To summarize, a significant number of planters maintained that banknotes would stimulate commerce and avoid crises while not provoking inflation.

A large number of landowners wished to restore Finance Minister Souza Franco's policy of 1857, which had permitted banks to issue banknotes up to the value of their paid-in capital, backed by bonds.[40] Banks would purchase Brazilian government bonds with their capital and subsequently issue notes up to the value of these bonds. These notes would be redeemable in paper money at sight. If a bank did not have enough paper money to honor its banknotes, the bonds could be sold to provide liquidity. The system of banknotes convertible into paper money, greenbacks, had functioned well in the United States since the beginning of the Civil War, when that country suspended metal convertibility. Although by 1878 the United States had legislated a return to convertibility in gold, it would actually only put this into effect the following year.

More radical individuals proposed allowing banks to issue notes equal to double or even ten times their capital invested in government bonds.[41] An issue larger than one to one would have been hugely inflationary. The planters realized that even issuing notes equal to once the capital invested in bonds would add significantly to the circulating medium. The total circulating medium at the time of the congress, including paper money, banknotes, and precious metals, stood on the order of 200,000 contos, or £20 million, while bonds outstanding exceeded 300,000 contos. Planters hoped that a large amount of capital would in fact be invested in banks that would acquire bonds and then issue banknotes. This activity would monetize the national debt and place resources in circulation that would otherwise remain buried in "unproductive" bonds.[42]

The planters at the 1878 congress blamed the internal debt for their difficulties in borrowing money.[43] Although the planters whined about the lack of credit, they were in fact an unsatisfactory risk. Planters' own actions to protect themselves, such as making mortgages virtually impossible to foreclose, gave bankers little incentive to lend to them. A banker or other investor not wishing to acquire imperial bonds had other opportunities to place his funds: railroad bonds, interest-bearing local bank deposits, foreign exchange drafts or bonds, and urban real estate. The availability of these alternatives made investors unlikely to accept the risk of illiquid planters whose lands could not be foreclosed. Moreover, the public debt served a purpose in and of itself. If investors had not purchased its bonds, the government would have had to resort to the printing press, increase taxes, decrease expenses, or borrow from abroad, all actions the planters might have condemned. At the congress, Prime Minister Sinimbú heard a request to lower the interest on bonds.[44] His successors did so, reducing the annual rate from 6 percent to 5 in 1887. Although this measure economized resources for the treasury, it did not make it easier for the planters to borrow, precisely because they constituted an unacceptable risk.

From the laments of the planters at the congress of 1878, one has the impression that they formed a distressed minority! In fact, as one of their number candidly observed, "There are three types of planters: the capitalists, the comfortable ones, and those who suffer. The capitalists buy bonds."[45] Wealthy planters from the Paraíba Valley purchased bonds, urban real estate, or financed their sons' plantations in São Paulo rather than reinvest in the valley. Many placed their funds in commerce as silent or active partners.[46] At least one, João Evangelista Teixeira Leite, established a banking house.[47] The wealthiest planters moved their principal residence to the city of Rio, where they intermingled their fortunes and their families with those of the urban elite's lawyers, politicians, and merchants.[48] Urban capitalists, whether their wealth came from coffee, trade, the professions, or the government, tended to want a strong, stable milreis. Planters in the newer "frontier" areas desired abundant credit and paper money. Thus the planter class at the congress can be divided between those who were already wealthy, those who were in the process of enrichment, largely in western São Paulo Province, and those who were fighting to avoid poverty, primarily the smaller Paraíba Valley landowners.

From the struggling planters of the Paraíba Valley and the rising coffee barons of São Paulo came the cry "Monetize the internal debt."[49] The money locked into bonds could go to "agriculture, banking, commerce, industry, railroads."[50] If the government would substitute either private banknotes or even treasury paper money for these bonds, a sixth of the budget—which went to interest payments—would be saved and all of a sudden there would be sufficient funds in circulation.[51] In the event, substituting paper money for the whole government debt would triple the circulating medium, causing intense inflation. The imperial politicians left this measure to the Republic . . .

The Sinimbú government enacted no changes in credit policy in spite of the recommendations of the Agricultural Congress. The planters and other

members of the elite who favored conservative financial regulations still held
the upper hand. By 1878, however, a considerable number of planters desired
change. These reformers advocated the establishment of rural credit banks
that would borrow money abroad in order to fund mortgages; they asked the
government to guarantee the foreign debt of these institutions. The soft-
money planters also sought to organize banks of issue that would lend to agriculture by creating banknotes. These planters suggested that these banknotes
would be convertible not into gold but into paper money, the supply of which
could be expanded by the government. Thus, these notes would be backed
not by gold but rather by bonds of the public debt, as was the case in the
United States and as had been the case in Brazil under Souza Franco. At the
time of the Agricultural Congress, the United States had not yet returned to
convertibility, which it did the following year, against strident protests from
indebted farmers. Brazilian soft-money interests felt that the bond-backed
banknotes would be a means of transforming the "unproductive" national
debt into productive loans.

When the planters at the congress demanded "capital and workers," by
"capital" they understood banknotes and rural credit banks, and by "workers"
they meant enforcing harsh labor contracts and encouraging immigration.
Successive governments would have to satisfy these demands for "capital and
workers" or face the hostility of important segments of the rural elite.

Chapter 5 Abolition

A decade before abolition, the coffee planters could imagine neither agriculture without coercion nor a solution to their problems that did not call for large government spending. With honorable exceptions, the planters refused to use local labor and demanded European or Oriental workers. Planters convinced themselves that slaves, once freed of the lash, would not work. The landowners wanted the state to pay for the immigrant workers' passage and then force them to labor long hours at the lowest possible wages. The planters also wanted the state to guarantee the foreign borrowings of rural credit banks; if, as experience suggested, the planters failed to discharge promptly these obligations, the state would have to pay. Not all contemporaries displayed enthusiasm at this extraordinary transfer of wealth to the planters. As the editor of the *Rio News,* a paper that represented the commercial interests, complained: "It must be patent to the most superficial observer that duties have reached a maximum, and some new sources of revenue must be discovered. To impose upon one class, the merchants, the obligation to support a class notoriously improvident, and to a considerable extent loaded with debt, is a gross injustice. Let the planter contribute something, in Heaven's name, to relieve the country upon which he has so long been little more than a load and to the advance of which he is an obstacle."[1] In fact, some 75 percent of public revenues came from duties (see the appendix). Indeed, planters did enjoy sufficient political power to pass the costs of government on to other groups.

Prime Minister Sinimbú's Liberal Party had assumed power in 1878 a few months prior to the Agricultural Congress on a platform that included the institution of a land tax in order to induce planters to either cultivate or sell unused estates.[2] That the Liberals expressed such an idea illustrates that at least some politicians realized that Brazil had several options regarding fiscal policy and land tenure. Although Sinimbú abandoned the land tax in short order, others voiced the need for such a measure as part of a general policy to create a free middle class of rural proprietors, as in the United States and France.[3]

> What Brazil needs most is free, intelligent labor; not a class which are free in name while as helpless and degraded as the slave, but a class of laborers which will be small property owners like those which have contributed so largely to the prosperity of the northern and western sections of the United States. To attain this result there must be a radical change in the colonization laws which will permit the immigrant to settle where he pleases, acquire property, and enjoy every privilege of Brazilian citizenship; and there must also be such a revision of the land and taxation laws as will enable him to easily acquire property and to claim full protection from the government in all the privileges growing out of such ownership. When this is done, it will then be found that Brazil has already a sufficient number of laborers to supply all present demands. . . . To neglect them, is simply increasing the number of idlers, paupers, and criminals, which is already too large for the security of life and property.
>
> —*Rio News,* June 5, 1879

Echoing the words of one of the planters at the Agricultural Congress, this article in the *Rio News* reflects a faith in the use of Brazilian laborers, once social and institutional barriers to their advancement could be eliminated.[4] Free poor Brazilians of all races avoided manual labor as degrading slaves' toil. When the poor man did work the soil, he found that the planters used every device, including debt peonage and violence, to avoid paying the contracted wages. Even after abolition, we have repeated examples of the flogging of immigrants and freedmen; workers fleeing the plantations could be hunted down with dogs.[5] If, in spite of everything, the poor man accumulated funds to buy a small plot of land, he found all sorts of obstacles to perfecting his title. Finally, public education for the less affluent proved scarce to nonexistent, thus barring upward mobility in the coming generation. Optimistic observers such as the novelist and senator viscount Taunay or Robert Lamoreux of the *Rio News* hoped that abolition would by itself provoke changes leading to a new, more egalitarian Brazil. Certainly emancipation did hold out a chance for progress. Still, the great landowners stood armed and ready to fight for their properties and to prevent freedmen and immigrants from gaining access to land of their own. The image of Brazil's planter elite held by the *Rio News*—and by many merchants, professionals, and military officers—could hardly have been more negative.[6] In language reminiscent of a contemporary revolutionary tract, the editor of this organ of the commercial community declared:

> For the greater part of crime and disorder existing in Minas Gerais and other parts of the empire, there is one prominent cause for which the great land proprietors are directly accountable. The practice of keeping about every large fazenda [coffee farm] a number of loafers called "capangas," who are very often nothing less than hired assassins, has been the occasion of crimes innumerable already and is unquestionably the cause of a great part of the robberies and murders which are occurring in every part of the empire today. The present state of affairs in the interior is a legitimate result of this species of feudal vassalage—a state of affairs more in accord with the middle ages than with the present era of civilization. . . . No efforts are made to break up these enormous partially cultivated estates in order to build up an industrious, law-abiding population of small proprietors; no effort is made to turn these idlers and cut-throats into laboring men, and but feeble efforts to bring them to justice for their misdoings; no effort is made to keep the freed blacks in the country and away from the cities where they are over-stocking the labor market and increasing the vagrant and criminal classes.
>
> —*Rio News,* August 15, 1879

Ruled by such men, could Brazil expect social change in the wake of abolition?

During the decade following the Agricultural Congress, the preparations for abolition dominated Brazil's politics and its finances. Throughout the years, right up to abolition, the financial conservatives maintained control, and issuing new banknotes remained prohibited. Coffee prices remained relatively low from the Mauá crisis in 1875 to 1885, reflecting the worldwide Great Depression. Since the decline of coffee production in the Paraíba Valley was offset by the expansion of São Paulo, total Brazilian output remained roughly constant during these years. The Great Drought of 1878 in the Northeast caused Prime Minister Sinimbú's government to substantially increase the circulating medium by issuing paper money to spend on railroads and other public projects in the region.[7] Although the circulating medium then contracted slightly during the five years prior to 1885, there were no financial crises at all during this period. As the world economy recovered after 1885, both the volume and the price of coffee improved. The milreis, at its parity of 27 pence in 1875 and as low as 20 pence during the difficult years that followed, began to climb in 1885 and approached par by abolition.

The Liberal Party, in office (1878–1885) after the Agricultural Congress, although financially orthodox, took steps to assist the planters.[8] In 1879, as a direct consequence of the congress, Sinimbú passed legislation to force free laborers to "honor" their work contracts. Two years later, Prime Minister Saraiva issued decrees implementing the law of 1875, which authorized the government to guarantee the return of foreign capital invested in rural credit banks and central sugar mills. Sensitive to the possibility for abuse, the cabinets in power between 1881 and 1889, both Liberal and Conservative, disbursed under guarantees for relatively few central sugar mills.[9] In fact, several of the guaranteed mills turned out to be failures, and a good number of successful mills were built without official assistance. In 1882, the government sanctioned the statutes of the Banco de Crédito Real do Brasil and the Banco de Crédito Real de São Paulo, the two largest rural credit banks after the Banco do Brasil.[10] The same year Parliament decreased the imperial export tariff from 9 percent to 7, partially complying with the demands made at the Agricultural Congress.[11] In a competitive world market for sugar, cotton, and coffee, the reduction of these export duties went directly to the planters' bottom line.

Also in 1882, evidencing the onset of Brazil's first round of industrial expansion, the government permitted joint-stock corporations—except for banks, insurance companies, food wholesalers, religious entities, and foreign concerns—to organize without the specific approval of the Brazilian Parliament.[12] Law 3150 of November 4, 1882, went partially against the spirit of the 1860 Law of Obstacles. Article 2 provides for limited liability for all shareholders. Article 3 requires that 100 percent of the capital be subscribed and that 10 percent of the capital be deposited with a bank or qualified individual for a corporation to commence activities. Article 7 stipulates that shares be nominal until they are fully paid in, at which time they may be converted into bearer shares. Shares may not be traded until 20 percent of the subscribed amount is actually paid in. For five years after an investor sells his shares, he remains liable to complete the amount originally subscribed. This article thus prescribes "reserved liability." In England, reserved liability continued a common practice for banks until 1878, when the City of Glasgow Bank suspended, and shareholders, many of whom had paid in only a fifth of their subscribed capital, had to produce the remaining four fifths or see their assets seized and auctioned. Under Law 3150, all Brazilian corporations had reserved liability, a feature that may have reduced willingness to purchase shares, but the drawbacks of reserved liability could be avoided if investors paid in all their capital within a short period. Another negative aspect of this law appeared in article 13: Recipients of fraudulently declared dividends were liable to repay these amounts for a period of five years—but this provision, too, was not as drastic as it sounded, since it specifically exempted good-faith shareholders in due course. Accordingly, Law 3150 constituted a major step forward in instituting practices that were standard in the industrial countries.

While the Liberals enacted their reforms, the financial situation of the Paraíba Valley planters deteriorated. In 1884, as abolitionist sentiment swelled, the Banco do Brasil ceased extending loans for which slaves served as collateral. With old coffee bushes and exhausted land, these planters had no other source of credit. Financiers could not be induced to make direct loans to the Paraíba Valley planters under any circumstances; almost half of the Banco do Brasil's mortgage portfolio was already over two years past due.[13] Though in dire economic straits, the coffee growers of the Paraíba Valley maintained considerable political influence, as half of Brazil's coffee still came from this region. They made it known that they wanted the ministry to do something to increase the availability of credit. By a law dated July 18, 1885, the Liberal government institutionalized the practice of lending public money directly to banks in time of crisis. Following the terms of the law of 1875, enacted after Mauá's collapse, this wise legislation established a limit of 25,000 contos, equivalent to £2.5 million, per bank, and directed banks to secure their drawings with government bonds, thus guaranteeing that no public funds would be lost in the process. In effect, this measure caused a temporary increase in the money supply, partially monetizing the internal debt, as the planters had requested at the Agricultural Congress. The 1885 law may be seen as a step toward establishing a beneficial system of bond-backed banknotes. Knowing they could always borrow against their securities portfolio in times of trouble, banks could increase their loans to the commission merchants, who in turn could lend to the planters.

Meanwhile, sentiment to free the slaves gained momentum. Since the termination of the slave trade in 1850, even the most vehement slaveholders realized that it was only a matter of time until emancipation, since the plantation economy continued to grow while the slave population declined. As early as the 1850s, a large part of the army's officer corps favored abolition.[14] The United States' abolition of slavery in 1865 left Brazil as the major slaveholding country in the world. In 1871, Brazil passed the Free Womb Law.

The abolitionist campaign in Brazil began in earnest in 1880, almost a decade after passage of the Free Womb Law. By this time slaveholding had declined in the North of Brazil as a result of large sales of slaves first to Rio de Janeiro and Minas Gerais and later to São Paulo. The Great Drought of 1877–1878 had lowered the price of free laborers in the North to the point where they became less expensive to maintain than slaves.[15] Many formerly independent individuals, their farms ruined by the lack of rain, offered their labor for any price, while the larger planters, also hit by the drought and competition from beet sugar, reduced their demand for workers. In 1881, to avoid a further decline in the slave population of the North, the coffee provinces imposed a prohibitive tariff on the interprovincial slave trade. Hard-line slaveholders in these provinces did not want to let slavery become a sectional issue; they wanted the northern elite to remain committed to the survival of this institution. The northern provinces of Ceará and Amazonas freed their slaves in 1884.

Between 1871, when the Free Womb Law was passed, to 1883, there had been 87,000 manumissions and 132,000 deaths of slaves. Slaves and *ingenuos,* children born to slaves after September 28, 1871, but under the control of their parents' owners, numbered 1,500,000 in 1883, or some 13 percent of the total population. Meanwhile, abolitionists noted a wave of 40,000 European immigrants to Argentina in 1883, which was several times the number of immigrants coming to Brazil.[16]

The Liberal cabinet of Prime Minister Manoel Pinto de Souza Dantas wished to undertake additional measures to hasten abolition, but he was unsuccessful, so he turned power over to a fellow Liberal, José Antonio Saraiva. When Saraiva, too, failed to push through reforms, Pedro II called on a hardline slaveholder, the baron of Cotegipe, to form a Conservative government, in August 1885. Cotegipe's principal objective was to preserve slavery as long as possible. His first legislation appeared to be another concession—he freed all the sixty-year-old slaves. Yet few bondsmen reached this age, and those who did often became a burden to their masters.

While he staved off the abolitionists, Cotegipe granted three of the requests voiced by the planters at the Agricultural Congress of 1878. He renegotiated the interest on the internal debt from 6 percent down to 5 percent.[17] This important act decreased the state's expenses and diminished the attractiveness of the public debt as an investment. Planters hoped that funds would be diverted from bonds to banks that would lend them money, but they hoped in vain, as many had become unacceptable credit risks. Finance Minister Francisco Belisário Soares de Sousa, a Paraíba Valley coffee planter, passed a law exempting sugar from the export tariff altogether.[18] This measure benefited the planters around Campos, in the province of Rio, an abolitionist center, as well as those of the Northeast, whose support the slaveholder government desperately needed. The Cotegipe ministry also made a gesture toward modification of the mortgage law.[19] Slowly the rural credit banks could begin to consider granting mortgages that were secured by land, although the information available indicates that most of the loans extended at this time were in fact secured by urban real estate.[20]

The divisions within the planter class between financially conservative large planters and soft-money indebted smaller farmers, apparent during the Agricultural Congress, continued. Belisário sought to please both the wealthy planters, who wished for a stable currency, and his struggling partisans in the Paraíba Valley. In his 1887 ministerial report, he suggested the time had come to reestablish banks of issue.[21] A true financial conservative, Belisário proposed that the banks should issue banknotes convertible only into gold.[22] The previous year he had negotiated, with the Rothschilds, as usual, a £6 million external loan on favorable terms, and gold was flowing in owing to buoyant exports of coffee and rubber.[23] The total circulating medium stood slightly above 200,000 contos, or £20 million, at an average exchange rate of 24 pence, 3 pence below official parity. Belisário hoped a bank of issue, established with a large share of foreign capital, could place enough gold and gold-backed banknotes in circulation to set Brazil on a true gold standard for the first time.[24] The international situation appeared favorable. In 1878 and 1879, respectively, France and the United States had resumed convertibility, following wartime suspensions, and in 1881 Italy returned to convertibility, a move that was facilitated by massive foreign borrowings. All these states adopted the gold standard, although they had had bimetallic standards prior to suspension.

In the recent past, planters had benefited from Brazil's nonadherence to the rules of the gold standard. When coffee prices had been at their cyclical lows, as in the period from 1875 to 1885, the milreis had been devalued relative to sterling. The planters' revenues in terms of milreis declined little or even remained constant, as each pound sterling of exports brought them a larger number of milreis. Planters' costs in local currency rose by less than the devaluation of the milreis. The fall of the milreis socialized the planters' losses in that the urban importing groups had to pay higher prices in local currency for goods produced abroad. By 1887, this process was operating in reverse: as the milreis appreciated, the cost of imported goods declined for urban workers and others whose incomes were in milreis. Debts assumed in milreis rose in value relative to exports that generated hard currency. In order to please exporters as well as borrowers, Belisário suggested reducing the parity from 27 to 24 pence.[25] Once the rate reached 24 pence, Belisário hoped to avoid a further rise in the Brazilian currency by going on the gold standard at this rate. Once the mechanism of the gold standard kicked in, greater exports would cause an expansion of the circulating medium rather than an increase in the rate of the milreis relative to sterling.

A major turn of events in 1887 left the Cotegipe-Belisário government on the defensive and prevented it from enacting any reforms, financial or otherwise. The number of slaves had fallen by this time to less than 1 million, through death, manumission, and flight; meanwhile the flow of immigrants, especially from Italy, surged precisely in 1886 and 1887.[26] Many of the planters from São Paulo came to see the combination of abolition and heavy immigration as their only chance for survival. The balance of power shifted abruptly in May 1887 when the Paulista leader, Antonio Prado, Cotegipe's minister of agriculture, resigned from the cabinet to join the abolitionist movement. A large number of his fellow Paulistas also became emancipationist, leaving the planters of the Paraíba Valley alone in their support of the ministry.

This division within the elite allowed other groups to become active in the political process. The officer corps had been frankly abolitionist since the 1850s, viewing slavery as both immoral and an obstacle to industrialization, but faced with a unified elite, the military could not bring its force to bear. In 1887, encouraged by civilian abolitionists, including members of the elite, the officer corps had a series of noisy confrontations with the Cotegipe ministry. In the same month that Antonio Prado resigned, the army came within a step of executing a coup d'état. At this time, senior officers announced that the army would no longer hunt for runaway slaves.[27] Urban dwellers also made their feelings heard by the elite through repeated and clamorous street demonstrations. Slaves now found it much easier to escape the plantations, as they had the active assistance of members of the elite, officers, and townsmen.

The Cotegipe ministry staggered on from May 1887 to March 1888. Many masters followed the example set by Antonio Prado and freed their slaves. Francisco de Paula e Souza, a leader of the Paulista planters, wrote at this time:

"I have liberated all of them, and bound them to the property by means of a contract identical to the one I have with the foreign colonists and that I intend to have with those I will hire."[28] Slaves of less enlightened planters fled from the land in unprecedented numbers. The same planter noted, with some exaggeration, concerning the fate of other plantations, "Eighty of every hundred were deserted while the blacks went to the cities or followed wicked seducers." In those months, the need to gather in the crop reached panic levels: "Nobody was thinking of a contest between the old laborers and the new. There was room for everyone." The army and the citizens of Rio became ever more vocal in their demands for emancipation, while Cotegipe relied more and more on the police to subdue the abolitionists. The violence that permeated the slaveholding interior now came to be used against the residents of the towns and cities. In August, the ailing Emperor Pedro II departed for Europe, leaving his daughter Isabel in power as regent. For several months the princess-regent resisted changing the government in spite of its untenable situation. Finally, in March 1888, an incident involving police brutality toward a naval officer forced her to accept Cotegipe's resignation. Princess Isabel appointed João Alfredo Correia de Oliveira as the new prime minister.[29]

A Conservative from Pernambuco, João Alfredo took office with a mandate to abolish slavery. A less radical abolitionist could hardly have been found. João Alfredo, who had freed the slaves on his sugar plantation as recently as June 1887, had held all the major political positions before becoming prime minister: provincial president, deputy, senator, cabinet minister, and councilor of state. The most unusual part of João Alfredo's political career came after the fall of the monarchy, when he refused to participate in republican politics. There were few other monarchists who held such strong principles.

In April, the month after he assumed the portfolio of finance and the presidency of the council of ministers, João Alfredo borrowed £6 million from the Rothschilds at the most advantageous rate thus far obtained by Brazil.[30] The prime minister took this money to have funds on hand to meet any financial emergencies resulting from abolition. Planters and merchants urged him to borrow more. Many felt, as did Belisário, that foreign loans could place gold permanently in circulation and thus simultaneously expand the money supply and maintain the value of the milreis. The appreciation of the milreis following Belisário's £6 million loan of 1886 and João Alfredo's borrowing, combined with rising coffee prices, tended to confirm this belief. João Alfredo, however, correctly viewed the strength of the milreis as a temporary phenomenon. He predicted that as the exchange rate climbed, foreign private debt would be liquidated; gold would flow out, and Brazil would be back where it started in terms of the quality of the circulating medium, but now with a high level of official external debt.[31] He observed that whereas Italy had recently succeeded in placing gold in circulation by massive foreign borrowing, this tactic would not work in Brazil, which, not being an industrialized country, suffered from commodity cycles.[32] Whenever the price of coffee fell, the demand for milreis would decline proportionately and would force down the value of the Brazilian currency.

Even as the milreis appreciated, contemporaries perceived tightness in the money market caused by the need to pay salaries to immigrants and freedmen. In January of 1888, just before leaving office, Belisário had advanced 10,000 contos to the Banco do Brasil as capital, an action of questionable wisdom, as this institution had been privately managed and controlled since 1866.[33] Belisário also invoked the 1885 law that permitted the government, during periods of crisis, to lend up to 25,000 contos to any bank that could provide imperial bonds as security. Praising the Brazilian way of furnishing liquidity to the banking system, the *Rio News* stated on January 24, 1888: "It is evident that the money market in Rio is in so delicate a condition, that a trifle might precipitate a crash. We know and recognize, that the authority held by the treasury to issue up to 25,000,000$ in paper money upon the deposit of securities is likely to palliate, if not entirely avert, anything like such crises as we have seen in England and the United States in our own day."

In the same edition the *Rio News* noted that by this time industry had become an additional and significant demander of credit. Belisário's renegotiation of the internal debt interest from 6 to 5 percent, the *Rio News* concluded, had encouraged investment in textile mills, banks, and other enterprises. The newspaper felt that Brazil in fact had already achieved self-sufficiency in coarse fabric. Thus, even before João Alfredo took office, many of the preconditions for the Encilhamento bubble had appeared. Immigrants and freedmen required at least partial payment in currency, and the number of immigrants was expanding rapidly. The growth of this "mass market" provided opportunities for industrialists. High coffee earnings and the peaceful resolution of the labor question supplied the economy with capital and optimism.

Two months after assuming power, João Alfredo secured passage of abolition by an overwhelming majority on May 13, 1888. The only dissenters were the delegation from the province of Rio de Janeiro. Planters all over the country feared that the freedmen would abandon the plantations and that crops would rot for lack of harvesting. Some even feared social upheaval.[34] In fact freedmen harvested the first post-abolition crops in São Paulo until the planters replaced them with "hard-working" immigrants. The 1887 census showed 700,000 slaves, a number that does not include adolescents born after the Free Womb Law, who worked as slaves of their parents' masters as well as individuals freed conditionally upon years of future labor. Ruy Barbosa estimated the total post-abolition number of salaried workers at 1,300,000, so freedmen were still vital to the money economy at abolition.[35] Once the immediate crisis subsided, the problems of the freedmen were promptly forgotten, even by the abolitionists.[36] In the Paraíba Valley, freedmen were given the dubious opportunity to sharecrop exhausted bushes.

The abolition law did not include a provision for indemnification of former slaveholders, and this caused a large number of Paraíba Valley planters to turn hostile to the regime. First these planters fought a campaign for indemnities and laws to force freedmen to work; when they realized that they would not receive satisfaction, many became republicans.[37] In response, former slaves formed the "Black Guard of the Princess" to defend the monarchy from their ex-masters. Republicans complained that the Black Guard violently interrupted their peaceful meetings.[38] On the other hand, freedmen suffered violence at the hands of their former masters.[39] Before emancipation the slaveocrats had accused abolitionists of republicanism; now the shoe was on the other foot. Demonstrating his awareness of the exploitation of laborers in Europe, the abolitionist leader José do Patrocinio wrote in the *Cidade do Rio* on July 4, 1888, "From August 20, 1885 to March 7, 1888, the reptiles Belisário and Coelho Bastos [the police chief] filled the *Jornal do Commercio* with articles to show how Abolitionists were simply Republicans, Anarchists, Communists. . . . Slaveocrats devourers of men and monopolizers of the land! We swear, Brazil will not be your Ireland."

On the other hand, João Alfredo knew he had to do something for the planters if he wished to remain in office. The Paulista landowners now demanded subsidies for immigration and greater local autonomy. During the empire, the governors, called provincial presidents, were appointed by the cabinet. The Paulistas wanted the provincial presidents elected and sought control over public lands in their province as well as a greater retention of taxes collected in São Paulo. The planters of the Paraíba Valley, for their part, insisted upon compensation for their former slaves. Most planters in both regions wished for an increase in the money supply.

During the same month as abolition, May 1888, João Alfredo summoned a bipartisan committee, led by a Conservative, viscount of Cruzeiro, and a

Liberal, viscount of Ouro Preto, to draft a law reestablishing banks of issue. While this committee prepared its legislation, the prime minister resolved to lend public funds to planters through the existing banks. As his predecessor had been slow to purchase the freedom of slaves, João Alfredo found 4,000 contos in the government's emancipation fund available for his loans. Between August and October, the government signed agreements with the Banco do Brasil and the Banco da Bahia to lend funds—ultimately 18,000 contos—to planters for terms of six months to five years.[40] The government engaged to provide half of these funds interest-free to banks that would disburse a like amount and charge 6 percent annual interest on the total; the prevailing interest charged by commission merchants to planters was around 12 percent. In practice, the banks lent the government's money but did not supply any of their own. Disbursements attained 4,300 contos by the time João Alfredo left office.[41]

Meanwhile, predictions of doom to the contrary notwithstanding, Brazil prospered after abolition. Optimism took hold of the planters as coffee prices continued rising. Foreigners, impressed by Brazil's peaceful solution of the labor question, increased the volume of their loans and equity investments, causing further appreciation of the milreis.[42] A number of new industries, especially textiles, expanded to take advantage of the recently created market of wage-earning rural workers, both immigrants and freedmen.[43] The need to pay rural workers as well as the desire to invest in new projects resulted in an increased demand for capital, and interest rates rose significantly, so that even urban merchants paid 10 percent.[44]

Under these auspicious circumstances, the legislature followed the recommendations of the Cruzeiro–Ouro Preto committee and passed Law 3403 on November 24, 1888, which authorized banks of issue. This measure proved to be similar to the Souza Franco system of 1857: Souza Franco adopted the contemporary United States practice of allowing banks to issue banknotes to the extent of their capital backed by government bonds. Banks earned interest on their capital twice, once on the bonds and once on the loans generated by delivering their banknotes to their borrowers. Although somewhat inflationary, the system worked well in the United States. During the generation between Souza Franco and João Alfredo, deposits had grown substantially in the United States, making banknotes a much smaller proportion of funding for banks. In 1863, the United States legislature imposed federal inspection over banks of issue and reduced their issuing capacity to 90 percent of capital. João Alfredo's law permitted Brazilian banks to issue notes only to two thirds of their capital and required them to hold a reserve equal to 20 percent of bank-notes outstanding in cash. In the industrial countries, a rule of thumb held that banks should keep in cash a sum equal to one third of their liabilities. For reasons discussed in chapter 3, Brazilian banks generally maintained cash at a much lower level.

Since the Bank Charter Act of 1844, banknotes of private banks had been in constant decline all over the world. The French gave the Banque de France a near monopoly of banknote issues as early as 1848. Germany followed suit, granting the Reichsbank a quasi monopoly in 1875, and the use of private banknotes dwindled in the United States in the face of federal paper currency. João Alfredo thus went against the global trend.

The 1888 law introduced a factor present neither in Souza Franco's system nor in that of the United States. It authorized the government to issue a special class of bonds with an interest rate of $4\frac{1}{2}$ percent per annum, a rate inferior to the standard 5 percent. Banks wishing to issue would have to purchase these bonds at par to the extent of half of their issue. As the regular 5 percent bonds traded under par, the acquisition of these bonds would result in a considerable capital loss, perhaps equal to two years' interest on these bonds.[45] The remaining half of the issue could be secured by delivering to the treasury standard 5 percent bonds purchased at the market price. The U.S. and Souza Franco arrangements both provided for the purchase of standard bonds at prevailing market rates. The 1888 law differed in that it required that the interest on the 5 percent bonds delivered as security be reduced to $4\frac{1}{2}$ percent. Law 3403 does not discuss the termination of issue rights. Apparently if a bank renounced its issue rights or liquidated, it would receive back from the treasury $4\frac{1}{2}$ percent bonds, thus incurring a loss on this part of its security as well—for these bonds would have to be sold at a discount to the standard 5 percent ones.

The loss resulting from the bond purchases would discourage a banker from issuing notes unless he felt certain that he would be in business for a sufficient time to recover his original loss. The 1888 law provided no such comfort for it also established as an alternative to bond-backed issues the possibility of issuing banknotes backed by and convertible into gold. Such banknotes could be issued for up to three times a bank's capital. Souza Franco had also provided for issuing notes up to three times capital convertible into bullion. As the exchange rate during that minister's tenure generally stood slightly below par, bankers could not issue convertible notes at that time. Souza Franco's enemies passed a law in 1860 that obliged the banks that had issued with bond backing to redeem their banknotes in gold. In consequence, these bankers sustained an immediate loss, and they all subsequently renounced their issue rights or went out of business entirely. When João Alfredo's law passed, the milreis had just returned to parity, and there was a good deal of pressure on him to go on the gold standard. Under these circumstances, an institution issuing notes backed by bonds could find itself in the same predicament as Souza Franco's banks.

The 1888 law demonstrated a preoccupation with inflation. It limited the total issue to 200,000 contos, an amount equal to the outstanding paper money. No individual institution could issue more than 20,000 contos. Furthermore, a sum equivalent to half the securities tendered as collateral for the issues (that is, the sale of the new 4½ percent bonds) would be used to burn paper money. Accordingly, the maximum theoretical increase of the circulating medium would be 50 percent.

When João Alfredo promulgated the enabling decree for his law on January 5, 1889, he determined that the 20,000 and 200,000 limits applied to banks regardless of the type of backing they employed. Ouro Preto, the coauthor of the 1888 law, complained that the global limitations should affect only bond-backed issues.[46] Contemporaries attacked João Alfredo for being too restrictive, especially in his interpretation of this clause.[47] In fact, during his remaining five months in office no bank availed itself of the issue law. João Alfredo did not think Brazil could go on the gold standard.[48] It appears that outside influences rather than internal convictions caused him to include the gold-backed alternative in his law. Bankers, fearing that the milreis might shortly fall under par, refused to issue convertible notes that they might have to redeem at a loss.[49] The bond-based system, which is the principal subject of the 1888 law, if honestly administered, would have provided an excellent mechanism for the controlled expansion of the circulating medium. The loss discussed above in connection with the collateral bonds as well as a fear of the repetition of the Souza Franco experience—the forced redemption in gold of bond-backed notes—discouraged financiers from taking advantage of the 1888 law.[50] Thus, the banks and the country lost an outstanding opportunity to effect an orderly transition to the new labor system.

The law of November 24 passed together with the budget for 1889. João Alfredo proposed to spend no less than 10,000 contos, equivalent to £1 million, to promote immigration, a major departure from the policy of his predecessors.[51] Other features of this law included authorization to negotiate a new tariff treaty with the United States to give Brazilian sugar a privileged position in that market, higher protection for locally produced raw materials, and elimination of the tariff on fertilizers. The planters should have been pleased.

Although João Alfredo, in one year, had accomplished abolition without bloodshed, enacted the empire's first immigration subsidy, instituted the empire's first direct agricultural loans, and authorized the establishment of banks of issue, many within the elite felt he had not moved fast enough. The Paulistas criticized him for not disbursing the immigration funds with sufficient speed.[52] They now insisted upon more local autonomy, for they wished to keep a greater share of the taxes collected in São Paulo as well as to elect the provincial president and to control public lands within the province.

At a critical juncture, August 1888, Pedro II returned from a period of convalescence in Europe. Observers noted that his health had not been restored. Over the following months the elite concluded that in fact the emperor no longer ruled. Princess Isabel and her husband, the French count d'Eu, had become the real monarchs. Isabel's Ultramontanism angered the Paulistas, who wished to encourage immigration from non-Catholic countries. She personally held up a bill to permit civil marriage that had already passed the Senate.[53] Citing specifically his discontent with immigration policies, Antonio Prado resigned from João Alfredo's government, where he also held the portfolio for agriculture, on the last day of April 1889.[54]

Parliament convened a few days later. During the month of May, a historian can sense how the elite consensus grew, rejecting not only João Alfredo but the monarchy as well.[55] Like the Paulistas, the Rio merchants thought João Alfredo had progressed too slowly in the direction of the promised reforms, especially concerning banking.[56] The army, which had played an important role in the final stages of the abolitionist campaign, felt that the imperial government, with its nepotism, had become an obstacle to development.[57] The officers also had corporate grievances, such as low pay, slow promotions, and the lack of pensions for the cripples, widows, and orphans produced by the Paraguayan War.[58] Finally, the planters of the Paraíba Valley, who had been the mainstays of the throne, abandoned the ministry and the monarchy that had first decreed abolition and then refused to pay indemnities for the loss of their slaves.[59] João Alfredo, through the agricultural loans and the banks of issue, tried to placate the Paraíba Valley planters. However, they joined with their enemies of the Liberal opposition to elect the brother of the former minister Belisário, Paulino de Sousa, president of the Senate. João Alfredo resigned.

The monarch's difficulty in appointing João Alfredo's successor revealed the gravity of this crisis. Three Conservatives and a Liberal all tried and failed to form a government. Finally the Liberal viscount of Ouro Preto, a financial expert with a combative personality, organized a government in the knowledge that it might very well be the empire's last.[60] Ouro Preto planned a radical departure from the conservative financial policies of his predecessors.

Although all the governments under the empire through and including João Alfredo's may be considered financially conservative, the imperial finance ministers had by no means been immobile. We have noted a respectable number of reforms during the years preceding abolition, and João Alfredo's ministry initiated several highly significant measures that affected immigration, agricultural loans, and banks of issue. Although few ministers contemplated resolving the problems caused by abolition through, for instance, massive expenditures on the education of freedmen, the late imperial governments proved quite sensitive to the needs of the landholding elite. In normal times, João Alfredo might have been celebrated as an energetic reformer. Governing during the most critical period of transformation of the century, however, he proved unable to deliver all the reforms necessary to provide a smooth transition to free labor.

Chapter 6 The Encilhamento

The extended ministerial crisis and the unprecedented failure of four leaders to form a government seemed to persuade many members of the elite that the Brazilian Empire had become politically bankrupt. Prime Minister Ouro Preto received a rather unfriendly reception in the Chamber of Deputies when he presented his program in early June of 1889. Two deputies turned openly republican and shouted, "Down with the monarchy!" to Ouro Preto's face. Although the prime minister handled himself well, the volume of shouting indicated that only half the members of the imperial Chamber of Deputies still defended the monarchy.[1] The Conservative majority passed a vote of no confidence, and shortly thereafter the emperor dissolved the legislature and called an election for August 31. It is rather difficult to capture the excited spirit of these days; though no one proved willing to die for the empire or for the Republic, the politicians took the issue of the form of government rather seriously, for their offices depended upon it. The *Rio News,* edited by an American and not openly partisan, described the situation a week after the confrontation with Ouro Preto in the Chamber of Deputies.[2]

The political situation is at last assuming a definite and definable state, and the crisis is for the present at an end. The immediate effect has been a serious loss to the crown and the ultimate result will unquestionably be a radical change in the form of government, but how soon this will occur can not easily be foreseen. Were Brazilian republicans as resolute and courageous as they are declamatory, the republic would be declared before the year closes; but as they are not, the course of events depends largely upon accident. It is entirely within the bounds of possibility that the apathy and temporizing policy thus far dominant in imperial circles will lose the empire almost without a struggle and at the moment when least expected, while on the contrary a prompt change from this negative policy to one of vigorous repression, attended by a generous grant of political privileges and reforms, would postpone the inevitable change for many years to come. If the crown and the dominant class would recognize this fact and the wisdom of this policy of repression and reform, and then seek to prepare the way for the future republic by educating the people for self-government, the future of Brazil would be assured; but instead of this the current of national life will be diverted by temporizing obstructions and makeshifts until the revolutionary force breaks through every barrier and overwhelms all. The future Brazilian republic will be an anarchy, a despotism of ignorant mobs and unscrupulous chiefs.

Ouro Preto agreed with this observer that only far-reaching reforms could save the monarchy. This leader from Minas Gerais, like João Alfredo, came from the inner circles of the imperial political elite. After serving as finance minister in Sinimbú's cabinet, he received lifetime appointments to the Senate and the Council of State. The new president of the council belonged to the progressive wing of the Liberal Party. In opposition during the 1870s, Ouro Preto advocated financial and educational reforms in articles, books, and speeches. His enthusiasm for reform even called into question his commitment to the monarchy at that time. Once in office, though, Ouro Preto became a mainstay of the throne and remained a monarchist until his death.

Since the emperor and Princess Isabel blocked political reforms, Ouro Preto devoted most of his efforts to restructuring public finances and the banking system. The greatest danger to the monarchy came from São Paulo. At this time the wealth of São Paulo Province had grown to the point where it visibly challenged that of Rio de Janeiro for first place.[3] Antonio Prado and his fellow Paulistas demanded federalism: the election of provincial presidents, the end of senators' serving for life, provincial control over public lands, and greater retention of local taxes. The Paulistas, although devout Catholics, also sought to separate church and state, which they felt would encourage Protestant immigration. In his declarations after assuming power,

Ouro Preto expressed his support for these political demands, although he took no steps to implement them.[4] Pedro II opposed federalism, and his daughter defended the Catholic church against disestablishment; she placed one of her favorites, the baron of Loreto, in the new cabinet, naming him minister of the empire, with jurisdiction over religious affairs.[5]

Planters in the province of Rio de Janeiro as well as southern Minas Gerais abandoned the empire because Ouro Preto could not indemnify them for their lost slaves. The merchants of Rio had attacked the João Alfredo government for its financial conservatism, although they proved to be more favorably disposed to the new prime minister.[6] Courted by the civilian republican press, the army displayed hostility to Ouro Preto from the start of his administration.[7] The officers' aims, in addition to the redress of corporate grievances such as poor pay, were the modernization of Brazil by means of overthrowing the nepotistic political elite and the promotion of industrialization. The army, discontent for many years, became politically dangerous as a result of encouragement by civilian republicans.[8]

For support the prime minister could count on the majority of the elites of the Northeast, his province of Minas Gerais, outside the Paraíba Valley, and the South.

Although the new government faced a disadvantageous political situation, economic conditions could not have been more favorable. Ouro Preto assumed office amid general prosperity, with the exchange rate above its 27-pence parity. The achievement of abolition without violence and without a collapse of plantation agriculture left all members of the elite, except the ruined landowners of the Paraíba Valley, in a state of extreme optimism. The first post-abolition coffee crop commanded excellent prices and yielded a volume greater than expected, and the 1889 harvest, which would begin in a few months, promised to be even better in both regards. It had been demonstrated that immigration could replace slavery and even surpass it as a source of labor. The number of immigrants to São Paulo Province rose from 5,000 in 1884 to 92,000 in 1889.[9] All of a sudden, the labor shortage in that province appeared to be much less a problem than pessimists had feared. Recognizing Brazil's fine prospects, foreigners increased both trade and long-term credit, forcing up the value of the milreis and placing a considerable amount of gold in circulation for the first time in twenty-five years.[10] Internal credit and liquidity increased in tandem. Investors in the stock market made sizable profits, encouraging others to invest, and share prices rose, as is often the case when people feel a new era of abundance has begun.

Ouro Preto hoped to take advantage of this favorable situation, combined with a radical financial policy, to restore the planters' allegiance to the monarchy. Although he could neither indemnify the planters of the Paraíba Valley for the loss of their slaves nor ultimately grant the Paulistas the federalism they demanded, he could attend to other requests, especially subsidized immigration, loans to agriculture, and the creation of banks of issue. He began to spend money on immigration immediately.[11] Within a month of assuming office, Ouro Preto also changed the regulations to permit banks that backed their issues with gold to issue convertible banknotes in value of up to three times their capital—without an upper limit to this capital.[12] This liberalization was praised by bankers, although, with one minor exception, the only bank that issued notes under this decree was the Banco Nacional, a recipient of other generous privileges.[13]

Ouro Preto maintained close relationships with three of the principal banking groups, the Banco do Brasil, the Banco Internacional, and the Banco de Crédito Real do Brasil. The Banco do Brasil, although no longer controlled by the government, was dominated by politicians. From August of 1888 to his death in May of the following year, the baron of Cotegipe presided over this institution; he was succeeded by Senator Manoel Pinto de Souza Dantas.[14] The Banco Internacional, with substantial French capital, had the Portuguese-born count of Figueiredo as its chief executive. Francisco de Paula Mayrink, of Austrian extraction, was president of the Banco de Crédito Real do Brasil and the Banco Predial and enjoyed extensive contacts with politicians as well as planters. Mayrink's two banks made him the seventh most important banker in Brazil at this time, in terms of the financial resources he controlled.[15]

On June 28, 1889, a scant three weeks after his appointment, Prime Minister Ouro Preto signed agreements with Mayrink to extend loans to planters for one to five years against mortgages, chattel mortgages on equipment, or crops to be harvested.[16] Following João Alfredo's initiative, Ouro Preto pledged to provide a sum to the banks interest-free, and the banks bound themselves to match this amount and lend the total at 6 percent interest per annum. Where João Alfredo in one year contracted 18,000 contos in agricultural credit and the banks had disbursed 4,300, Ouro Preto in five months contracted no less than 172,000 contos and the banks disbursed 26,000.[17] In all, Ouro Preto made agreements with seventeen institutions, some of which appear to have been created for the sole purpose of taking advantage of the government's interest-free money. He must have known of abuses in the system, but in his preoccupation with winning friends for the monarchy, Ouro Preto looked the other way. When several of the banks, including the Banco de Crédito Real do Brasil, had disbursed all the treasury's resources, they returned to the government to ask for more official funds instead of lending their own funds as agreed. Ouro Preto granted additional sums to a number of these banks, leaving observers in doubt as to the honesty of his original intentions regarding their participation with their own resources.[18]

The *Rio News* raised a dramatic protest as soon as Ouro Preto opened the doors of the treasury to the planters.[19] A week later the newspaper sounded a warning to Ouro Preto not to imitate the dangerous banking practices prevalent in Argentina—which shortly would lead to a major crash there:[20]

There is now a very dangerous epidemic raging in this country and the River Plate republics, the peril of which can not be overestimated—the creation of *crédit foncier* banks for the distribution of unnecessary loans to an improvident class. It is not a question of encouraging or aiding agriculture, but rather a purpose of extending assistance to unworthy speculators and men who are seeking to carry on large enterprises on borrowed capital. It is not intended to assist small farmers, for we have known such loans to be refused by the banks, but to furnish cheap capital to politicians and speculators who live in the cities and waste more than their estates can produce.

In spite of his reputation for fiscal conservatism and his dedication to the gold standard, Ouro Preto provoked a false boom, the *Encilhamento*.[21] The prospect of interest-free funds from the government induced the formation of a number of new banks, while those already in existence sought to increase their capital to become eligible for greater sums of public money. The value of bank stock under these circumstances rose rapidly. Fortunes could be made in a few days. The predominance of bank shares traded in the stock market can be seen in the figures in table 2, "Capitalization of the Rio Stock Exchange."[22]

Table 2   Capitalization of the Rio Stock Exchange—Book Value of Shares Outstanding in Contos on December 31, 1889.

Banks	572,000
Railroads	176,000
Insurance companies	35,700
Navigation	26,000
Textiles	25,600
Central sugar mills	9,000

Source: Amaro Cavalcanti, *Resenha financeira, do ex-império do Brasil.* Rio de Janeiro, 1890, 355.

Of the value of bank shares, 250,000 contos represent stock in institutions established in 1889 and 126,000 represent new stock issued during that year by banks already in operation. Fourteen of the forty banks doing business at the end of 1889 had been founded that year. The only industry listed in table 2, textiles, absorbed a minor fraction of the capital in the stock exchange. In the eloquent words of the *Rio News* of September 30:

> Not only has the rage for new banks gone beyond all reasonable limits, but even the old banks have caught the fever and are rushing in to increase their capital and extend their responsibilities. Beyond the new speculative transactions, which interest the brokers more than the banks, we can not see that the business here has increased so very much. . . .
>
> We see gigantic companies organized to boil soap, make candles, forge nails, manufacture buttons, and do all sorts of things good enough in themselves but better carried on by means of small companies with small investments of capital. The absurdity of the schemes does not concern the speculator, however, and he subscribes for large blocks of stock, without a vintem [a coin of 20 reis, or half an English penny] at his back, just as eagerly as though large dividends are to be paid.

The agricultural loans themselves added liquidity to the Rio market. Through the factors, banks lent government monies to planters, who had difficulties meeting short-term obligations to the same bank. No new cash actually went to the planters; instead, the short-term debt was paid by means of a book-keeping entry and a mortgage was established in its place.[23] The planters were happy because they found themselves with long-term mortgages instead of immediate liabilities.[24] The lending bank's net result was to have cash and a mortgage in place of a past-due short-term advance. This cash could then be lent wherever the bank pleased, including in the cities, and for whatever purpose, including the purchase of bank stock.

Ouro Preto obtained the funds for the agricultural loans from the issue of 100,000 contos of imperial bonds. Since the 1878 Agricultural Congress, the planters had expected banknote issues backed by bonds that in practice would have monetized the public debt, forcing into circulation capital previously "immobilized" in bonds.[25] Ouro Preto's plan should not have been inflationary as it withdrew from circulation, through the placement of bonds, an amount equivalent to the government's contribution in the agricultural loans. In fact the prime minister's "national" loan raised 90,000 contos, as the bonds were sold at 90, carrying coupons of 4 percent in gold rather than milreis. Of this 90,000, 26,000 were actually disbursed to the banks on the planters' behalf, while 22,000 were employed to reduce the public short-term debt.[26]

Over half of the interest paid on the gold, or "national," loans went to recipients in London, which suggests that the majority of these obligations were
purchased by foreigners or by Brazilians with funds abroad.[27] Comparing the
sums provided planters and short-term note holders with the share of the "national" loan subscribed by domestic capitalists, the effect of this loan should
indeed have been neutral in terms of the money supply. By way of measuring
the loan's potential impact, the total external debt at this time stood at £30
million, or 270,000 contos, while the internal debt, including this loan,
reached 540,000 contos (equivalent to £60 million).[28] The circulating medium
consisted of 200,000 contos in government paper money and banknotes plus
another 90,000 contos in gold.

Taking advantage of the favorable economic environment with the milreis
over par, Ouro Preto renegotiated with the Rothschilds £20 million of the
£30 million external debt, substituting 4 percent obligations for those of 5
percent.[29] Although no additional gold came into the country as a result of
this loan, with good coffee earnings the amount of specie in circulation
reached £9 million, or almost a third of the total circulating medium.[30] Once
the milreis achieved its parity of 27 pence, debtors preferred to discharge their
obligations in sovereigns and other gold coins, as these became less valuable
than milreis paper money. The placement of this relatively great amount of
gold into circulation caused a major expansion of the circulating medium and
the money supply. Thus, with the milreis above parity, the expansionary effects of the classical gold standard operated on the Brazilian economy.

Ouro Preto firmly believed in the gold standard, and he hoped he could
institute that standard in Brazil. In September, he reached an agreement with
the count of Figueiredo, president of the Banco International, to convert this
institution into the Banco Nacional, a gold-based bank of issue. The new
privileged bank, which had important foreign shareholders, notably the
Banque de Paris et de Pays-Bas, began with a capital of 90,000 contos. As it
had the authorization to issue up to three times this amount (270,000 contos, a sum greater than all outstanding paper money and banknotes), contemporaries felt that the Banco Nacional would receive a monopoly on banknote
issue, making it the local equivalent of the Bank of England.[31] In regard to
this quasi monopoly on issuing banknotes, Ouro Preto proved more in keeping with the worldwide trend toward government-controlled circulation
than was João Alfredo, who advocated multiple banks of issue. The Banco
Nacional's shares traded at a large premium from the start.[32] Ouro Preto established a schedule over five years for this institution to replace the paper

money outstanding with its own banknotes convertible into gold. The government pledged to issue bonds with 4 percent interest in gold rather than milreis in return for treasury money redeemed, an excellent proposition for the bank.

This attempt to establish the gold standard constituted another form of aid to the planters. The planters had seen their purchasing power in local currency decline since the milreis started to appreciate during the mid-1880s. Indeed, Belisário had considered lowering the parity to 24 pence to prevent the milreis from rising beyond this point. With the milreis at 27 pence, Ouro Preto could keep the milreis from appreciating further by having a bank freely issue banknotes at this level. Ouro Preto, as well as many planters, feared an overly strong milreis much more than a weak one.

Although applauded at the time, the gold-backed banknote issue was doomed from the start. As soon as coffee prices fell, Brazil would probably face a large balance-of-payments deficit, meaning that gold would flow out of the country, and the bank would lack the specie to honor its notes. In fact, long before coffee prices collapsed, a political crisis provoked a flight of capital from Brazil, causing the Banco Nacional to cease issuing. This crisis began on November 15, 1889, with the proclamation of the Republic.

Despite the widespread support Ouro Preto received from the financiers and merchants of Rio's Rua do Ouvidor, he failed to meet the demands of the Paulista coffee planters.[33] Rather than promote federalism, as they wished, the prime minister rigged the August elections for the Chamber of Deputies in the traditional manner. His pet banks assisted in this effort by making loans to those who supported the government. The new Parliament, which had already begun preliminary meetings shortly before the military coup, seemed to offer nothing to the Paulistas. Although some of the Paraíba Valley planters participated in the Encilhamento speculations, they remained hostile to the government. The officer corps also expected no significant reforms from Ouro Preto. Republican civilians continued to play barracks politics, helping to provoke one military incident after another.[34] When Marshal Manoel Deodoro da Fonseca surrounded the ministry on November 15, no one in Rio rose to the defense of the government or the monarchy. The provincial presidents of Minas and Bahia tried to organize resistance in their capitals but gave up the next day when the emperor peacefully departed into exile.

Marshal Deodoro's provisional government rewarded the groups that had brought the Republic into being. The Paulistas immediately obtained the separation of church and state, and they achieved their federalist objectives through the new constitution.[35] The officer corps won a large salary raise as well as accelerated promotions and an increase in the size of the army.[36]

The republican government had just as much desire to placate the planters of the Paraíba Valley as the monarchy did, and consequently continued Ouro Preto's loans to agriculture.[37] The new administration also wanted the support of commercial interests and the small but growing industrial sector. Lacking a financial background, Marshal Deodoro gave complete freedom to his finance minister, Ruy Barbosa. Barbosa faced a situation more difficult than that of his predecessor because the military coup had unsettled the foreign bankers and merchants. Brazil's leading financiers, the Rothschilds, refused to consider loans until elections and the reestablishment of legitimate government. The Banque de Paris et de Pays-Bas refused to extend credit to its affiliate, the Banco Nacional.[38] Foreign merchants as well as wealthy Brazilians, fearing political and monetary instability, sent large amounts of gold out of the country.[39] In a month, the exchange rate fell from its par of 27 pence to 24 pence. The stock market bubble collapsed.[40]

Unlike his colleagues in the provisional government, the man in the finance ministry had turned republican only a few months before the coup. Ruy Barbosa (1849–1923) began his political career as a Liberal Party deputy from Bahia under the protection of Prime Minister Souza Dantas. During the Ouro Preto government, Barbosa achieved notoriety as editor of the *Diario de Notícias,* attacking the incumbent for abuses that turned out to be less significant than those he would later commit as minister of finance. As a member of the opposition, Barbosa courted the military and encouraged them to assume power by force. Twenty years later, Barbosa had his moment of glory in the "civilian campaign" when he lost the presidential elections to Marshal Hermes da Fonseca, Deodoro's nephew. Ironically, Barbosa accused Marshal Hermes of trying to establish a military dictatorship. In fact, Hermes came to power by the ballot box, whereas Barbosa's government ruled by force. In any case, Barbosa has become a hero in popular Brazilian historiography, perhaps for his part in the "civilian campaign." His actions as finance minister appear rather short of heroic.

With the Encilhamento bubble in apparent collapse, Ruy Barbosa attempted to continue Ouro Preto's gold-backed banknotes with several banks of issue. However, the Brazilian bankers perceived that with declining exchange, these convertible issues would be unprofitable.[41] On December 17, Barbosa ordered the banks to effect their issues within ninety days or forfeit their contracts. When this measure proved ineffective, Barbosa turned to

Francisco Mayrink.[42] This gentleman, president of the Banco de Crédito Real do Brasil and of the Banco Predial, had received generous favors from Ouro Preto, and in fact had been arrested immediately after the proclamation of the Republic. Quickly ingratiating himself with the new rulers, Mayrink convinced Barbosa to establish banks of issue backed by bonds.

The concept of bond-backed banks of issue made a good deal of sense. The *Rio News,* among others, called for this measure.[43] Contemporaries remembered Sousa Franco's promising start in 1857, and João Alfredo had provided for bond-backed issues as well as gold-backed ones in his law of November 24, 1888.[44] For the banks, these banknotes, exchangeable into paper money rather than gold, were protected from the effects of devaluation. When a bank used its capital to purchase bonds that served as the guarantee of its issue, it found that this capital earned interest twice: once on the bonds and once on the loans generated by the banknotes. For the economy as a whole, the effect of these notes would be somewhat inflationary, as funds that previously would have been absorbed by the public debt were freed to enter circulation. Kept within reasonable limits, however, these banknotes would stimulate economic activity without causing a major depreciation of the currency. The flight of gold following the establishment of the Republic had led to a contraction of the circulating medium. Bond-backed notes could neutralize this deflationary tendency and save the business community and the Republic from a severe embarrassment.

Unfortunately, the execution of Barbosa's credit policy left a good deal to be desired. As originally promulgated, Barbosa's bank reform of January 17, 1890, Law 165, gave Mayrink's bank the right to issue 200,000 contos, an amount equal to the sum of paper money and banknotes in circulation at this time. Mayrink received the exclusive right to issue banknotes in Rio de Janeiro, São Paulo, Minas Gerais, Paraná, and Santa Catarina. Two other regional banks of issue, based in Salvador in the Northeast and Porto Alegre in the South, obtained the privilege to issue 150,000 and 100,000 contos, respectively. This law stipulated that the three banks could issue banknotes backed by the internal public debt. To issue 200,000 contos, Mayrink would have to purchase between two fifths and two thirds of this debt (depending whether or not the domestic gold loans are included), a movement that would certainly upset the market. In a table that Franco presented utilizing data from the *Jornal do Commercio,* only 33,000 contos of this debt were traded from November of 1889 to December of 1890.[45] Apparently no one supervised this bank, which admitted to issuing 50,000 contos of banknotes by September of 1890.[46]

Clearly Mayrink issued notes without backing; he literally printed money. Within two weeks, public pressure forced Barbosa to decrease Mayrink's limit to 100,000; a month later, he had to reduce the privilege still further, to 50,000.[47] The banks of issue won by Law 165 permission to undertake real estate development and conduct commercial and industrial enterprises.[48] Although contemporary German banks notoriously engaged in the latter type of venture, Brazilians recognized the dangers of banks' distancing themselves from their essential commercial lending function. Evidently a conflict of interest could arise between a banker's needs as an investor in an industrial corporation and his responsibility to protect his depositor's money. Furthermore, the German banks had lost the power to issue banknotes in 1875.

The banks of issue received via article 3 of Law 165 a number of concessions and privileges: free land from the government; preference, under equal conditions, for obtaining contracts for the construction of all government railroads and public works projects; preference for contracts to develop mines and adjoining rivers and canals; preference for immigration contracts; and the right to expropriate lands necessary for the implementation of these concessions. In return for these privileges, the interest banks would earn on the government bonds deposited to guarantee the banknote issues would be reduced immediately, from 5 percent to 2 percent. Within the following two years the interest paid to the banks would fall to zero. Clearly this stipulation made the bankers less than eager to make their deposits, although of course they did take advantage of the concessions offered in article 3.

Barbosa reformed the 1882 corporation law on the same day that he regulated the banks of issue. Law 164 of January 17, 1890, followed closely the wording of Law 3150 of November 4, 1882. Once again, banks, insurance companies, food wholesalers, and foreign corporations needed prior government approval for limited-liability status. The separation of church and state meant that religious bodies no longer required official permission to incorporate. The crucial articles 2, 3, 7, and 13 continued similar to those in the 1882 act. As in 1882, 10 percent of the capital must be deposited with a bank or qualified individual and 100 percent must be subscribed before a company could begin operations. An investor must pay in 20 percent of his shares before he can trade them. Reserved liability survived, although in attenuated form. Under Barbosa's measure, the liability of a seller of shares terminated not in five years, as in 1882, but when the shareholders' meeting approved the annual accounts. Thus, current holders as well as recent sellers of capital could be required to pay in the full capital subscribed if the company went into bankruptcy.

As noted previously, in the case of the 1878 failure of the City of Glasgow Bank in the United Kingdom, investors had to pay in the balance of their subscribed capital. In Britain, this liability of the shareholders was regarded as a guarantee for depositors.[49] In Brazil, however, many shareholders refused to pay in their shares when called and instead "*roeram a corda*" (literally, "chewed off the leash").[50] Whereas in England the goods of stockholders who did not meet their obligations would be seized, in Brazil, stockholders could walk away with impunity.

A number of Barbosa's contemporaries considered his decree of January 17 to be a scandalous act of favoritism. In spite of an understanding within the provisional government that all measures would be discussed and voted prior to promulgation, Barbosa published the bank-reform act with the prior knowledge only of President Deodoro.[51] Three ministers—the war minister, General Benjamin Constant, Agriculture Minister Demetrio Ribeiro, and Justice Minister Campos Sales—threatened to resign. They felt that Mayrink had received enormous advantages without offering the state anything in return. If not properly overseen by the very minister who had just given him privileges, Mayrink could provoke a severe inflation and corresponding devaluation of the currency.[52] Justice Minister Campos Sales, opining that Ouro Preto's pet banks had won the election of August 31 for the Liberal Party, demanded a bank of issue for his state of São Paulo.[53] Barbosa conceded São Paulo its bank in exchange for the support of the Paulista republicans. Agriculture Minister Demetrio Ribeiro registered his protest against both the substance of the January 17 decree and the high-handed manner of its announcement. When President Deodoro and Finance Minister Barbosa refused to make changes, Ribeiro tendered his resignation, and left the government on the next day. Although Benjamin Constant also could not be convinced to accept the banking decree, he remained in the cabinet for the sake of stability.

After the decree of January 17, the Encilhamento bubble, which observers felt had burst with the fall of Ouro Preto, gained a second wind.[54] Mayrink's bank placed large numbers of its banknotes in circulation. Following the example of the United States greenbacks, which carried portraits of President Lincoln and his treasury secretary, Salmon P. Chase, Mayrink printed notes bearing the likeness of Finance Minister Barbosa. The banker also underwrote the shares of numerous ventures that turned out to be frauds. He subscribed shares with his own banknotes while the gullible public paid with real money. With the increased liquidity provided by the banks combined with excellent coffee sales abroad, the stock market and the economy resumed the spirit of euphoria that Ouro Preto had stimulated six months previously. With all this apparent prosperity, businessmen disregarded the warnings of the former agriculture minister Demetrio Ribeiro, the *Gazeta de Notícias,* and other critics. Like "voodoo economics" in our own day, unorthodox policies may be acclaimed for some time—until the inevitable results become obvious. As Demetrio Ribeiro predicted, the banks expanded the money supply rapidly, provoking an immediate decline in the exchange rate in spite of the boom in coffee and rubber exports. Brazilian banks lent against the security of their own stock, a practice roundly condemned by prudent bankers as well as by Souza Franco back in 1857. Mayrink's bank also employed the funds that should have gone into agricultural and commercial loans in financing speculators and underwriting frauds. Perhaps worst of all, against contemporary norms, the government did not verify the backing for the issues. In effect, Mayrink's bank created notes based on nothing.[55]

Pressured by the count of Figueiredo's Banco Nacional and the Banco do Brasil, now chaired by Barbosa's former protector, Manoel Pinto de Sousa Dantas, on March 8, 1890, the minister granted these banks the privilege of issuing banknotes up to twice the value of their capital, to a limit of 50,000 contos each. These issues were to be gold-backed but not convertible into gold—a contradiction in terms. A nonconvertible issue is, in effect, not gold-backed. This decree gave the banks the means to create 50,000 contos each— taken together, a sum of money equal to half of the circulating medium of the entire country. Adding Mayrink's 50,000 limit, ostensibly backed by bonds but in fact also unbacked, the three large banks could almost double the circulation at will. Nonconvertible issue, confined to notes of the Banco do Brasil, had been used to good effect as an emergency measure in 1857 and 1864. But Barbosa's policy may be considered irresponsible because he encouraged an expansion of unbacked, nonconvertible notes during a boom rather than during a crisis, the difficulties of November–January having passed, and because he intended his decree to be permanent rather than temporary.[56] The privileged banks should have delivered gold to the treasury equal to half their banknote issues. Then if the banks should relinquish their issue privileges, the treasury would have to return the gold, regardless of the exchange rate at that time. Under normal banking practice, gold-backed notes would have to be redeemed in specie, a situation that would maintain the exchange parity until the banks' gold supply ran out. Under Barbosa's arrangement, the banks did not redeem in gold, so the exchange rate continued to fall.

Barbosa's actions could hardly be described as disinterested. Immediately after his tenure as finance minister he held directorships in Mayrink's companies.[57] In August of 1890, Mayrink awarded Finance Minister Barbosa—still in office—a luxurious mansion. The *Rio News* commented: "When the minister of finance accepts a valuable residence from Mr. Mayrink and a few of his intimate associates, all of whom have just received exceptionally valuable privileges from the minister's hands, the outside world will experience no slight difficulty in making the transaction look quite innocent and straightforward. In this selfish, wicked world, men do not give away $100,000 to a public official through patriotism or personal admiration."[58]

Also in August 1890, Barbosa gave Mayrink's Banco dos Estados Unidos do Brasil the right to double its issue to 100,000 contos, which was equal treatment with the Banco do Brasil and the Banco Nacional; the additional 50,000 of banknotes became gold-backed but nonconvertible, an extraordinary privilege for a privately owned bank in time of peace and prosperity. A few weeks later, Barbosa extended the privilege of nonconvertible gold backing to four smaller banks: the bank in São Paulo, which Minister Campos Sales had championed; the Banco da Bahia; and the issue banks of Recife and Porto Alegre. By the end of September, according to the report of the ministry of finance, the circulating medium consisted of 170,000 contos of paper money and 120,000 contos of banknotes, as compared to 180,000 contos of paper money and only 30,000 contos of banknotes at the start of the year. Mayrink's bank accounted for 50,000 contos of banknotes officially but may in fact have printed a greater volume of paper. In nine months, the circulating medium expanded 40 percent, a huge change following two decades of stability.

Ruy Barbosa pursued the mutually exclusive goals of sustaining the milreis while keeping Mayrink and associates happy. By September, even Barbosa recognized that something had gone wrong. Back in May, he had terminated the aid to agriculture program after disbursing some 14,000 contos, as compared to Ouro Preto's 26,000.[59] That month, to maintain the exchange rate, which had fallen considerably, he began collecting part of the import tariff in gold. By October, as the exchange proceeded downward to 22 pence per milreis, he decided to levy the entire tariff in gold. At this time he issued a decree by which he sought to curb the worst abuses of the stock market. On October 13 he amended the January 17 law, which permitted companies to function after only 10 percent of their capital had been realized. The new decree required that 100 percent of a firm's shares must be subscribed and 30 percent must be paid in at the start of operations. The new decree stipulated that 40 percent of capital had to be realized before shares could be traded. Directors wishing to commence operations and wishing to start negotiating shares required a declaration from an existing bank that these funds in fact had been deposited. The *Rio News* and the *Gazeta de Notícias,* which had criticized the government continuously since the January 17 decree, praised Barbosa for this attempt at reform. On October 20, the *Rio News* noted:

> If the minister would now compel the payment of the whole subscribed capital before a company can apply for a loan, if he will forbid the declaration of dividends on imaginary profits, the watering of stock, fantastic valuations, and all that, he will do still more toward bringing us once more into a normal state of commercial and industrial development. And then let us have the officers and directors of these companies made individually and collectively responsible to the fullest extent of their fortunes and personal liability, for all that may happen through deception, fraud, and maladministration, and then we shall have some security against absolute bankruptcy and national discredit.

This article lists some of the abuses practiced by the organizers of the Encilhamento. As the use of jargon such as "watering of stock" indicates, Brazilian scoundrels had European and American examples of fraud from which to copy. Typically, several respected bankers, merchants, lawyers, and politicians would draft a statute of a company to undertake a specified activity such as banking, railways, or textiles with a capital in excess both of the real needs of the company as well as the possibilities of the future shareholders. If possible, the founders would obtain a government concession, such as a land grant, to give some intrinsic value to the venture. The concession could be contributed to the company in lieu of the organizing group's share of the capital. The promoters next would sell shares to the public. Generally only 10 or 20 percent of this capital would be paid in at the outset, the remainder falling due at some indefinite time in the future. In this fashion, a company could be fully subscribed with a 10,000 conto ($5 million at the prevailing exchange) nominal capital and only 1,000 contos in cash.

The directors of the new enterprise would open their accounts by paying 5 percent of the total issue, or 500 contos, to the founding group that included these directors. But 5 percent of the nominal capital amounts to no less than 50 percent of the capital actually paid in. To create a favorable climate for calling up the remaining 90 percent of the subscribed capital, the directors would then use the other 500 contos of cash to purchase the company's stock on the exchange. This would cause the enterprise's share price to rise, thus attracting further investor interest. As soon as possible, the directors called up another 10 percent, or 1,000 contos, that they now needed to pay their own salaries and to begin operations. The young venture required a headquarters, which the organizing group sold to the company for considerably more than its real value. After a semester in business, the directors declared a sizable dividend to further increase the value of their shares. As the company had no profits, the dividend also came out of the capital paid in. After disbursing directors' salaries and dividends, purchasing its own stock, and acquiring overpriced assets from its founders, the concern would again find itself without cash. The directors would call up the next 10 percent of the subscribed capital and so on until the investors caught on to the fraud. By this time, of course, the founders had disposed of their shares at a notable advantage.

The viscount of Taunay's celebrated novel, *O Encilhamento,* written just after the events described, provides a fair glimpse of life during the bubble. The work shows in detail the means that "pillars of society" used to defraud their clients and the public at large. The only major inaccuracy we have detected in this account is that Taunay, a monarchist, blames the Republic for the Encilhamento. In fact, the scenes of frenzied buying and stock manipulation could also apply to the period of the viscount of Ouro Preto. (We highly recommend this classic to those interested in feeling the spirit of the Encilhamento.)

Barbosa's attempt to control the bubble through the decree of October 13 met with slight success. The pace of new incorporations slowed during the two months following this measure, but banks began to issue fraudulent receipts for the 40 percent of a new company's capital that had to be placed on deposit before trading in the shares could commence. Having discovered this expedient, the leaders of the Encilhamento established new records for incorporation in the period beginning in January 1891.[60]

A few weeks after the October 13 decree, recognizing that the banks did not possess the gold upon which their banknote issues were based, Ruy Barbosa proposed to allow them to use the government gold loans as backing.[61] As the government by this time encountered mounting difficulties in meeting its gold obligations, these bonds traded at around 70 percent of face value.[62] Accordingly, allowing banks to issue up to double the face value of these securities was highly inflationary. Also in November, under increasing criticism from the press and others, the leaders of the Encilhamento staged a massive demonstration in favor of Ruy Barbosa and national industry with the participation of their workers. Taunay noted in *O Encilhamento* that the laborers appeared ashamed at their role in this farce, as other observers hostile to the bubble agreed.[63]

While they organized their rally, Mayrink and his associates continued to found new, largely fictitious enterprises. Ironically, in view of events a decade later, Mayrink at this time underwrote the initial public offering of the future finance minister Joaquim Murtinho's Banco do Rio e Matto Grosso.[64] The banks controlled by Mayrink and Figueiredo continued to issue banknotes to be lent to their own and their associates' ventures. Both institutions now had large portfolios of unrealizable loans to fraudulent or incompetent companies. In an attempt to eliminate competition and form a single, almost monopolistic, bank of issue, these two gentlemen proposed an alliance. Barbosa readily agreed, abandoning his ideal of a plurality of banks of issue. On December 7, the minister recognized the merger of the Banco dos Estados Unidos do Brasil and the Banco Nacional to form the Banco da República, confirming the new institution in the privileges of its predecessor banks as well as the issue rights of the Banco do Brasil, which had sold this facility to Mayrink and his partners. The Banco da República was authorized to issue 50,000 contos backed by bonds that the old Banco dos Estados Unidos do Brasil already had placed in circulation. In addition, the minister gave the Banco da República the privilege of issuing not twice but three times the 150,000 contos of remaining capital (50,000 each of the Banco dos Estados Unidos do Brasil, the Banco Nacional, and the Banco do Brasil) in "gold-backed" notes that would be convertible only if the milreis remained above par, 27 pence, for a whole year—an extremely remote possibility by this time, since the Brazilian currency had fallen to 20 pence. As under the original January 17 decree, Mayrink, president of the new entity, found himself with the ability to double the circulating medium at his will.

Ruy Barbosa was not the only one who granted extraordinary privileges to the speculators. His colleague in the ministry of agriculture, Francisco Glicério, distinguished himself by his energetic alienation of public lands and concession of valuable immigration contracts. The *Jornal do Commercio,* the *Gazeta de Notícias,* and the *Rio News* continually denounced these practices.[65] Glicério's grants were perverse, in that they obliged immigrants to purchase land from the privileged companies, which provided no services, rather than acquire farms cheaply from the government, as in the United States. The large planters benefited indirectly from these privileges, as immigrants had to work longer for wages in order to accumulate capital to purchase land. Speculators also profited from the generous bounties they obtained from the government for transporting the unfortunate immigrants.

In tandem with financial turmoil, Brazil experienced considerable political instability as well. Early in 1890, the army increased in size, a move that was accompanied by mass promotions and almost equally massive retirements within the officer corps. For several months, the government refused to set a date for elections to the Constituent Assembly, leaving everyone guessing as to the length of the military dictatorship. Finally, in February, the war minister, General Benjamin Constant, declared his support for early elections, and President Deodoro da Fonseca set the date for September 15.[66] In April, Constant left the War Ministry for the newly created Education Ministry. Contemporaries viewed this transfer as a means of removing this idealistic professor in the military academy from his powerful position, although he fervently believed that only education could transform Brazil.[67] Unfortunately, Deodoro closed this ministry nine months later, following Constant's illness, resignation, and death. No other serious reforms of Brazil's woefully backward educational system were even attempted during the remainder of the military government. His replacement in the War Ministry, Marshal Floriano Peixoto, assumed Benjamin Constant's role as leader of the younger reforming pro-industry officers. Floriano Peixoto maintained a low profile in 1890 while consolidating his power. The government meanwhile repeatedly faced charges of authoritarianism from the press.[68]

Elections to the Constituent Assembly did take place on September 15, 1890, and it convened on November 15, the first anniversary of the proclamation of the Republic. The peaceful election of this body as well as the prospects for a democratically elected executive brought a feeling of relief to the elite. Combined with Ruy Barbosa's October attempt to rein in the Encilhamento, the election of the Constituent Assembly led to a slight recovery of the milreis. Foreign observers also expressed their satisfaction with a return to legitimate government, although they practically ceased investing, because of the unstable monetary situation.[69] The suspension of operations of a leading British merchant bank, Barings, the month the assembly convened also discouraged potential foreign investors, while serving as a warning to Brazilian speculators. Barings's embarrassment occurred when it underwrote a large issue of Argentine bonds that could not be sold because of a financial crisis in that country. Although an important study views the withdrawal of foreign capital as a cause of Ruy Barbosa's difficulties, we understand the repatriation of resources to be largely a consequence of the uncertain political and economic conjuncture.[70] This repatriation of foreign investments was accompanied by Brazilian capital flight, reinforcing the argument that internal problems, not external shocks, caused Brazil's crisis.[71] Incidentally, the decade of the 1890s witnessed a series of financial crises characterized by sharp outward movements of capital. The United States and Australia both suffered such events in 1893. Italy abandoned the gold standard in 1894. The fact that crises occurred in several areas in different years tends also to support the idea that these panics originated from excesses in the capital-importing countries rather than from a shortage of surplus funds in the United Kingdom and the other capital exporters.

Rio de Janeiro and São Paulo states did not experience the Encilhamento the same way. The Paulista Republican Party (PRP) elected one of its members, Prudente de Morais, as president of the Constituent Assembly and confirmed itself as the leading political force in the country. The Paulistas won the right to retain a greater share of taxes collected in the state of São Paulo, including the export tariff, control of public lands, and election of the governor. The planters of São Paulo had already received from the provisional government the separation of church and state, as well as an immigration policy favorable to them. The first year of the Republic witnessed continued real economic growth in the state of São Paulo. The harvesting of the profitable third post-abolition crop, now largely done with immigrant labor, provided an additional burst of liquidity to the Paulista economy. Many planters expelled freedmen from their plantations to make way for "hard-working" Europeans. Coffee planting and railroad construction proceeded briskly. Apparently additional funds reached the countryside, facilitating at least partial cash compensation for workers. A number of banks and industrial companies established themselves during São Paulo's Encilhamento. A stock exchange was organized in 1890, closed before the end of the bubble the following year, and reopened definitively in 1895.[72] São Paulo's banks showed restraint compared to the ones in Rio de Janeiro, generally limiting themselves to short-term commercial transactions. Whereas the Rio-based Encilhamento rested on fraud, the growth of the São Paulo economy, paced by real coffee revenues, proved much more durable. As late as 1888, Rio collected more export tariffs than São Paulo did, but three years later, São Paulo generated twice the revenues of Rio.[73] Supported by this material strength, the PRP now wanted to elect Prudente de Morais as the first constitutional president of Brazil. Unfortunately, the Generalíssimo, Deodoro da Fonseca, and several of his brother officers had acquired a taste for political power. The Generalíssimo also wished to be elected president.

All the ministers of the provisional government, except for General Benjamin Constant, had won seats in the Constituent Assembly. Shortly after the

installation of this body, several members of the government, including Campos Sales of the PRP, almost resigned in protest against Deodoro's refusal to
punish military officers for their part in sacking a monarchist journal.[74] In
consequence of this confrontation, the ministers rarely met with the Marshal
Deodoro. Absorbed with the constitutional proceedings, they appear not to
have taken much note of Barbosa's December 7 merger decree. Barbosa found
himself in an increasingly uncomfortable position, having lost the confidence
of Deodoro without ingratiating himself with the PRP. On January 20, 1891,
as the constitution passed its first reading, the provisional government resigned, and most of its members entered the PRP camp.

Deodoro formed a new government composed largely of former monarchists from the Northeast, led by the baron of Lucena. During the monarchy
in 1886, Deodoro had served as the chief military officer in the province of
Rio Grande do Sul under Lucena as provincial president. This friendship continued into the Republic, to which Lucena adhered immediately. Allied to the
sugar planters of Pernambuco, Lucena had neither republicanism nor indus-
trialism in his past.

A month after Lucena took office, on February 24, the constitution became
law and the following day the Constituent Assembly elected a president of the
Republic for a term to run through November 15, 1894. Deodoro narrowly defeated Prudente by threatening to use military force and bribery—the funds,
courtesy of the leaders of the Encilhamento—to convince undecided congressmen.[75] Marshal Floriano Peixoto, with the support of both presidential
candidates, became vice president. The PRP entered into frank and increasingly hostile opposition to Deodoro and Lucena. The exchange rate, which
had recovered in response to good news in September and October, declined
steadily as a consequence of a series of unfavorable developments: the Baring
suspension in November, Barbosa's inflationary bank reform of December,
Lucena's appointment in January, and the threatened coup of February.

Price rises accompanied the declining exchange rate, provoking the lower
and middle classes of Rio, who participated in frequent antigovernment
demonstrations. One of the leaders of the labor movement, Augusto Vinhaes,
a federal deputy and naval lieutenant, proclaimed in the *Gazeta de Notícias:*[76]

> Hunger is making itself felt among the poor classes of this capital. . . .
>
> One should not take advantage of the good nature and patience of this people.
> They do not constitute an ethnographic exception; they are patient, it is true, but
> this patience may wear itself out, and, as the illustrious congressmen know, what
> has brought peoples to revolution has generally been hunger. . . .

Salaries in fact have increased but this increase has been arithmetical while the prices of necessities have grown geometrically.

It is said that the companies and industries in general have developed significantly in a short period of time. I agree; but no one can guarantee that these industrial companies and banks shall continue to prosper in the same degree in the years to come if, that which is now fictitious does not transform itself, thanks to prudent and energetic measures of the authorities, into brilliant truths.

Violence in the streets of the capital became much more common than it had been under the monarchy.[77] So many Portuguese immigrants returned home to Portugal during the Encilhamento that the cessation of their remittances helped provoke a major financial crisis in that country.[78] Thus Lucena began his administration in a difficult political situation. Like Ouro Preto and Ruy Barbosa, he tried to sustain a weak, illegitimate government through the granting of financial favors.

The British ambassador described Lucena as a "plunderer" at the beginning of his rule; Lucena went on to fulfill the diplomat's expectations.[79] He stepped into Barbosa's friendship with Mayrink and provided this banker and his associates with further concessions. Lucena also befriended the count of Leopoldina, whom he assisted in the formation of a fraudulent railway empire. Given the possibilities for enrichment, it is significant that Lucena chose the Ministry of Agriculture for himself rather than the Finance Ministry, which he entrusted to Tristão de Alencar Araripe. The latter, in an attempt to curb some of the abuses of the Encilhamento, sought to impose a 2 percent tax on dividends in excess of 12 percent per annum and a 3 percent tax on futures transactions with stock. The power of the leaders of the Encilhamento forced Araripe to withdraw his measures immediately.[80] Speculators could continue to pay high dividends out of the paid-in capital of a new enterprise as well as sell futures on shares they did not own.

The press had been highly critical of Lucena's predecessor at the agriculture ministry, Francisco Glicério. Around the time of Lucena's accession, the *Jornal do Commercio* amassed documentation demonstrating Glicério's misdeeds. Summarizing the attacks of the *Jornal do Commercio*, the *Rio News* charged:[81]

It is idle to urge that the provisional government is not responsible because it was a dictatorship; it might do many things on that warrant, but certainly not the wholesale confiscation of the public domain, nor the wholesale dissipation of the national revenue in jobberies such as immigration contracts, banking privileges and guaranteed private enterprises. However deeply we may regret it, and however

much we might wish to conceal the facts, it cannot be gainsaid that this first year of
so-called republican rule has been the most corrupt and inefficient this country has
ever known. . . . Some weeks ago [December 19] the *Jornal* published a list of railway grants by this same government aggregating over 20,000 kilometers with an
aggregate guarantee capital (30,000$ per kilometer) of 600,000,000$ and a nominal interest charge of 36,000,000$ a year. That in itself was enough to unsettle all
confidence in such a government and should at once have led to a strict investiga-
tion. . . . According to the figures collected by the *Jornal* no less than 210 land
grants have been made which cover an area of 30,691,000 hectares, or 76,727,500
acres or 119,887 square miles—an area nearly equal to that of Great Britain and Ireland (121,115 square miles). . . . If now we add to this the 330 immigration contracts
which the minister celebrated, which involves the introduction of no less than
1,415,750 families, say 7,078,750 individuals, we have a climax of administrative
jobbery and recklessness for which it will be difficult to find a parallel. The "assisted
passages" which the government undertakes to pay, average about 50$ per capita. If
we add to this the premiums offered, the maintenance and transportation of immigrants after arrival, and the other purely government expenses connected with the
work, the average will reach 100$ for every man, woman, and child brought into
the country.

Although Lucena rescinded some government concessions, he made many
of his own.[82] During the second quarter of 1891, prices on the stock exchange
began to fall. Subscribers who had paid in between 10 and 40 percent of the
value of shares refused now to come forth with the remainder, forfeiting their
original investment. The banks, especially the Banco da República, continued
to place banknotes in circulation to support the stock market. Having lent
heavily on the security of stock and other uncertain collateral, most banks had
already become insolvent.

The consequences of the irresponsible issue of banknotes did not take long
to make themselves felt. During the third quarter of 1891, the milreis collapsed
to 14 pence, just two thirds of its value when Lucena assumed power some six
months before. Industrialists who had ordered machines abroad did not have
sufficient milreis to pay for them when they arrived. Industries dependent
upon raw materials also suffered. The citizens of Rio, a large part of their budgets spent on imported items, found their cost of living doubling while their
salaries barely increased. Strikes and riots became ever more common.[83] As
coffee prices remained high, internal factors, especially excessive banknote issues, must be blamed for the decline of the Brazilian currency, as contemporaries perceived.[84] Banknote issue had increased the demand for imports as

well as the supply of milreis competing to buy scarce exchange. Many commercial and industrial firms simply closed their doors.

Lucena fought the symptoms of this crisis by printing more banknotes. In September of 1891, now Finance Minister Lucena proposed to Congress that it authorize the Banco da República to issue up to 600,000 contos again without real backing. This bank already had almost 300,000 contos of notes outstanding, an increase in the circulating medium of some 50 percent during Lucena's tenure. Upset with the decline of the milreis, disgusted with the revelations of swindles on the stock market, and unhappy with President Deodoro's autocratic behavior, the opposition, led by the PRP, refused this increase. On November 3, in part due to this refusal, Deodoro and Lucena executed the so-called "stock exchange coup," closing Congress and establishing a dictatorship.

Deodoro's arbitrary government lasted but twenty days. Since the marshal's questionable victory in the indirect presidential elections the previous February, the PRP had tenaciously opposed him in Congress. The Paulistas considered Deodoro to be a centralizer, and they blamed him for the inflation that had accompanied the Encilhamento. Immediately after the coup, the PRP began to organize a counterattack in collaboration with the navy and with dissident army officers, including the vice president, Marshal Floriano Peixoto. Meanwhile, the middle and lower classes of Rio de Janeiro, seeing their living standards decline rapidly, took to the streets. A railroad strike first isolated the capital by land.[85] A few days later, the navy severed the president's sea communications with the rest of the country, and part of the local army garrison rebelled. Even the country's financial agents in London abandoned Lucena. The Rothschilds refused to extend further credits to the Banco da República, in spite of the finance minister's offering government deposits with these bankers as security. Rothschild regretted to inform the minister that these funds were necessary for upcoming interest payments on bonds.[86] An article in *The Times* of London attests to the importance of the Rothschild denial of credit as the Banco da República was the last remaining seller of sterling in the Brazilian market at the close the bubble.[87] On November 23, 1891, Marshal Deodoro, Brazil's first president, resigned, and Vice President Floriano Peixoto took his place. The Encilhamento was over. Floriano promised a return to orthodox financial policies.

In the two and a half years' duration of the Encilhamento the exchange rate fell from 27 pence to below 12 pence. Accustomed to a milreis that fluctuated in a narrow band between 20 and 27 pence, most people were caught by surprise by this abrupt movement. Investors in government bonds saw their assets lose half of their value. Importers received machinery and raw materials for which they now needed more than twice as many milreis as when these goods had been ordered. City dwellers, major consumers of imported goods, saw their standards of living decline dramatically. Many members of the middle classes lost significant sums of money when they purchased fraudulent stock from bankers they considered the pillars of society. With this financial mismanagement came arbitrary government, demonstrations, coup, and countercoup. The new political institutions lost credibility because of their association with the Encilhamento.

To balance these negative consequences, defenders of Ruy Barbosa cite one positive feature of this period: the growth of industry.[88] This aspect of the Encilhamento must be considered in comparison with the years immediately preceding and succeeding it. Beginning around 1880, various industries arose to satisfy the consumption demands of salaried workers and a small middle class, especially in Rio de Janeiro and São Paulo. Textiles led this first burst of industrialization, followed by leather goods, food processing, and building materials.[89] Light industry expanded continuously under the conservative financial system of the empire as well as under the conservative republican governments that succeeded the Encilhamento. Neither Ouro Preto nor Ruy Barbosa nor Lucena had been associated with industrial interests before they took office, and none of these three were ever considered industrial leaders.[90] The finance minister most identified with industry, Serzedello Correia (1892–1893), advocated a return to orthodox finances. He insisted that industrialists needed stable currency in order to calculate their costs. To the extent that industry developed between 1889 and 1891, this growth was a byproduct of subsidized immigration and easy-money laws enacted to win support from planters and merchants. Without question, the demand from immigrants and from the recipients of the bank loans stimulated industry.

Equity capital most decidedly did not go into industrial ventures as a result of the expansion of the stock exchange during the Encilhamento. Industrials were almost insignificant among the traded companies, compared to banks and railroads.[91]

Ouro Preto, Ruy Barbosa, and Lucena, like their pre-Encilhamento predecessors, used tariffs principally to generate revenues. Ruy Barbosa in fact discarded the draft of a moderately protectionist tariff that Ouro Preto prepared just prior to his fall.[92] Only after the collapse of the bubble did a government arise that consciously employed tariffs to defend one key industry, textiles,

Table 3   Machinery Imports from the United
Kingdom, by Five-Year Period (in £ Millions)

1870–74	1.1
1875–79	1.0
1880–84	2.2
1885–89	2.3
1890–94	3.9
1895–99	2.3
1900–04	1.9
1905–09	4.1

Source: Richard Graham, *Britain and the Onset of Modernization in Brazil,* Cambridge, 1972, 331–332.

from foreign competition, without regard to the revenue consequences of this
measure. Significantly, all of the finance ministers of the Encilhamento period
as well as all those who served Floriano Peixoto supported the Blaine-
Mendonça Treaty with the United States, which allowed Brazilian sugar duty-
free U.S. entry in exchange for conceding U.S. industrial exports a similar
privilege in Brazil. Between the interests of the sugar planters and those of the
industrialists, Brazilian politicians knew which to choose. The Blaine-
Mendonça Treaty, negotiated under Ouro Preto and Ruy Barbosa, was promulgated in February 1891 by Lucena and continued until the United States
abrogated it in 1894.[93] Although criticized by the Brazilian press at the outset,
this agreement proved highly beneficial to the local sugar interests, which as a
consequence enjoyed a great increase in their sales to the United States.[94] In
fact, Brazilian industrialists did not suffer because American exports to Brazil
failed to expand.[95]

Imports of machinery from the United Kingdom provide one indirect in-
dication of industrial growth. Table 3 shows that machinery purchases increased significantly during the 1880s and rose again during the five years that
included the Encilhamento and the Floriano Peixoto administration, and declined in the years of retrenchment that followed. Significantly, machinery
never made up more than one tenth of total imports from the United Kingdom during this period. As the Encilhamento took place during the prosperous phase of the coffee cycle, industrial imports might have been nearly as
great without easy money.

The Encilhamento ministers did not hold industrialization as a priority or
even as a major objective. Easy money favored industry in the short run but
probably proved neutral or worse in its medium-term effects.

The Encilhamento bubble began when Ouro Preto, seeing the monarchy in danger, tried to buy the support of discontented planters by making large sums of money available to them. He employed two devices: agricultural loans and convertible banknotes. As a financial expert, Ouro Preto knew that convertible banknotes would only function in Brazil during the periods of high coffee prices that permitted the milreis to rise to parity.[96] He must have hoped that prices would remain strong long enough for him to win the planters back to the monarchy. The agricultural loans constituted an even more dubious expedient. In fact, he provided banks with interest-free loans so they could make subsidized advances to the planters. Most of these credits were to be repaid in five years, by which time either the monarchy would have fallen or regained its past vigor. Probably most of these loans would in practice not be discharged, causing a significant transfer of resources from the population in general to the landowners. In that interest was paid, funds that should have been used for public purposes went to benefit privileged banks; after all, the government made interest-free loans to these institutions.

The second phase of the Encilhamento proved to be even more irresponsible than the first. Ouro Preto at least insisted upon the convertibility of banknotes, and funded the agricultural loans with sales of bonds. His successor permitted banks to create money at will with no backing. Ruy Barbosa tried to continue Ouro Preto's gold-backed banknotes but failed as the exchange rate fell below parity. Bankers refused, understandably, to issue notes with a purchasing power of 24 pence that could be redeemed in gold worth 27 pence.[97] The republican finance minister experimented briefly with bond-backed banknotes. When the banks did not deliver the bonds that should have served as security for these issues, Barbosa allowed the issue of nonconvertible gold-backed notes. In other words, he permitted banks to print money. By the time he left office, the banks had issued notes equal to over half the circulating medium at his accession. This immense sum represented a transfer of resources from the Brazilian public to the privileged banks and their preferred clients.

The last phase of the Encilhamento, presided over by the baron of Lucena, lasted from January to November of 1891. Lucena, like Ouro Preto and Ruy Barbosa, found himself in a weak political situation. He served a president who had just been elected by threatening a coup; the most powerful political group, the PRP, opposed him from the outset, and the populace of Rio proved hostile. The baron continued expanding the supply of unbacked banknotes to maintain a stock market known to be artificially inflated and a banking system reputed to be bust. When he could no longer obtain Congress's approval for further issues, he tried to use force and was overthrown by the Paulistas and their military allies. Maintaining shaky governments through easy money did not work.

That three successive and very different governments maintained the Encilhamento leads one to wonder whether the bubble was unavoidable. The following circumstances prevailed throughout the life of the Encilhamento. Abolition required an increase of the money supply in order to pay at least a portion of the agricultural workers' salaries.[98] The peaceful enactment of abolition and high coffee prices combined to create an optimistic feeling within most agricultural and business circles. Abolition and immigration together greatly broadened the market for light industrial goods. Ouro Preto, Ruy Barbosa, and Lucena all had to do something to placate the planters and to win supporters for their fragile governments.

Given this conjuncture, all three ministers granted valuable privileges to the agricultural elite, including interest-free loans, subsidized immigration, and public lands. All three effectively increased the liquidity of the economy by permitting banks of issue. Under these conditions, some upward movement of the stock exchange appears to have been inevitable as banks and industry expanded in response to the burgeoning market of immigrants, freedmen, and city residents. The three governments erred in the quantity of additional liquidity, in the lack of supervision of both issuing banks and the stock exchange, and in their unprincipled distribution of public lands and contracts. As contemporaries quickly saw, these mistakes could have been avoided. Post-Encilhamento governments reined in the growth of liquidity, limited government concessions, and regulated the stock market. The damages caused by the Encilhamento in fact made it possible for financial conservatives to regain control of the state in relatively short order. It is hard to escape the conclusion that the worst abuses of the bubble could have been avoided, using economic instruments available at this time, had the country enjoyed more responsible leadership.

Chapter 7 Orthodox Reaction:
The Unsuccessful Phases

Vice President Floriano Peixoto's accession to the presidency in November 1891 marked the beginning of an orthodox reaction in monetary policy (throughout his presidency Floriano insisted on using the title of vice president). Issuing banknotes ceased; the exchange rate leveled off after two years of decline; and the stock market was allowed to fall to its real value. However, Brazil suffered for another ten years before true monetary stability could be achieved. Floriano missed the opportunity to contain the money supply because he became involved in an expensive and probably unnecessary civil war. An external shock, the fall of coffee prices, prevented Floriano's civilian successor, Prudente de Morais Barros (1894–1898), from resolving the financial crisis. Only the recovery of the coffee market combined with tough fiscal and monetary policies allowed Prudente's successor, Campos Sales (1898–1902), finally to return the country to a stable monetary situation, a full decade after the Encilhamento.

Floriano Peixoto took office as president on November 23, 1891, with three broad objectives: industrialization, financial stabilization, and, above all, the consolidation of the Republic. The "consolidation

of the Republic," which appeared to cynics to be nothing more than the sub-
stitution of Deodoro's followers by those of Floriano, compromised the vice
president's financial plans.

All the governors, save Lauro Sodré of Pará, collaborated with Deodoro's
"stock market coup." Even before the countercoup in the capital, a group of
officers and civilians forced the governor of Rio Grande do Sul, Julio de Castilhos, to step down. Floriano, soon to be known as the "iron marshal," was determined to remove all the remaining governors even though the Constitution
did not provide him with the necessary legal instruments. By March of 1892,
military-inspired rebellions had deposed every one of the collaborators. While
this was taking place, Deodoro's partisans and the leaders of the Encilhamento
did not remain passive. They enjoyed ample financial resources. Ruy Barbosa
continued in the Senate, while Francisco Glicério, a federal deputy, played a
prominent role in that chamber, along with the bankers Mayrink, the count of
Figueiredo, and Matta Machado, among others. Within a month of Deodoro's
fall, the Encilhamento leadership instigated a minor military revolt, and within
two months a major one. In this second incident, rebels seized the two forts
controlling the entrance to Rio de Janeiro's harbor. When the senior officers
who organized the uprising failed to appear, the forts surrendered. Busy depos-
ing the governors, Floriano chose to hush things up while placing a close watch
on the real leaders.[1] The following week, at the end of January, Mayrink resigned the presidency of the Banco da República and Ruy Barbosa announced
his withdrawal from the Senate,[2] but Mayrink and the count of Figueiredo
continued to have representatives on the board of the bank, and those who opposed Floriano prepared for another trial of strength.[3]

In February, rumors again circulated that the speculators would overthrow
Floriano.[4] The nation seemed headed for chaos as several of the incumbent
governors resisted being deposed by force of arms while bandit groups dominated the countryside.[5] The railroad workers went out on strike. Not surpris-
ingly, the price of the external debt collapsed to 60 percent of face value. (This
debt had been placed during the last years of the empire at 90 percent or
higher.) The Paulista Republican Party (PRP) had hoped that Floriano would
respect the Constitution, which required the vice president to hold elections if
the president did not complete at least half his term.[6] Like many other soldiers in similar circumstances, Floriano decided to give his own interpretation
to the Constitution, asserting that its transitory dispositions stipulated that
the first president and vice president would serve until November 15, 1894.
The PRP acquiesced to this bending of the law in return for control of São

Paulo and the appointment of one of their number, Francisco de Paula Rodrigues Alves, as finance minister. An experienced politician, Rodrigues Alves had governed the province of São Paulo under the empire and continued his career under the new regime as though nothing had changed.

Rodrigues Alves represented the coffee planters of his state. Greatly increased production—thanks to good soil, new railroads, and immigrant labor—combined with high international coffee prices and a weak milreis had led this group to experience some excellent years and it had become relatively well capitalized. Under these circumstances, most of the Paulistas accepted a reduction in the supply of credit in exchange for a stable financial system with less inflation. In essence, the PRP now wished to return to the pre-abolition status quo in terms of finance. By this time, the finance minister no longer had to concern himself with appeasing the coffee planters of the Paraíba Valley because this sector had declined significantly in force. Many planters had turned to sharecropping exhausted plants or had abandoned coffee in favor of cattle ranching, and the landowners of Rio de Janeiro, though not totally without influence, lacked the overwhelming importance they had enjoyed a scant two years previously.[7] Also, by this time the Paulistas considered the transformation to free labor complete. Europeans had largely replaced the former slaves, who often were forced off the plantations. Apparently sufficient liquidity reached plantations so that salaried labor functioned.

Rodrigues Alves questioned the efficacy of the agricultural credits, declaring that virtually all the banknotes and rural loans had remained in the city of Rio.[8] His adversaries argued that the increased liquidity in the capital benefited the planters. Merchants and factors with greater access to bank credit could provide more financing to the planters. As the planters' credits and debits resided in the factors' books in Rio, the planters could have received a good volume of resources without the banknotes' ever leaving the city. Looking back on the Encilhamento from the vantage point of 1903, the industrial leader, colonel, and former industry minister Serzedello Correia observed that a significant portion of the expansion of coffee during the early 1890s in São Paulo could be attributed to easy money.[9]

These observations to the contrary notwithstanding, on the evidence one must agree with Rodrigues Alves that rural credit did not help much. In spite of extensive credits, the Paraíba Valley coffee plantations collapsed. Western São Paulo Province, with less financial help, had expanded "miraculously," given excellent land, high world coffee prices (from 1886 to 1895), and mass immigration from Italy. Subsidized government loans and excessive banknote

issues, rather than saving the planters, had increased corruption, created inflation, and left the country disillusioned with its new republican leaders. Neither
the bursting of the bubble nor the political instability of Floriano's government diminished the optimism of the São Paulo planters. Two months after
Floriano assumed power, the Paulista railroad purchased the Rio Claro–São
Paulo Railway Company from British interests for a financed purchase price
equal to 15 percent of Brazil's annual exports. The Paulista railroad's shareholders were largely local planters, led by none other than the former agricultural minister Antonio Prado.[10]

Rodrigues Alves set about increasing revenues, decreasing expenses, and talk-
ing to foreign bankers, who had not made any loans to Brazil since the proclamation of the Republic. He sought to get a law passed prohibiting the Banco da
República and others from increasing their banknote issues. Although this measure passed the Chamber of Deputies, Mayrink still enjoyed sufficient influence
in the Senate to prevent a quorum from examining this bill prior to adjournment.[11] Thus even after the failed coup of January, the Banco da República retained its privilege of printing money. By this time, the institution apparently
felt it prudent, at least temporarily, to refrain from exercising this power.

Rodrigues Alves could not allow the insolvent Banco da República to fail because of the distress this event would cause. Invoking the banking law of 1885
to its full extent, he extended a credit of 25,000 contos each to the Banco da
República and the Banco do Brasil. During the month of February alone, the
former institution availed itself of 6,500 contos of this facility.[12] Rodrigues
Alves administered this rediscount honestly, insisting that the borrowing banks
deliver government bonds as security. The Banco da República could furnish
these bonds, whereas many of the smaller institutions had nothing to offer
other than the uncollectable loans and worthless stock in their portfolios.[13]

The origin of the Banco da República's government bonds has its own
story. This bank should have deposited gold at the treasury to secure its issues.
Ruy Barbosa allowed it to substitute government bonds for gold. Lucena went
one step further, permitting Mayrink's bank to deliver depreciated railroad
bonds in return for the release of the government obligations.[14] Furthermore,
Lucena had lent a total of £2.5 million in gold to the Banco da República, the
Banco de Crédito Popular, and the Banco Emissor de Pernambuco instead of
demanding the delivery of gold to secure their issues. The *Gazeta de Notícias*
of March 16, 1892, the *Rio News* of March 8, 1892, and the *Jornal de Commercio* of January 13, 1892, all concluded that these banks in fact had not
deposited the legally required gold and government bonds that should have

provided security for their issues. The banks had printed money.[15] Since these banknotes had no other backing, Rodrigues Alves perceived that, one way or another, the government would have to assume control over and responsibility for these pieces of paper, which had become the national currency.

The Banco da Bahia's experience was different from that of the Banco da República. The former, one of the two surviving banks established during Souza Franco's administration, had received João Alfredo's contract to extend agricultural loans in the North. In January 1890, Ruy Barbosa passed over the Banco da Bahia, giving the issue privileges in Bahia to a smaller institution. In September, he reversed himself and granted the Banco da Bahia the privilege to issue up to twice the value of its gold deposited at the treasury up to 10,000 contos. Apparently the Banco da Bahia actually deposited 2,000 contos in gold coins at the treasury and issued 4,000 contos in banknotes. By early 1892, as the Brazilian currency had fallen to less than half its parity against sterling, this privilege had lost its value. In May, this bank delivered 4,000 contos in paper money to the treasury and received its gold coins back.[16] Even by observing the law, the Banco da Bahia made a substantial profit from its issue privileges.

Mayrink and the other leaders of the Encilhamento resolved not to surrender control over their "printing press" without a fight. The count of Leopoldina, who had milked the railroad empire he created under Lucena, faced bankruptcy if additional government assistance did not come forth. He financed a conspiracy to overthrow Floriano that included several prominent politicians, financiers, and military officers.[17] On April 6, thirteen general officers of the army and the navy published a declaration calling for Floriano to hold elections for president as the Constitution demanded. Floriano, supported by the vast majority of the officer corps, counterattacked by retiring the offending generals. A few days later, some five hundred protesters marched on the presidential palace; they were counting on the participation of the 7th Infantry Battalion, which supposedly had been suborned by Leopoldina. This battalion never arrived, and the vice president faced the demonstrators from behind a position that was reinforced by three infantry battalions as well as artillery and cavalry units. With this superiority, he easily disbursed the invaders and arrested their leaders, including Leopoldina and Matta Machado. Some forty conspirators—congressmen, bankers, journalists, and military officers—were banished to unhealthy villages on the upper Amazon. Leopoldina went into bankruptcy, and the road to financial reform seemed to be cleared.

Rodrigues Alves continued his struggle to balance the budget and gain control over the currency. The collapse of the Encilhamento bubble had left the country in a liquidity crisis. Even genuine and relatively conservative commercial and industrial companies found themselves in tight circumstances. Importers who had ordered raw materials and machinery from abroad lacked the resources to pay for goods whose milreis price had more than doubled. Some politicians and politically active military officers wanted to defend national industry. Reflecting the PRP's priority, stabilizing public finances, Rodrigues Alves opposed the campaign for "aid to industry," which became highly vocal at this time. On April 12, 1892, the *Rio News* blamed the speculators of the Encilhamento for this attempt to reopen the floodgates of the treasury and praised Rodrigues Alves for his efforts to avoid further subsidies: "Never perhaps in the history of Brazil has it been so necessary to have a man in charge of the treasury who was not afraid to do nothing." As a spokesman for foreign interests, the word of the editor of the *Rio News* cannot of course be accepted as gospel; on the other hand, in view of the excesses of the Encilhamento, his skepticism regarding the motives of those advocating government subsidies may be justified.

In April, Rodrigues Alves appointed a committee to make recommendations regarding "aid to industry."[18] The chairman of the committee was Paulino de Sousa, spokesman of the Paraíba Valley planters, who had been the principal beneficiaries of Ouro Preto's "aid to agriculture." One of the committee members, viscount Guahy, president of the Banco da República, afforded the leaders of the Encilhamento representation on the committee. It seemed that Floriano now had his erstwhile enemies as allies. The remaining three members of the committee were two journalists, including the editor of the *Jornal do Commercio,* and the former senator Souza Dantas, now president of the Banco do Brasil. The committee published its findings in May. It proposed that the government issue bonds and pass the resources obtained by the sale of these instruments through the banks to industry.[19] The bankers of the Encilhamento would now have additional funds at their disposal. They could lend them not necessarily to the most efficient enterprises but rather to those in which they already had interests.

In May Congress also convened. Floriano presented the legislators with an ambitious list of objectives: tax reform, aid to industry, banking reform, railroad development, educational expansion, eradication of yellow fever in the capital, and the establishment of a new capital in the central highlands.[20] Unfortunately, he also made a decision at this time that would undermine all his positive efforts. Following the deposition of the governors and the retirement of the thirteen generals, politics throughout most of the country had returned to normal, but in Rio Grande do Sul the situation became chaotic. In June, Floriano restored Julio de Castilhos to the governorship of that state. Although Castilhos had supported Deodoro's coup and had been overthrown in consequence, he had been a republican long before the fall of the monarchy. In Floriano's opinion, no other republican figure had the force to maintain order in this state, where former imperial politicians still enjoyed great popularity.[21] Hundreds of Castilhos's enemies, both sympathizers of the Republic and those of the fallen regime, found it expedient to retire to Uruguay when he returned to power. From June on, Floriano's patronage of Castilhos became a major national political issue.

Floriano Peixoto, the "iron marshal," had placed Rodrigues Alves in the finance ministry because he needed support from the PRP while he consolidated his power. An economic nationalist, Floriano wanted to do something to help "legitimate" industries that had been organized before and during the bubble and found themselves in financial difficulties. When Rodrigues Alves demonstrated his opposition to providing the banks with additional resources, Floriano made Serzedello Correia, the minister of industry, transport, and public works, his chief financial adviser. Shortly thereafter, in August, Rodrigues Alves resigned and Serzedello Correia took over as finance minister.[22] A military intellectual and a leading spokesman for the industrialists, Serzedello led the debates in favor of "aid to industry" that dominated the congressional session from May to November of 1892.[23]

In June, in line with the recommendation of the committee that Rodrigues Alves had appointed, a follower of Floriano's proposed to the congress a 100,000-conto bond issue to save industries. The Rothschilds telegraphed their apprehension that such a measure would reignite inflation.[24] Other critics of the bond issue also charged that it would cause prices to rise. Recalling the painful experiences of the Encilhamento, these foes of aid to industry argued that subsidies and privileges were in and of themselves unfair, corrupting, and inefficient.[25] National industry absorbed resources that could be used more profitably elsewhere, while the tariffs imposed to protect industry hit the poor consumer hard. One opponent of aid to industry even suggested that import tariffs be partially replaced by an income tax, the burden of which fell more heavily on the rich, whereas tariffs oppressed the poor.[26]

Ironically, though both Rodrigues Alves and the Rothschilds voiced their unhappiness with aid to industry in June, it was in June that the finance minister and the bankers brought Brazil back to the international debt market for the first time since the establishment of the Republic. Together they issued £1 million of nine-, twelve-, and fifteen-month government obligations. Potential lenders could not be convinced to advance new long-term credits to Brazil, as the Republic's outstanding debt traded at a substantial discount.[27]

A leading spokesman for national industry, Senator Amaro Cavalcanti, from Rio Grande do Norte, denounced the Paulista industrialists who combated the aid measure in order to destroy competition from other states.[28] Cavalcanti told his colleagues to ignore the Rothschilds' warning; the English bankers concerned themselves only with the strength of the milreis and Brazil's balance of payments, not with the Republic's progress, he charged. The senator observed that, as a general rule, tariffs by themselves should be sufficient to protect industry and constituted a more nearly impartial and honest mechanism than subsidies. After giving examples of effective use of both tariffs and subsidies in other countries, he concluded that the errors of the previous governments made the exceptional recourse to subsidies necessary on this occasion.[29]

During the congressional debate, a consensus developed in favor of the unification of banknote issues under government control, But there was strong disagreement as to how this end should be accomplished. Leopoldo de Bulhões, a future finance minister (1902–1906), and other financial conservatives wanted the government to become responsible for all banknotes issued in return for assuming the gold and bonds that backed these issues. As a second step, he hoped the government would actually reduce the quantity of paper money in circulation.[30] Although they wanted paper money to replace private banknotes, Bulhões and his group desired the banks to remain private. He denounced what he termed "state socialism," fearing that a government-owned bank would crowd out private initiative.[31] Other congressmen wanted the Banco da República nationalized without compensation to the shareholders, while deputies influenced by the bank sought compensation for its stockholders for the loss of the privilege of issue. Leite e Oiticica, a prominent critic of the aid campaign, observed that the capital of the Banco da República was 130,000 contos, whereas its debt to the government stood at 150,000, and therefore the state owed nothing to the shareholders.[32] In fact, with its unrealizable portfolio, the bank probably had a negative net worth at this time. Leite e Oiticica noted that the bank had borrowed gold from the government at 27 pence per milreis but had the effrontery to want this gold computed at a rate of 19 pence per milreis for purposes of compensation for the backing taken over by the government—which in any case proved greatly insufficient.[33]

In essence the congressional session of 1892 evolved into a three-cornered contest among the leaders of the Encilhamento, Floriano, and the PRP. The latter wished for the government to assume responsibility for banknotes and opposed both compensation for the bank shareholders and loans to industry. Floriano, Serzedello, and the young officers who followed them wanted government control, if not outright ownership, of the banks of issue and aid to industry. The men of the Encilhamento, represented in the Chamber of Deputies by Francisco Glicério and Matta Machado, who returned with the other banished conspirators in August, advocated aid to industry and struggled to retain control over their banks as well as to receive consideration for their lost issue rights. Echoing the thinking of Rodrigues Alves in particular, the PRP in general, and the foreign business community, the *Rio News* (November 1, 1892) feared the bankers of the Encilhamento would have their way as Congress approached the date of adjournment:

> It has been largely the fault of the government that these banks have been allowed to issue currency without making the deposit in the treasury required by law, and it has also been in fault for permitting them to speculate in all sorts of tricky companies, to the serious risk and eventual loss of their capital and other assets. Banks of issue perform a public service of great importance, and the older nations of the world have found it necessary to hold them to a very strict account for all their operations, to prohibit stock speculations, and, in the United States, they are even prohibited from investments in real estate. Here no restrictions whatever were enforced. Some of the "wildcat" banks have devoted their whole attention to buying and selling their own shares. All of them became promoters of bubble companies, nearly all of them permitted their directors to draw out their capital for speculative purposes, all of them advanced cash on speculative and insecure paper, and all of them have lost heavily. And of all these speculating and badly-managed banks, the Banco da República was one of the worst. It was the duty of the government to remedy the evil as far as it could, and to protect the public from loss so far as the currency emitted by these banks is concerned. Instead of this, the Chamber of Deputies, many of whose members are shareholders in this bank, now votes that the government shall not assume a liability fully incurred, and that the Banco da República shall not only continue its own emission but shall have the emission of all the other issue banks!

Deadlocked between friends and foes of industry and proponents and opponents of the bank, Congress adjourned without passing either reform. Among the few significant acts to arise from the 1892 session was a law, backed by the Paulista planters, authorizing the immigration of Chinese and Japanese workers. Shortly thereafter, immigration from Asia, particularly from Japan, became significant. The budget that emerged from this session included substantial allocations for immigration. In one aspect, this budget represented a victory for the pro-industry forces in that it provided a high level of protection to one leading industry, textiles. For the first time, tariffs had their revenue purpose subordinated to that of stimulating industry.[34]

The Chamber of Deputies passed Floriano's banking reform bill, but the Senate rejected it. As soon as the legislators left town, however, the iron marshal decreed this measure on his own authority. On December 17, 1892, he merged the Banco da República and the Banco do Brasil to found the Banco da República do Brasil. The successor institution assumed the responsibility for the banknotes of the predecessor banks, and the decree prohibited all banks from issuing more banknotes. The federal government appointed three of the new institution's nine directors, including the president and the vice president. Sousa Dantas, president of the Banco do Brasil, became the first chief executive of the merged bank and the Paulista (PRP) politician Francisco Rangel Pestana, whom Serzedello had previously attempted to make president of the Banco da República, became vice president. These gentlemen both enjoyed reputations for financial orthodoxy. As the president had a veto over all bank activities, the federal government assumed virtual control over the Banco da República do Brasil. From this point it was but a small step— one that was taken in 1896—for the government itself to assume responsibility for all banknotes and return to a system of treasury money only. The experiment with private banknotes had ended. The merger decree proved to be a compromise. On the one hand, the Encilhamento bankers kept their shares in the bank that the government now committed itself to support. On the other hand, they lost control over this institution and received no compensation for the loss of their issue rights.

As part of the merger decree, Floriano and Serzedello gave the Banco da República do Brasil permission to issue 100,000 contos' worth of 5 percent twenty-year bonds guaranteed by the government and acceptable as legal tender for the payment of taxes. The bank could lend these bonds to industrial companies, which in turn could pass these instruments to their creditors. The original creditors avoided holding these bonds as an investment, selling them at a discount to individuals with tax liabilities. Since he employed bonds rather than paper money, Floriano considered this measure to be free of inflationary effects. The bonds did help some industries, although the bank of course lent these instruments to firms in which it had an interest.[35] Financial conservatives condemned this measure as well as Floriano's arbitrary, unconstitutional means of enacting it.[36]

Criticism from financial conservatives notwithstanding, Serzedello believed in the gold standard. He felt that industrialists could not plan their costs in periods of fluctuating exchange rates.[37] Although a declining exchange rate tended to give local industry a price advantage, he felt that there were many factories dependent upon imported raw materials which would see their supplies increase unpredictably in price. Furthermore, the manner in which Congress assessed the tariffs made the effective duty lower when the milreis fell. Serzedello praised Ouro Preto, hoping he could eventually return to the imperial minister's system of convertible banknotes.[38]

After a little over a year of sound management under Rodrigues Alves and Serzedello, business confidence started to recover, in spite of the political instability.[39] The exchange rate, which had declined continuously during the Encilhamento and had dipped below 12 pence by the fall of Deodoro, leveled off under these two ministers and began a modest recovery early in 1893, reaching 13 pence. Brazilian external debt also regained a portion of its value. In São Paulo, new industries continued to appear. A contemporary observer might have been cautiously optimistic about the country's immediate future.

At this juncture, Serzedello achieved a major success. Winning the confidence of the Rothschilds, he negotiated the placement of the Oeste de Minas Railroad loan, the only bond underwritten during the military government.[40] The bankers had been quite sensitive to both political and economic uncertainties. Under the empire, the Rothschilds had undertaken large issues for Belisario, João Alfredo, and Ouro Preto, but they closed their doors to the Republic until it held elections. In November 1890, when the Constituent Assembly convened, the house of Barings suspended as the result of underwriting Argentine bonds that became unsellable due to the crisis in that country. The Rothschilds had taken a leading role, together with the Bank of England, in rescuing Barings. Under these circumstances, Brazil's bankers had no desire to accept the risk of Deodoro's government, which appeared to be just as financially irresponsible as Juarez Celman's had been in Argentina. Immediately after assuming office, Rodrigues Alves had resumed the dialogue with the bankers. They, however, remained skeptical of Brazil's administration, fearing that further inflation would result from the "aid to industry" campaign in the middle of 1892. Only after Serzedello's bank merger decree did the bankers adopt a favorable view of the Republic.[41] The Rothschilds' customers, on the other hand, took a less sanguine view of Brazil's credit, taking only £2.5 million of the £3.7 million Oeste de Minas bond. To sell the remainder of this issue, the bankers convinced Serzedello to use the treasury's funds to purchase existing bonds at a discount, thereby raising the market value of all Brazilian debt.[42] While the British bankers attempted this manipulation, Serzedello entered into conflict with Floriano.

Although Floriano and Serzedello agreed on the need for protecting local industry and returning the state to stable finances, they clashed on Floriano's Rio Grande do Sul policy. In February of 1893, eight months after Floriano restored Julio de Castilhos to the governorship, hundreds of Castilhos's enemies returned from exile in Uruguay to invade Rio Grande do Sul. Floriano, rather than mediate, continued to give Castilhos his full support, the latter's violence notwithstanding. Serzedello felt he could neither balance the budget nor attract foreign capital while disbursing the current level of military expenses. Relations between Floriano and Serzedello deteriorated. Serzedello resigned from the government at the end of April, in protest against war spending he considered futile, inflationary, and illegal.

At this point, Floriano had to choose between monetary stability, the stimulation of industry, and the desire to keep Castilhos in power in Rio Grande do Sul. Rather than seek a compromise in the South, the iron marshal allowed Serzedello and Navy Minister Custodio de Melo to leave his cabinet. The latter organized a strike among the admirals, several of whom refused to serve as Floriano's navy minister, but Floriano carried on with the war despite the hostility of the navy and only unenthusiastic support from the PRP. This struggle proved to be among the most violent in Brazilian history—hundreds of prisoners had their throats slit.[43] The new finance minister, Felisbello Freire, attempted no financial innovations. He sustained the federal troops with the printing press. The milreis, which had stabilized under Rodrigues Alves and Serzedello Correia, resumed its downward movement. Standards of living in the capital declined further while violence and unrest increased.[44]

In September, five months after Serzedello's resignation, the fleet joined the rebellion in the South and almost succeeded in overthrowing Floriano. For half a year the citizens of Rio de Janeiro had hostile warships shelling them from within Guanabara Bay. Until foreign navies intervened, the port also suffered under blockade. Despite his extreme nationalist rhetoric, from the first day of the revolt, Floriano pleaded repeatedly with the foreign ambassadors to protect the city and break the blockade.[45] Although rumor had it that the United States backed the Republic and that the United Kingdom supported the "monarchist" rebels, both powers remained relatively passive. As the legal incumbent, Floriano received the assistance of some American businessmen who helped organize a mercenary fleet to come to his aid.[46] Floriano's appeals to the Rothschilds for a new bond could not be attended as the market remained obviously closed to a country suffering from financial stress and civil war. The English bankers recommended that Floriano seek the good offices of the United States president to mediate the conflict.[47]

While a rebel army advanced toward São Paulo from the south, Floriano's partisans staged a witch hunt in the capital, imprisoning political enemies and physically assaulting Portuguese merchants whom the populace blamed for the inflation.[48] Many members of the elite, like Mayrink, fled to Minas Gerais, which did not impose martial law, or abandoned the country entirely, as Ruy Barbosa wisely did.[49] Street crime increased in the capital. Economic and political problems acted together to give the impression that Brazilian society might fall apart.

With the naval revolt, Floriano's dependence upon the PRP for men and money became nearly absolute. Although he had hoped to have Governor Lauro Sodre of Pará or Julio de Castilhos elected as his successor, Floriano had to accept the PRP leader, Prudente de Morais, in order to obtain the necessary resources to overcome the rebels. With the rebel fleet still anchored in Guanabara Bay, Prudente de Morais won the presidential elections, held on March 1, 1894.

Shortly thereafter the government's fortunes improved dramatically. The mercenary fleet recruited in the United States made its way toward Guanabara Bay. The naval rebels, unable to obtain supplies, scuttled their vessels in Rio's harbor on March 13 while their overextended comrades in Paraná found themselves forced to withdraw south. By May, Floriano's armies regained control of Paraná and Santa Catarina, executing a considerable number of prisoners, including civilians, in the process. The war in Rio Grande do Sul degenerated into a guerrilla struggle in August, when the chief rebel general fell in combat. Now that Floriano was less dependent on the PRP, many wondered whether he would relinquish power to the Paulista oligarchs, whom he loathed.[50] Governor Bernardino de Campos of São Paulo maintained his armed forces in readiness. On November 15, 1894, with the fighting in Rio Grande do Sul not yet over, Prudente de Morais became the first civilian president of Brazil. Floriano, disgusted with the prospect of returning power to the planters, did not bother to attend the inauguration.

Prudente de Morais suffered at the hands of contemporary critics.[51] From the military regime he inherited a bankrupt Republic, discredited by the swindles of the Encilhamento and by the violence of Floriano's partisans in the South. The war continued in Rio Grande do Sul, while the army, dissatisfied with the "restoration of the oligarchy," still looked to Floriano for leadership. Prudente also found a hostile Congress dominated by Francisco Glicério, the "constable of the Republic." Even Prudente's vice president, Manoel Vitorino Pereira, conspired incessantly against him. On top of all these problems, the coffee trees planted in São Paulo after abolition began to bear fruit, causing a sharp drop in the international market and a decline in government revenue.

Prudente recalled Rodrigues Alves to the Ministry of Finance. Together they set out to balance the budget. By July of 1895, Prudente had negotiated the end of the war in the South, which had been the principal cause of inflation during Floriano's administration. The iron marshal's death in June 1895 had eliminated a major obstacle to peace. As the budget figures demonstrate, Prudente managed to lower military expenses with each year he held office.[52] Peace helped restore confidence, and that year, Prudente issued his only external bond, underwritten, as usual, by the Rothschilds. Given the unstable situation of the world credit market at this time—Italy had just abandoned the gold standard and J. P. Morgan and the Rothschilds had barely saved the United States from the same fate—the negotiation of this bond represented a major accomplishment.

Rodrigues Alves also managed to place a large internal bond issue. In spite of their losses on the internal debt instruments purchased before the Encilhamento, investors had regained confidence in the government's ability to sustain the milreis. Prudente perceived that the Brazilian currency needed to achieve stability in order to attract additional foreign capital as well as to stimulate Brazilians to invest.[53] To this end he pursued a policy of deflation. In November 1894, when he became president, the total money in circulation (government and Banco da República notes) was 708,000 contos, or over three times the amount on November 15, 1889, when the Republic was established; in 1894 the milreis stood at 10 pence, as compared to 27 pence in 1889. Two years later, the circulation fell to 678,000.[54]

Despite general agreement that the exchange rate must not fall further, many influential voices opposed Prudente's policy of revaluation. J. P. Wileman's *Brazilian Exchange: The Study of an Inconvertible Currency*, published in 1896, argued persuasively against against any attempt to regain parity. Wileman suggested adopting the current rate of 10 pence and maintaining this level principally by reducing government expenditures.[55] He criticized Prudente's incineration of the circulating medium. Wileman believed there existed two separate factors influencing exchange: the balance of payments and the size of the circulating medium. He recognized that, absent changes in the former variable, a reduction in the circulating medium must raise the value of the milreis. He feared that such a rise would harm the lower classes and give an unfair benefit to wealthy creditors.[56] He noted further that both a declining and a rising exchange rate harmed the poor, the former because wages lagged far behind devaluation and the latter because revaluation immediately created labor friction, wage reductions, and redundancies.[57] Wileman's reasoning bears an uncanny resemblance to that of Poincaré, who chose a new, lower parity when he returned France to the gold standard after World War I. History proved kinder to Poincaré than to his British contemporary, Chancellor of the Exchequer Winston Churchill, who went back on the gold standard at the old parity, thereby creating an immediate and persistent unemployment problem.

Supporters of revaluation argued that individuals who lent to public and private borrowers had seen the real value of their financial assets shrink to little over a third since the establishment of the Republic. They felt that fairness required that the currency return to parity. Wileman disagreed, noting that loans and government bonds had changed hands during the course of the devaluation, so revaluation would not favor the original creditors. Furthermore, many bonds had been issued, especially during wartime, at large discounts, meaning that revaluation would deliver a windfall to current holders.[58] Finally he observed that internal prices had appreciated by less than the devaluation, so creditors had not lost as much as they appeared to have lost.[59] Later Wileman contradicted himself on this point, noting that prices tend to catch up with devaluation in the longer run.[60] Wileman blamed the devaluation largely on two finance ministers, the monarchist viscount of Ouro Preto and the republican Ruy Barbosa.[61]

Wileman wanted Prudente to hold the circulating medium constant. He advocated augmenting government revenue through the reimposition of a gold tariff, which had lapsed after Ruy Barbosa left office, as well as the institution of an excise tax. He also wished to reduce expenses to eliminate the federal deficit. He opposed foreign borrowings, arguing that Brazil, unlike more responsible debtors, tended to waste resources.[62] Wileman called the president's attention to Brazil's balance of payments, which he felt had moved abruptly into the red in 1890, not as a result of trade but rather of increased immigrants' remittances, Brazilians' expenses abroad, and capital flight.[63] As Wileman wrote, the trade balance, which had been the most positive portion of the balance of payments, slipped into deficit. For the remainder of Prudente's administration, the balance of payments replaced the growth of the circulating medium as the cause of the Brazilian currency's decline.

Unfortunately for Prudente, the coffee trees planted during the years of euphoria following the abolition of slavery started to produce just as he took office. Surplus production led to the fall of coffee prices, and trade declined along with customs revenues, the principal source of government income. Planters fired workers, so immigration slowed, diminishing the growth of the national market for light industrial goods. Commercial and industrial firms experienced liquidity problems, while political and military unrest continued. For the first time since the Rothschilds became the country's principal bankers, the Brazilian government lacked the exchange to service its debt. Prudente had less room to maneuver in attempting to respond to this crisis than did his pre-Encilhamento predecessors. The Encilhamento, followed by Floriano's wartime inflation, made the issue of banknotes, as in 1857 and 1864, quite unacceptable to the elite. The banking system, with its unrealizable Encilhamento loans, lacked the means to expand credit. Furthermore, the government could not direct funds toward capital projects (except through unpalatable inflationary devices) because it saw its income decreasing in proportion to the contraction of foreign trade.

In spite of the unfavorable international conjuncture, Prudente decided to avoid increasing the liquidity of the economy. Remembering the problems caused by the inflationary Encilhamento, he followed a course of monetary stability if not outright deflation. Only during his final two years in office, when coffee prices declined further, did Prudente find himself forced to reverse his original policies and print a modest sum of paper money.

During the 1896 session of Congress, Prudente and Finance Minister Rodrigues Alves had as their principal objectives the reduction of expenditures and the assumption of the Banco da República's banknotes. Congress, still influenced by the bank, refused to enact the law whereby the government would assume the outstanding banknotes. With the decline of coffee prices, Prudente found his constituents, the Paulista coffee planters, demanding advances from the government.[64] Resisting tenaciously, the president and his minister avoided compromising their program with these new handouts, and as the need for immigrants had declined, they succeeded in removing the immigration subsidies from the 1897 budget. By October 1896, Rodrigues Alves found it necessary to deny rumors of a general moratorium in the Brazilian market. He wrote the Rothschilds:

In consequence of the fall in Coffee and the withdrawal of Coin, there has been re-striction in business in the market. Some Coffee brokers, having made large ad-vances to the growers, have felt difficulties through the fall in prices and payments by some merchants have been suspended in very small number, whilst in other cases arrangements have been made with the creditors. Interested parties sought to gain time by the proposal of a plan of moratorium which was presented to the Chamber by a deputy of the Opposition. The idea of moratorium repelled by the market and in the press. The situation of the market is calm, all operating with pru-dence. Congress does not seek to increase taxes, thinks of reducing public expenses and studies to find means to strengthen credit without increase in the circulation. Sensible improvement in the collection of the revenue.

Commercial Association has resolved in General Meeting today to telegraph to the *Times* replying to its telegram with regard to the state of this market, repelling energetically the idea of moratorium. The Association has assured *Times* that, in spite of the delicate commercial situation, there is no justification for the exagger-ated news sent to London.[65]

In November 1896, the month that indebted American farmers almost placed William Jennings Bryan in the White House, Prudente had to take a leave of absence for health reasons. Vice President Manoel Vitorino Pereira appointed his own cabinet and enjoyed the support of Francisco Glicério as well as the vocal so-called "Jacobin" groups that had originally followed Flori-ano. Observers doubted that Prudente would return to power.

Vice President Vitorino immediately decreed that the government would assume responsibility for the Banco da República's banknotes, so that these instruments now became paper money. This bank continued heavily in debt to the government, so Vitorino correctly felt that compensation for the issue privilege was not in order. He set out consciously to "liquidate the Encil-hamento," although this objective did not prevent him from maintaining friendly relations with Mayrink.[66] To reduce expenses, he also tried unsuccess-fully to rent out the government railroads. The bankrupt Leopoldina Railway was conveyed to British interests in 1897.

During Vitorino's administration, his ally, Julio de Castilhos, resumed the per-secution of his federalist enemies in Rio Grande do Sul.[67] The Jacobins also be-came more active in attacking monarchist newspapers. When the Jacobins and the military heard that a force of five hundred regulars had been defeated by a group of "bandits" in the backlands of Bahia, they erupted in noisy demonstra-tions. Vitorino sent Moreira Cesar, a colonel who was notorious for slaughtering prisoners of war during the naval revolt, with 1,500 men to destroy the supposed "monarchists" in a remote town of Bahia state called Canudos.

As Moreira Cesar approached Canudos in the beginning of March, Prudente returned to Rio from his convalescence in Teresopolis. He resumed the presidency just in time to receive the shocking news of the colonel's defeat and death at the hands of followers of a messianic local leader named Antonio Conselheiro ("the counselor"). The officers and Jacobins exploded, wrecking the offices of monarchist newspapers, assassinating a prominent monarchist, and running uncontrolled throughout the capital. Although he and the former minister Campos Sales had been the only two men to sit in the imperial Chamber of Deputies as republicans, Prudente was insulted by the Jacobins and found himself forced to prove his republicanism. He made the most of this situation, which in fact gave him an opportunity to win control of the army and the Congress. First, he dispatched a force of four thousand men, led by another prominent follower of Floriano, General Arthur Oscar, to besiege Canudos. Then he prepared his own political offensive.

During his years in office, Prudente had patiently negotiated alliances with the governors of the larger states. Supported by their patronage and influence over congressmen, the president wrested control of Congress from Francisco Glicério in June 1897. Meanwhile he gradually won over the army, which had been openly hostile to him at the beginning of his term. Prudente improved salaries and, as a counterweight to Floriano's followers, restored the officers who had followed Deodoro.[68] The president overcame two revolts at the military academy, in 1895 and 1897, expelling unruly cadets. Finally he utilized the "war" of Canudos to give the officers a chance to defend the Republic against the supposed monarchist insurrection. Canudos fell in October 1897, when the soldiers of "civilization" slit the throats of the last captured "barbarians." The following month, as Prudente received the victorious troops at the Rio docks, an assassin attempted to kill him but instead stabbed his minister of war to death. Vice President Manuel Vitorino, Francisco Glicério, and other opposition leaders were implicated in the plot and fled the capital in the face of a violent popular reaction. From this point, Prudente consolidated the power of the presidency relative to civilian politicians as well as the military. In 1898 he secured the succession to his office of a fellow PRP leader, Manoel Ferraz de Campos Sales. The political situation regained the stability that had been lost with the fall of João Alfredo and the onset of the Encilhamento.

The Canudos campaign, deploying four thousand soldiers, or one fifth of the total of twenty thousand in the army, placed a considerable additional burden on public finances. By the end of the conflict, and with coffee prices continuing downward, the milreis reached 7 pence, its lowest level prior to World War I. Prudente's political success was in contrast to his financial failure.

Although the governments of Floriano Peixoto and Prudente de Morais were very different, in terms of public finance these two presidencies together form a period of unsuccessful orthodox reaction to the abuses of the Encilhamento. Also, both governments had blood on their hands. The massacre of thousands at Canudos, including virtually all male prisoners, occurred during Prudente's tenure, though it is certain that the president would not have ordered such a brutal response had he not been under extreme pressure. Floriano proved much more eager to use the sword. The spilt blood underlines another characteristic common to both Floriano's and Prudente's administrations: political instability. Floriano assumed power in reaction to Deodoro's coup d'état. He faced violent uprisings in early 1892 in addition to the fighting engendered by the deposition of the governors and by the naval revolt. Armed clashes in Rio Grande do Sul took place continuously from February 1893 to July 1895 and sporadically both before and after then. Prudente, in addition to the conflicts in Rio Grande do Sul and Canudos, had to overcome two revolts of the military academy. After Prudente subdued the military, the Jacobins, and Glicério's opposition, the Republic became a more peaceful affair.[69] Judged in political terms, Prudente's government must be considered a success. When he handed over the office of the presidency to his successor, Brazil was in a state of tranquillity.

Despite energetic actions and good intentions, both Floriano and Prudente failed to regain the financial stability lost during the Encilhamento. They both left office with a greater circulating medium and a lower exchange rate than when they came to power. Floriano made a promising beginning in his first year in office. The great expenses of the war in Rio Grande do Sul and the naval revolt made it impossible for him to eliminate the public deficit. A secondary cause for his inability to control inflation was his desire to protect national industry. He issued 100,000 contos' worth of bonds that practically functioned as paper money and that increased the circulating medium by over 12 percent. Prudente resolved the civil war but had to contend with an economic crisis caused by the fall of coffee prices. His successor, Campos Sales, had more luck with the international situation he encountered. This third orthodox government would finally restore financial stability.

Chapter 8 Stabilization

Between Campos Sales's election and his inauguration, it became clear that Brazil lacked the foreign exchange to pay the interest on its external debt. Since the Rothschilds had become the country's principal bankers in 1855, Brazil had never missed an interest payment.[1] In November 1897, with the bond market closed to Brazil and secondary prices highly depressed, Prudente negotiated a £2 million two-year credit from the Rothschilds, largely to meet immediate interest requirements.[2] As the Spanish-American War began, Prudente's government took advantage of the opportunity to sell off a completed warship and another one still under construction. The Rothschilds conducted an auction between the two combatants, which was decided in favor of the United States.[3] Under the advice of his industry minister, Joaquim Murtinho, Prudente struggled unsuccessfully to purchase and lease out the unprofitable railroad lines that enjoyed 7 percent government guarantees. The failure of the railroad reorganization early in 1898 convinced the Brazilian authorities that they would be unable to discharge their international obligations. Intent on maintaining the Republic's credit standing, Prudente and the president-elect agreed that the latter would go to London to negotiate an emergency advance from the Rothschilds. The resulting Funding Loan provided the Brazilian government with sufficient resources so that it would not have to remit exchange for interest payments for the next three years. Believing in the quality of Brazil's leaders, the Rothschilds acquiesced to forgo payments of principal for thirteen years. To obtain this loan, Campos Sales mortgaged the Rio customs house and promised not to issue any additional paper money. The pledge to mortgage the customs house proved to be a mere formality while Prudente was already engaged in the struggle to reduce the paper money in circulation. Although criticized at the time for caving in to the foreign bankers and not sustaining the national honor, Campos Sales succeeded in maintaining the ties between his country and the international community.[4] Investment funds flowed into Brazil throughout the three-year interest moratorium, demonstrating widespread confidence in Brazil's economic management.[5]

The immediate cause of this moratorium was the debacle of the coffee market, but the depletion of gold reserves during the Encilhamento and during Floriano's conflict in the South had left Brazil more vulnerable to adverse coffee prices than the country might have been otherwise. Had the Encilhamento not drawn in imports, and had Floriano not purchased large amounts of armaments abroad, the country would have had more gold on hand when the price of coffee fell in 1895.[6]

Campos Sales assumed office on November 15, 1898, with the Funding Loan already in place. Where Floriano failed to achieve financial stability for the country because of his war expenses, and Prudente failed because of the unfavorable coffee market, Campos Sales finally triumphed in restoring the national finances. He chose as his finance minister Joaquim Murtinho, a physician from Matto Grosso State whose family owned huge maté tea plantations and dominated the politics of that state. A controversial figure, Murtinho was accused of many evils, including quackery. In matters of finance, Murtinho proved to be both orthodox and firm. He balanced the budget. On the expense side of the federal accounts, Murtinho significantly reduced military spending. He kept the civil service payroll stable, and, according to a newspaper friendly to the government, actually fired several public employees for not going to work.[7] Along the same lines, he sought to limit the granting of public pensions, an especially scandalous practice whereby those in favor received large lifetime payments from an already bankrupted treasury.[8] Following upon important precedents set by Prudente's ministers, Murtinho also denied government loans to the planters.

Murtinho's greatest contribution to fiscal policy, however, may be on the income side of the national accounts. Although he failed to reduce the level of corruption at the customs house, Murtinho increased collection of taxes on imports, still by far the central government's major source of revenue, by charging a quarter of the tariffs in gold.[9] The Campos Sales administration imposed Brazil's first excise tax, principally on alcohol and tobacco, which generated approximately one tenth of federal income.[10] Murtinho rented several of the government railroads to private companies, converting a sizable expense into a source of revenue. None of these ideas may be considered particularly novel. The gold tariff had been frequently discussed during the empire and effectively used under Ruy Barbosa. Great Britain levied excise taxes for two centuries before Campos Sales did, while many contemporary governments left their railroads in private hands. Murtinho's accomplishment lies in his successfully executing these reforms in the teeth of powerful opposition.

As a consequence of his prowess in raising taxes, Murtinho could continue the deflation initiated by Prudente in spite of the inflow of capital from abroad. During his four-year term, 1898 to 1902, the circulating medium fell from 733,000 contos to 675,000.[11]

Campos Sales and Murtinho had the good luck that the coffee market recovered as they assumed office. The unit price for this commodity remained stable, but consuming countries considerably increased the volume of their imports. After the defeat of William Jennings Bryan in the American presidential election of November 1896, the economic situation in the United States, Brazil's principal market for coffee, improved significantly. The discovery of gold in Alaska, South Africa, and Australia at the same time helped reverse the world's deflationary trend, which had begun with the crisis of 1873.

Taking advantage of this favorable international situation, Murtinho negotiated an agreement with the Banco da República that he thought would set this institution on a firm foundation. The Encilhamento had left the bank with a large portfolio of uncollectable loans, most of which had been ultimately funded by public money. In March 1900, Murtinho offered to cancel 186,000 contos of the bank's debt to the government in return for a cash payment of 25,000 contos and a note for the same amount to be repaid over four semesters.[12] Since the start of the Encilhamento, the authorities had certainly behaved benevolently to the Banco da República and its predecessors. The 186,000 contos included 80,000 contos' worth of bonds that Floriano had issued as "aid to industry" but that in fact were used to bail out the bank. Another 40,000 contos represented Ouro Preto's agricultural loans to the bank's predecessor institutions, and the remaining 66,000 contos were advances made by successive ministers to provide the bank with liquidity.[13] Murtinho acknowledged the worthlessness of the bank's portfolio by accepting just over a quarter of the original value of the government loans. To strengthen private initiative, the state relinquished its right to name the president of the bank, a power it had retained since Floriano's decree of 1892.

The improvement of coffee export volumes allied with the contraction of the circulating medium led to an appreciation of the milreis. At 7 pence when the year 1900 began, the Brazilian currency rose constantly amid heavy speculation to 14 pence in July, before retreating to 10 pence in August. Murtinho committed an error at this point: he failed to set an exchange-rate target. Although Wileman among others made the case for not allowing the exchange to rise toward the old parity, Murtinho never disavowed the notion of returning to 27 pence per milreis. Writing at the end of Campos Sales's term, Federal Deputy Alcindo Guanabara claimed that Murtinho's objective in 1900 was an exchange rate of 12 pence and that he later changed course, wishing to attain the official parity of 27 pence—which would have been a disaster.[14] Wileman argued that a rising exchange rate distorted relative prices just as a falling exchange rate did, exacerbating labor friction while granting a windfall profit to creditors. Had the minister adopted a rate somewhat above the 7 pence exchange rate prevailing at his accession, the government would have diminished bullish expectations, thereby reducing volatility. He could also have expressly suspended the burning of the paper money to slow the milreis's ascent. To keep the exchange rate stable, Murtinho would have had to choose a new official parity, preferably between 10 and 12 pence, and, if the currency maintained itself at this level, to offer to issue freely. Such a policy would have placed Brazil on the gold standard but would have broken the government's promise to reduce the circulating medium.

Although the public blamed the foreign banks for the volatility of the exchange, the Banco da República also participated heavily in this speculation.[15] The downturn in the value of the milreis helped provoke a run on this bank that had been under private management since March. As in past periods of difficulties, the bank turned to the government for help. In July, Murtinho lent £400,000 to the bank.[16] As the terms of the Funding Loan precluded the issue of paper money, in August Murtinho offered a second loan denominated in sterling. He proposed an advance of £600,000, equivalent at the time to 18,000 contos.[17] The bank's management considered the amount too small and did not wish to incur an additional exchange risk, especially as the milreis had been declining. After a short delay, the bank took this loan. Early in September, Murtinho refused the directors' second request for a 50,000-conto loan. On the eleventh, they resigned and the bank closed.

When the Banco da República failed, it owed the treasury £1 million, equivalent to 30,000 contos, for the sterling loans, as well as 10,000 contos on deposit and the 50,000 contos that the bank had undertaken to discharge in March but had not actually paid.[18] Serzedello Correia, now a leading member of the finance committee of the Chamber of Deputies, defended the bank eight years after his merger decree. He observed that the Banco da República had 99,000 contos of deposits.[19] Against these liabilities, its assets included 18,000 contos in cash, 51,000 contos in federal and state bonds, and a large amount of stock, of which he mentioned only 10,000 contos of shares in the Santos docks.[20] These enumerated assets were 20,000 contos less than the deposits. On top of the deposits of course stood the bank's debt to the government. The bank in fact was completely worthless, or rather it had a negative worth.

As a condition for government assistance, Campos Sales and Murtinho insisted on the appointment of Otto Petersen, the manager of the German Bank, as a director of the Banco da República. Understandably, nationalist outcries joined the normal noises that accompany bank interventions.[21] Ironically, although Petersen's nomination aroused the antagonism of certain American and British interests, the English Rothschilds served as the conduit for negotiation between the Brazilian government and Petersen's employers, the Disconto-Gesellschaft, to grant him leave from the Brasilianische Bank.[22] Petersen did in fact take charge of the Banco da República for a number of months.[23] At first he tried to reopen its doors, but he had to suspend payments again within two days. All the other domestic banks suspended payments as well, leaving the economy completely without liquidity.[24] Only individuals with deposits in foreign banks or gold hoarded at home could pay for even the most trivial purchases. Commerce stopped for total lack of means of payment. This crisis proved to be worse than those of 1864 and 1875 because it affected virtually everyone. In 1864, the government had allowed the Banco do Brasil to issue banknotes, and in 1875, the ministry had issued paper money; in 1900, it could do neither for fear of undermining its stabilization program.

In spite of the limitations imposed by stabilization, Murtinho proved to be far from a passive spectator. In fact, within two days of Petersen's suspension, the minister presented a solution that maintained the government's credibility regarding inflation while providing a means to restore liquidity. He called his proposal a "liquidation plan," although he clearly intended to fortify the Banco da República rather than liquidate it. Murtinho offered an additional £1 million in cash. As the Funding Loan agreement prohibited the issuance of paper money, the government proposed to issue 100,000 contos of five-year bonds paying 3 percent that would be delivered to the bank to pass to its creditors. The state would also lend the bank 25,000 contos out of the paper money it had retired and charge the bank only 2 percent interest per year. As collateral for all of these credits, the government took all of the stock of the Banco da República and resumed the right to name its executive officers.[25] Within a period of only two weeks, the bank's stockholders agreed to the Murtinho plan, and the creditors also voted to accept the 3 percent government bonds as payment for their deposits at the Banco da República.[26]

The acute shortage of liquidity continued for a month after the bank's shareholders' and creditors' meetings, while the government prepared the bond issue. Overextended banking and commercial houses disappeared. In Rio, seven banks in addition to that of the Banco do República either reorganized or liquidated during 1900.[27] These institutions had carried uncollectable loans on their balance sheets since the Encilhamento. Contemporaries considered the crisis of 1900 the liquidation of the Encilhamento.[28] Incompetent and fraudulent institutions disappeared, but the more prudent banks reestablished themselves with relative ease. The Banco Commercial offered its creditors 25 percent cash, 25 percent in government bonds that could be sold without a loss as soon as liquidity returned, and the remaining 50 percent in three semi-annual notes paying 5 percent per annum, almost a full market rate.[29] The Banco Commercial's depositors accepted this form of repayment and suffered little if any loss. The financial crisis affected the state capitals as well as Rio. In Bahia, at least two banks, including the former bank of issue, went into liquidation. The Banco da Bahia signed an agreement with its creditors similar to that of the Banco Commercial and quickly returned to business as usual.[30] After the creditors of the Banco da República approved Murtinho's plan, even the share price of that institution recovered, reaching around half of its par value.[31]

On November 5, upon receipt of the 3 percent bonds, the Banco da República reopened.[32] Gradually liquidity returned to the economy paced by earning from exports, the repatriation of hard currency by Brazilians, and advances from foreign merchants.[33] During the crisis, the government's debt, both internal and external, lost its liquidity, like all other assets. With the reopening of the banks, the secondary market for government debt came back to life. In a short period of time, these securities traded at levels substantially higher than before the crisis.[34] The appreciation of the public debt represents the most sincere sign of contentment over Campos Sales's management of the bank crisis.

With coffee exports at record levels, the crisis of 1900 can only be attributed to domestic causes. The accumulation of bad loans during the Encilhamento as well as Murtinho's contraction of the money supply appear to be the two principal factors leading to this event. Murtinho has been censored for an overly orthodox response.[35] His refusal to create money contrasts with the actions of the finance ministers of 1857 and 1864, who allowed the Banco do Brasil to issue banknotes, as well as the government of 1875, which printed money to lend to that bank. On the other hand, we cannot forget that the experience of the Encilhamento placed real constraints on Murtinho. With the excesses of Deodoro's administration not such a distant memory, elite opinion feared easy money and largely supported the contraction of the money supply that occurred under Prudente de Morais, Campos Sales, and his successor, Rodrigues Alves. Moreover we should by no means consider that Murtinho remained immobilized by orthodox principles. In two days he prepared an innovative plan that resolved a good deal of the market's liquidity problems. His contemporaries in the United Kingdom even thought him a bit too permissive compared to their financial authorities.[36] Writing at the apex of the panic on September 25, the editor of the *Rio News* also berated Murtinho for not allowing the failed ventures to go to the wall, while praising him for resisting the temptation to resolve the crisis by printing money.

As Floriano Peixoto is remembered as Brazil's iron marshal, the political strongman who accepted no compromise, Joaquim Murtinho survives in Brazilian thought as the financial strongman. This reputation is justified. Murtinho executed genuine reforms, including the imposition of the excise tax, which increased government income and decreased expenses. He took a relatively hard position during the crisis of 1900, forcing the stockholders of the mismanaged banks to absorb at least part of their losses, while providing liquidity that avoided further negative effects for the economy as a whole. During and after the crisis, Murtinho fulfilled Brazil's part of the bargain with the foreign bankers; in consequence, capital from both merchants and investors flowed into the country. A high volume of coffee sales undoubtedly played a significant role in Murtinho's achievements, but his tenacity was equally central.

Successful tight-money policies, those that have been followed by periods of low inflation and high growth, have always received criticism for causing more suffering than necessary. Could a milder or more permissive stance have produced more prosperity in both the short and long term? This question is crucial to understanding 1900 as well as to guiding us in the present. What can be demonstrated is that, too rigid or not, Murtinho's tight money period contributed to a decade of spectacular development. In all probability, by stabilizing the currency and the public accounts, Murtinho made Brazil a more attractive market for Brazilian and foreign investors as well as a more hospitable destination for immigrants. This situation permitted Brazil to obtain more benefits from the prosperous world economy of the pre–World War I years than would most other industrializing countries.

If Murtinho is to be faulted, it is in connection with his exchange policy. By signaling that the government wished to return to the old parity of 27 pence, he encouraged speculation. The doubling of the value of the milreis in 1900 severely distressed borrowers and increased unemployment, even before the banking crisis. An announcement by the authorities that they opposed rather than supported this rise would certainly have made for a lesser change in the milreis accompanied by lower pressure on debtors. As a further measure, the government could have threatened to issue paper money once the currency rose to a new, lower parity. In any case an increase in exchange value from 7 pence to 27 would have been unprecedented and highly disruptive. The value of the United States currency did recover from a Civil War low of 39 percent of parity to par by the restoration of convertibility in 1879, but the process was accompanied by grave social distress.

It is highly significant that Serzedello Correia, who had been Floriano's finance minister, was one of Murtinho's principal supporters at this juncture. As the leader of the finance committee of the House of Deputies, Correia organized the passage of Murtinho's legislation. Correia, who was to be president of the Brazilian Industrial Center from its inception in 1904, felt stabilization to be a necessary precondition for economic development in general and industrialization in particular.[37] Although he favored increased government participation in the economy, including loans for both agriculture and manufacturing, Correia recognized that industry required a stable currency in order to prosper. An outspoken nationalist, he sought to limit foreign participation in sectors such as commerce and mining, but he favored Murtinho's policy for making Brazil an interesting market for foreign lenders by means of the country's meeting its financial obligations.[38]

The year after the crisis vindicated Campos Sales and Murtinho. Brazil resumed the payment of interest on its foreign debt as scheduled, on July 1,

1901. The government used its credit standing to obtain a new loan, twice the size of the Funding Loan, which went to purchase a number of foreign-held railroads.[39] This transaction saved the taxpayers money in that the interest on the new loan came to less than the guaranteed minimum payments set by the earlier railroad agreements. Following an idea that emerged during Prudente's administration, Campos Sales rented several rail lines to private companies, thus converting government expenses into government revenues.[40] This measure also was intended to reduce the role of the state in the economy.[41]

Murtinho's treasury report that year summarizes his thoughts concerning the government's place in the economy as well as his assessments of Brazil's relationship to the international financial system. Regarding the latter, the minister battled to honor the country's commitments to the investment bankers to obtain greater resources for public and private infrastructure undertakings.[42] Like the planters who took part in the 1878 Agricultural Congress, he also wanted to borrow from abroad to retire the internal debt in order to release funds for "productive" purposes.[43] Far from being a lackey of foreign interests, Murtinho took a strong stance on the different purposes of foreign and domestic investments; for example, he differentiated sharply between the role of foreign investments in railroads and in mines, saying:[44]

> Let us turn our attention to the exploitation of our mines.
>
> Even though capital for these undertakings may be supplied in part by foreigners, I think the exploitation should be made by domestic companies.
>
> Mines are very different from railroads, ports, and other activities, which, along with direct profits, provide indirect benefits of inestimable value.
>
> If a railroad or a port is owned by a foreign company, the direct profits of these ventures leave the country, but we enjoy all the indirect benefits that develop trade, industry, agriculture, and the other elements of civilization.
>
> The situation changes with mining which leaves no indirect benefits at all. . . .
>
> This is what is happening with us: our wealth, the gold of our Earth, is siphoned off outside of our country without any positive gain for us.

Further demonstrating his independence of foreign interests, Murtinho proposed at the worst point of the 1900 crisis that the banks that dealt with exchange should be prohibited from taking deposits.[45] He specifically exempted the Banco da República from this measure. Had Murtinho's bill passed, the foreign banks would have had to relinquish their local deposits in order to remain in the exchange business and would therefore have lost one of their two principal sources of profits. Murtinho showed himself quite willing by this act to make use of government intervention—seen by some as violating "liberal" financial principles—to further his policies, in this case the strengthening of the Banco da República.

Murtinho's treasury report demonstrates a balanced view of the government's role in the economy. Although criticized for doing too little to assist the bank's shareholders and creditors, Murtinho felt he was required to defend his actions vis-à-vis those who thought public funds should not have been used at all to bail out private interests.[46]

> But, Mr President, if we refused to follow the policies assumed until then regarding this credit institution, we did not have the right to abandon its creditors and shareholders.
>
> Two motives, one moral, the other social, obliged us to intervene.
>
> From the moral point of view, we could not forget that the government was mostly to blame for the madness at the stock exchange and for all the economic and financial confusion accompanying the devaluation of our currency.
>
> It was the government that authorized the issue of bank notes which generated these acts of insanity whose colossal losses became concentrated in the portfolio of the Banco da República.

Murtinho made available credits to the bank equal to about one third of the total circulating medium of the country, hardly the workings of a dogmatic opponent of government intervention.[47] His liquidation plan for the Banco da República do Brasil explicitly proposed only to liquidate the "old portfolio."[48] A new government bank arose out of the wreckage of the failed institution, with Murtinho's blessings. Clearly he intended neither for the state to withdraw from banking nor for the government to retire entirely from the railroad business. Murtinho rented out some of the railroads to private companies, but he supported the construction of new lines within the state sector.[49]

During a period that the growers felt to be one of overproduction, Murtinho defended himself from charges that he had not helped the coffee planters by trying to draw the line against state intervention. He noted that to overcome the current unsatisfactory prices, demand would have to expand while supply contracted, an observation that was irrefutable.[50]

> The process by which consumption expands is, however, by nature slow, and all efforts in this regard, even if we start immediately, will not affect the present crisis.
>
> Accordingly the reduction of supply has unfailingly to come from a selection that will eliminate the weakest allowing only the survival of the fittest.

I have been branded a barbarian for defending this doctrine, as if I were the creator of this law of nature and as [if] I could prevent it from being enforced.

It has been argued here that this law does not apply to human societies, but this is a time when its manifestations become ever more intense and ever more visible.

And in spite of its harshness, this is the law par excellence of progress, and when a society does not have this law rule its trade, its industries, its agriculture, and its other human activities, then all its social classes will be comprised of inferior beings and the society will degenerate.

Without a doubt, we should alleviate the sufferings that come from its effect; but it would be madness to oppose or try to prevent its action.

A century later, Murtinho's fear of being taken for a barbarian by the elites strikes one as somewhat ironic. While this elite enjoyed the material advantages of the twentieth century, most of Brazil's other "citizens"—freedmen, immigrants, and squatters—lived in barbarian poverty. Neither Murtinho nor his critics considered that the state had obligations to these groups as well as to the coffee planters. At least, to his great credit, Murtinho struggled to avoid delivering the keys to the treasury to one interest.

Murtinho received some of the sharpest attacks from the foreign merchant community, suggesting he was nobody's puppet. Just months before the resumption of interest payments on the international debt, the *Rio News* charged:[51]

Minister Murtinho's great defect as a financier is his narrowness. He seems to be utterly incapable of grasping the idea that the real interests of the national treasury depend on the prosperity of the country. In his opinion every vintem extorted from an impoverished people is so much net profit. Taking office when the country was suffering from prolonged financial and commercial depression, he proceeded at once to aggravate the situation by heaping upon the already overtaxed people new and exceedingly oppressive burdens. In this way he has woefully depleted the most valuable sources of public revenue, recklessly destroyed an immense amount of private wealth and completely paralyzed energies which would in a few years have furnished ample means for meeting all reasonable demands of the national treasury.

This line of criticism, echoed in more recent times, is that the government should exert itself more in reducing expenses rather than in increasing income. In the case of Murtinho, this attack appears to be refuted by the budget figures. Almost half of his budgets went toward the payment of the debt, a use of funds that the foreign community surely could not fault. The second greatest recipient of public resources, the Ministry of Industry, Transportation, and

Public Works, found its funds greatly reduced by Murtinho and Bernardino de Campos, his immediate predecessor as finance minister, under Prudente de Morais. Bernardino de Campos eliminated subsidies for immigration and Murtinho rented out railroads to the private sector and slowed construction on new state lines. The third area of government outlays was defense. Under Prudente de Morais and Campos Sales, spending on the armed forces declined continuously, even to the point where the army's ability to maintain order could be considered impaired. The navy actually sold a number of its newest vessels.[52] As we have seen, Murtinho endeavored to reduce spending for civil and military pensions. Finally, Murtinho avoided the large expense that did not appear on the budget: loans to planters. The landed interest's complaints notwithstanding, the Campos Sales administration resisted the temptation to provide agricultural loans. While hardly free of abuses and corruption, the Campos Sales government did as good a job of controlling expenses as could be expected, given the values of the Brazilian elite.

The foreign community faulted the government in which Murtinho participated for high-handed actions, including the deportation of a foreign merchant without due process.[53] These businessmen resented corruption at the customs house that many felt had increased substantially since the advent of the Republic.[54]

The merchants saw the government's taxation measures as unfair. Wealthy planters still paid no land or income taxes, whereas both the customs and the excise taxes weighed heavily upon merchants, many of whom were foreign. Not only the *Rio News* but also the *Cidade do Rio,* spokesman for the freedmen and the poor in general, denounced the injustice of Murtinho's fiscal reforms. The *Cidade*'s editor, José do Patrocinio, wished to institute an income tax instead of the excise tax.[55]

Although one may feel strongly that stabilization's advantages outweigh its costs, costs do certainly exist. A government must try to distribute these burdens, both the increase in taxes and the decrease in benefits, upon its constituents as fairly as possible. Like every other policy at this time, the stabilization program favored the large planters in that additional taxes were imposed on others, especially the merchants and the final consumers. It could hardly have been otherwise in the Brazil of 1900. The planters' contribution came indirectly, through the appreciation of the milreis.

Foreign businessmen complained that prices in sterling became high by international standards during the stabilization phase.[56] Prices in milreis barely declined, even though, by 1901, the milreis, at 12 pence, bought twice as much

British currency as it had during the worst days of Prudente's administration. In principle, this phenomenon should have been favorable to the merchants, many of whom were importers. Planters should have been the group most opposed to the appreciation of the milreis, as they received less local currency for their exports. Yet the majority of planters supported Murtinho during his tight-money administration, calculating that financial stability and access to the international credit market would bring them more advantages than easy money and moratorium. Only when financial stability appeared to be safely achieved, and when the exchange rate rose further, to 16 pence, with no upper limit in sight, did the planter consensus turn against the appreciation of the value of the milreis. This change in the consensus occurred in 1906, at the end of the term of Rodrigues Alves, Campos Sales's successor.

To summarize, the stabilization plan depended upon both a favorable world conjuncture and a determined government. Excellent coffee export volumes provided the government with significantly higher revenues and supplied the economy with greater liquidity. The determination of the administration won the support of Brazilian and foreign investors, who brought their capital into the country. A forceful minister also managed to obtain substantial—if unfairly assessed—additional income as well as major economies in public spending. Although taxation and the contraction of the money supply together forced a number of weaker corporations and farms into bankruptcy, the overall impact on the economy appears to have been highly beneficial. A more equitable division of the burdens of stabilization would undoubtedly have been much healthier for the economy; Murtinho did what appeared to be possible.

EPILOGUE

On November 15, 1902, Campos Sales handed the office of the presidency over to his chosen successor, the former finance minister Rodrigues Alves. Rodrigues Alves received a prosperous economy with a rising exchange rate. The long crisis, which had begun with the Encilhamento and continued through Floriano's war and, further, through the coffee depression under Prudente, finally came to an end. Optimism ruled. While maintaining a tight fiscal policy, Rodrigues Alves rebuilt the center of Rio, adding an opera house, museums, and other imposing public edifices. He also eradicated yellow fever, an important milestone that helped make the capital livable. At the end of 1905, the liquidation of the Banco da República terminated. The bank had in fact functioned throughout this period.[57] Rodrigues Alves and his finance minister,

Leopoldo de Bulhões, recapitalized the bank, dividing its equity among the old shareholders, the government, which received stock in lieu of its loans, and new shareholders, who effectively contributed cash to the bank. This institution, renamed the Banco do Brasil, came under the control of the state, where it has remained for a century. At least at its inception, the new Banco do Brasil held to highly conservative banking practice, even though politics played its usual role in determining the recipients of loans.[58]

At this time, buoyed by a strong world economy and increasing coffee consumption, the milreis socialized the planters' profits in the same manner as the devaluation had socialized their previous losses. From a low of 7 pence under Prudente, the average yearly exchange rate reached 12 pence under Campos Sales and advanced to 16 pence as Rodrigues Alves's administration came to an end in 1906. The cost of living fell significantly for urban dwellers. Planters, on the other hand, found their export earnings purchasing fewer milreis. A similar, though milder, appreciation had occurred in the late 1880s. On that occasion, Finance Minister Francisco Belisário Soares de Sousa considered reducing parity from 27 to 24 pence to prevent the milreis from rising beyond the latter value. His government fell before he could execute this change. Ouro Preto, assuming office a year later, with the milreis at par, chartered the Banco Nacional to issue banknotes convertible into gold. Had the Banco Nacional succeeded in implementing Ouro Preto's aims, the gold-standard mechanism would have prevented the currency from rising above 27 pence by more than the cost of transporting gold (the gold point). In 1906, Rodrigues Alves's advisers debated how far the milreis's value should be allowed to rise. As the official parity had never been lowered from 27 pence, bondholders and conservatives held for the maintenance of this level, but a number of planters demanded devaluation to 12 pence. When, in 1906, President-elect Afonso Pena announced that the value should be 15 pence, about one penny lower than the prevailing market rate, Rodrigues Alves passed the final decision over to him. Pena, in his first month of office, established the Conversion Office (Caixa de Conversão), which would freely exchange milreis for sterling at a rate of 15 pence. Thus, Brazil adopted the gold standard for the first time in 1906.

The planters, who had benefited from the flexible exchange system during the milreis's periods of weakness, came to support the gold standard during this phase of strong export earnings. The metallic standard placed a ceiling on the value of the milreis, which assured the planters higher incomes in terms of the local currency than they would have obtained had the milreis been permitted to float upward toward 27 pence. (From 1906 to 1914, Brazil enjoyed great prosperity while remaining on the gold standard.[59] In fact the government actually revalued the milreis to 16 pence. World War I caused Brazil to abandon the gold standard, but it returned to it in 1926, once again in order to stop the milreis from appreciating. Brazil's second experiment with the gold standard proved far less successful than the first, and ended once and for all with the advent of the Depression in 1930.)

The recovery of the coffee market at the turn of the century resulted in heavy plantings, renewed railroad construction, and the resumption of immigration. When the coffee trees flowered in early 1906, it became clear that the country would produce a harvest so large as to provoke the collapse of international prices. Taking advantage of Brazil's record as a good debtor, planters wished to borrow from abroad to remove the crop from the market. In February of that year, against Rodrigues Alves's wishes, the governors of São Paulo, Minas Gerais, and Rio de Janeiro signed the agreement of Taubaté, which established the framework for the "valorization" scheme whereby the supply of coffee was limited to keep prices high. When Afonso Pena took office in November, he threw the central government's support behind the effort to control the coffee market. During his term, the federal authorities borrowed millions of pounds sterling to finance the purchase and retention of millions of bags of coffee, with apparent success.[60]

Valorization signaled that the revulsion against state intervention, that elite position demonstrated after the Encilhamento, had run its course. In addition to valorization, Afonso Pena broadly favored increased government activity within the economy. The orthodox reaction to the bubble had triumphed to the point where its leaders could be retired.

Chapter 9 Reflections on Inflation

With the exception of the brief ministry of Bernardo de Souza Franco (1857–1858), the imperial elite had invariably followed conservative doctrine and policies regarding credit. The gold standard served as an objective for all the succeeding governments, although in practice the empire never adopted full convertibility. This conservative thinking did not, however, inhibit decisive action during periods of adversity. In particular, during the commercial crises of 1857, 1864, and 1875, the Paraguayan War, and the great drought of 1878, the government acted both rapidly and vigorously to increase the volume of paper money and banknotes in circulation.

With the approach of abolition, pressure arose from certain groups of planters to make available medium-term credit for agriculture. The two prime ministers in power after abolition, João Alfredo and the viscount of Ouro Preto, advanced funds to the planters through the banking system, and, taking advantage of a favorable international situation, permitted banks to issue banknotes convertible into gold. Ouro Preto, who governed during the final five months of the empire, sought to regain the planters' allegiance to the monarchy by lending them large amounts of public funds. Although these loans saved neither the declining coffee barons of the Paraíba Valley nor the monarchy itself, easy money provoked a speculative boom known as the Encilhamento.

After the proclamation of the Republic, the issuance of convertible banknotes became impossible because foreign merchants and domestic investors, fearing political disturbances, expatriated their gold, forcing down the value of the Brazilian currency, the milreis. The republican finance minister, Ruy Barbosa, attempting to win the goodwill of planters, merchants, and financiers, authorized privileged banks to issue banknotes backed by government bonds. This measure was a response to the repeated request of segments of the landowning class to monetize the national debt. In practice, the government lent these banks the funds that backed their issues while enacting regulations that facilitated fraud and speculation. Throughout 1890 the bubble grew. In the second quarter of the following year, under the ministry of the baron of Lucena, the stock market started to retreat. To save both the boom and his precarious government, Lucena encouraged the privileged banks to issue yet more banknotes. The resulting large volume of paper in circulation sucked in imports, causing the collapse of the milreis later in the year. By November 1891, the Brazilian currency, which had fluctuated in a relatively narrow band for sixty years, had fallen to less than half its parity.

That month, partially as a result of the frustration of their financial policies, Deodoro and Lucena executed a coup d'état. A civilian and military movement overthrew them within twenty days. Vice President Floriano Peixoto assumed office with the dual objectives of ending inflation and furthering industrialization. With his first finance minister, Rodrigues Alves, Floriano emphasized the former, whereas with his second, Serzedello Correia, he tried to direct resources to industry. In the end, Floriano achieved only mediocre results in both of these efforts because he took an intransigent position in a dispute in the state of Rio Grande do Sul that led to a war that ended up consuming most of the government's available funds and accelerated inflation.

The civilian government that took office in 1894 represented the interests of the São Paulo coffee planters and their allies. This administration drew three broad conclusions concerning the credit policies of the military regime. Massive medium-term credit to agriculture was inefficient and corrupting; subsidies, whether to agriculture, immigration, industry, or whatever, could not be administered honestly; finally, immoderate credit expansion by issuing banknotes generated instability and inflation, which far exceeded any benefits to agriculture, commerce, and industry resulting from increased liquidity. In consequence, the three successive Paulista presidents in office from 1894 to 1906 adopted orthodox monetary and fiscal policies. After a period of difficulty occasioned by low world coffee prices, the second Paulista administration, that of Campos Sales, balanced the budget, reduced the state's role in the economy, and placed the currency on a secure basis. From the end of his tenure in 1902 to the eve of World War I, Brazil experienced a true epoch of prosperity characterized by major expansion in both agriculture and industry.

Unfortunately, the benefits derived from Campos Sales's success accrued almost exclusively to the elite—for the landowners, the merchants, the industrialists, and the politicians, the period from 1900 to 1914 was a golden age of growth. Meanwhile, the vast majority of Brazilians continued to suffer the effects of a hostile land law, the government's indifference to education, and widespread corruption. For Brazil's future, one would hope that the advantages arising from financial stability can be shared more evenly by all groups within the population.

In widening our focus beyond the years preceding and following abolition, we may draw some broader conclusions regarding Brazil's inflation and its relations with the outside world. While the Portuguese court resided in Rio (1801–1820), the milreis's parity stood at 67 pence. By 1827, during Pedro I's Cisplatine campaigns, the Brazilian currency collapsed to 23 pence in consequence of military expenses, corruption, and financial mismanagement.[1] Peace, responsible governments, and the rise of coffee exports permitted the milreis to recover to 27 pence, a value that became the new official parity in 1846. Thus in 1889, some sixty-two years after the Cisplatine War, the milreis's exchange rate actually stood higher relative to sterling than it had been during that conflict. Throughout these sixty-two years, which include several periods of deflation, British prices probably declined.[2] The maintenance of parity with sterling therefore implies little or no inflation over two whole generations. After the Encilhamento, the milreis recovered once again so that in 1914, almost another generation later, the milreis stood at 16 pence, two thirds of its value in 1827.

Actual prices in milreis appear to have risen in spite of the maintenance of parity. The cost of certain foodstuffs increased by as much as 100 percent during the forty years between 1850 and the fall of the empire.[3] Rio de Janeiro real estate prices also increased considerably as the result of the rapid growth of the city. On the other hand, imported manufactured goods probably declined in unit price as a result of greater efficiency in the leading industrial countries.[4] In consequence, the cost of living must have increased by less than double during this period.

Salaries provide a reasonable measure of inflation. In 1825, two years before the milreis's downfall during the Cisplatine War, the salary of a captain in the Brazilian army stood at 60 milreis per month.[5] Officers received their first raise, to 80 milreis, thirty-two years later. In 1873, after an interval of sixteen years, Parliament increased captains' salaries to 120 milreis, but the executive did not put the new pay scale into operation until 1887, when it did so in a vain attempt to placate the largely abolitionist officer corps. These raises imply an approximate doubling in the cost of living during the course of the empire.

Even if we use officers' salaries rather than the milreis's relationships to sterling as a measure of inflation, a 100 percent increase over sixty years represents a pretty decent performance by contemporary standards. Over the past sixty years, since 1950, prices in the United States have increased by a factor of 5 or more. At least until World War I, it seems grossly unfair to consider Brazil as a country with a chronic inflation problem. From the end of the Cisplatine War until the start of the First World War, Brazil had but one bout with inflation: the Encilhamento.

When we look at the most advanced economies, we see that during the two centuries that preceded World War I, England, France, and the Netherlands enjoyed a period of unprecedented monetary stability. Following the example set by the Dutch early in the seventeenth century, England and France maintained the metallic content of their currencies without alteration from 1696 and 1726, respectively, until the French Revolution.[6] Before this, even these two rich states had recourse to the debasement of their coinage. The French Revolution brought with it the wild inflation of the "*assignats*" in France and the suspension of convertibility and inflation in Great Britain (see chapter 2). From Waterloo to the outbreak of World War I, both countries once again enjoyed absolute stability in terms of the metallic content of their currencies, with Britain quickly resuming convertibility at its prewar parity. The United States and the wealthier European states also maintained their parity to sterling and gold throughout the century preceding World War I.

To place Brazil's nineteenth-century performance in perspective, we should compare it not only to that of Britain and France but also to that of other nations in Latin America. Argentina's currency inflated relative to sterling no less then twenty times in the country's first half century of existence, while Colombia increased its prices one hundred fold by 1903.[7] In this context, nineteenth-century Brazil appears closer to Europe than to its Latin American neighbors.

A number of Brazilians saw the country's nonadherence to the gold standard prior to 1906 as a sign of inferiority. In fact, the flexible exchange system served Brazil's elite well, protecting it from the worst effects of crises while defending the incomes of planters in terms of the local currency.[8] A conservative French textbook of 1911 praises Brazil's pre-1906 flexible exchange rates as a means by which a nonindustrial economy could defend itself from external influences.[9] Three times—during the Paraguayan War, during the coffee recession of 1875 to 1885, and during the Encilhamento—Brazil's exchange rate fell considerably, to 17 pence, 20 pence, and 12 pence, respectively. On the first two occasions, the milreis subsequently returned to par. The excesses of the Encilhamento proved to be too great to permit a return for the third time. However, conservative governments eventually achieved a recovery to 16 pence. From the vantage point of 1911, one could conclude that Brazil had enjoyed almost a century of broadly successful financial management that avoided inflation while protecting the economy from the negative effects of commodity cycles and financial crises—again excepting the Encilhamento. Brazil's flexible approach may indeed have provided its merchants and planters with more assistance in times of panics than the more rigid British and American financial systems did.[10] In conclusion, we may suggest that, in terms of monetary and exchange policy, the Brazilian elite generally displayed a combination of prudence, creativity, and independence from the rules of the central economies.

From the fall of Pedro I to the outbreak of the First World War, Brazilian monetary management broke down but once—during the Encilhamento. Inflation, devaluation, redoubled corruption, and overall instability arose when successive weak governments, looking to buy support, abused the printing press. Inflation is a sign of governments attempting to undertake more than they can afford.

Appendix: Public Finance in Brazil

> I did send to you
> For certain sums of gold, which you denied me:
> For I can raise no money by vile means:
> By heaven I had rather coin my heart,
> And drop my blood for drachmas, than to wring
> From the hard hands of peasants their vile trash
> By any indirection. I did send
> To you for gold to pay my legions
>
> —Brutus to Cassius, *Julius Caesar,* act IV, scene iii

In these lines Shakespeare sums up the public finances of traditional societies. On the expense side, most of the funds go toward war. Taxes are levied by force on the tillers of the soil. When force proves insufficient to make income equal expenses, the coinage is debased. Through this classical expedient, inflation preceded paper money and banknotes by many centuries.

Brutus, high-minded, preferred to borrow gold from an ally (or his banker) than adulterate his coinage or squeeze his peasants. His concerns regarding his subjects reveal the transformation taking place in seventeenth-century England that led to the Civil War, the supremacy of Parliament, and taxation only by the consent of the elite. By this time, duties on international trade had replaced the squeezing of peasants as the state's major source of income.[1]

During the eighteenth century, especially in England, France, and the United States, thinkers clarified the principle that government rules through a compact with society. Taxes must be approved by the governed, and the government must promote the good of the entire population. An examination of the public finances of these states should reveal which groups really paid for government and which sectors benefited from government spending. Public finance provides one of the few reliable measures of the degree of social justice a society enjoys.

Public finance consists of the state's collecting and allocating resources. Taxes have usually made up the bulk of government income, although the rents of crown lands as well as booty often contributed to preindustrial exchequers, and today, the earnings of state-owned companies are important components of public income. Often, however, revenues fall short of allocations. In this case, the government may either borrow or create more money. Money can either be created directly, by debasing the coinage or printing paper money, or indirectly, by loans from the banking system. This appendix covers the strictly fiscal—tax and expenditure—aspects of public finance. In the real world, fiscal and monetary policies are closely related; an understanding of the fiscal framework in which the Brazilian government operated is essential to evaluating its credit and monetary policies. Conversely, monetary policy serves fiscal ends. As the financial crisis of abolition illustrates, public funds lent to privileged groups such as the planters without the expectation of repayment are identical to public subsidies of these elites.

For the first generation of its independent existence, which began in 1822, the empire of Brazil experienced both a depression in the trade in sugar and cotton, hitherto its major exports, and continuous civil strife. During the 1840s, a new commodity, coffee, achieved a dominant position in the world market, and this inaugurated a period of sustained economic growth that continues to the present day.[2] Coffee revenues permitted the imperial government to re-equip the army and suppress the regional revolts, the last of which ended in 1849. The year 1850 is highly significant as it marked the end of the slave trade, so we shall use this year as the start of this analysis. We conclude with 1901, by which time Brazil had recovered from the crisis of the 1890s.

Table 11 shows the budgets from 1845 to 1899 as supplied by official publications— *Orçamento da receita e da despesa* (Budget of receipts and expenses) and *Leis e decretos do Brasil* (Laws and decrees of Brazil). These figures appear to be reasonably accurate except for those gathered during the Paraguayan War, 1864 to 1870, and the Naval Revolt, 1893 to 1895, when the governments spent significant unappropriated funds on the armed forces.

The budgets reveal that prior to 1850 the maintenance of law and order counted as the Brazilian elite's chief preoccupation. The armed forces and the judicial system consumed virtually all the resources not destined to service the national debt (the principal item under the heading "Ministry of Finance"). After the army crushed the last internal revolt, in 1849, the political elite immediately turned its attention to what in the nineteenth century were called "improvements." Railroads and other public works fell within the Ministry of the Empire, which saw its budget triple in real terms during the 1850s. In 1855, the government guaranteed dividends on funds invested in the strategic Santos-Jundiaí Railway, destined to open western São Paulo Province to coffee growing.[3] Thus the Ministry of the Empire eventually remitted payments to investors in private rail lines outside its control and also provided subsidies to steamship companies. In 1862, the cabinet formed a separate Ministry of Agriculture, Commerce, and Public Works to execute developmental functions. Three years later, the government nationalized the Dom Pedro II, Brazil's most important railway, linking Rio de Janeiro to São Paulo. Within a decade, the Ministry of Agriculture, Commerce, and Public Works was spending more than the Ministry of War. Only the Ministry of Finance, which serviced the public debt, received greater resources than the ministry that built and operated the railroads. In 1893, President Floriano Peixoto changed its name to the Ministry of Industry, Transportation, and Public Works; by then it consumed 40 percent of the total budget, more than any other ministry.

The Great Drought of 1878, in the Northeast, caused the authorities to further increase the state's participation in the economy. The legislature approved 70,000 contos, a sum equivalent to £7 million, or half the budget of that year, for extraordinary assistance to the victims of the drought. Prime Minister Sinimbú used part of these funds to accelerate the construction of railroads in the Northeast and the remainder to purchase foodstuffs.[4] Despite the inevitable waste and corruption that took place while thousands of people starved to death, Sinimbú's efforts did provide significant relief.[5]

Another area of state involvement in the economy was the subsidies to immigration. During the 1880s, the provincial government of São Paulo began to pay passage for European immigrants in order to supply workers for the coffee plantations. To partially compensate the Paulista planters for abolition, João Alfredo, the prime minister in 1888, allocated 8,000 contos of the imperial budget toward subsidies for immigration. The governments of the Republic increased this spending, which reached a high of 21,000 contos in 1891, over one tenth of the national budget. From 1893 to 1896, immigration consumed 7,000 contos per year, but the subsidy came to an end in 1897 because of the fall of coffee prices.[6] Spending on immigration benefited exclusively the elite. Most of the funds went to contractors who obtained generous allowances per head and in return provided transportation for the immigrants that was of generally subhuman quality. Once in Brazil, immigrants remained confined and starving in government facilities until they could be delivered to their planter employers.

The Brazilian state spent little on the education of the immigrants, and in fact showed scant interest in training and educating native-born citizens, either. After 1862 the Ministry of the Empire, which included the Department of Education, was allocated only 7 percent of the national budget (see table 11). The provincial and municipal governments had relatively low incomes, so they depended on the imperial authorities for resources to devote to primary and secondary education. The elite's hostility to public education resulted in extremely low and scarcely improving levels of literacy throughout nineteenth-century Brazil. The only sectors of public instruction that received ample endowment were the legal and medical schools, which provided tuition-free higher education to the sons of the elite.

The budget figures suggest that the governments of the empire played a very active role in the economy and that the advent of the Republic did not produce any significant change in fiscal policy. The governments of the empire proved able to appropriate a fair portion of national income through taxation. We do not have precise numbers for national income, although some interesting attempts to quantify these figures have been made.[7] We do have available satisfactory statistics on trade, so we can compare public spending to exports.

Table 4   Government Budget as Percentage of Exports, 1835 to 1887

Fiscal Year	Budget[a] (000 contos)	Exports[b] (000 contos)	Budget as Percentage of Exports
1835–36	11	41	27
1840–41	19	42	46
1845–46	25	54	46
1850–51	26	68	39
1855–56	32	94	34
1860–61	48	123	39
1865–66	59	157	38
1870–71	83	168	49
1875–76	105	184	57
1880–81	116	231	50
1885–86	139	195	71
1886–87	138	264	52

[a] Figures from *Leis e Decretos do Brasil* for relevant years.
[b] Figures from Carreira, *História financeira e orçamentária do império no Brasil*, pp. 726–741.

Table 5   Government Expenditures as a Percentage of Exports After Abolition (in Thousands of Contos)

Year	Government Expenditures[a]	Exports	Expenditures as Percentage of Exports	Milreis Exchange Rate (Pence)
1888	147	273	54	27 (par)
1889	186	256	73	27 (par)
1890	221	326	68	21.5
1891	221[b]	574	39	16.0
1892	279	784	36	12.3
1893	300	706	42	11.7
1894	373	766	49	10.6

[a] Figures from *Orçamento da receita e da despesa* for relevant years.
[b] The accounting for the gold tariff eliminated the item "exchange difference" and kept both the revenues and the expenses for 1891 lower than they would otherwise have been.

During the period under analysis, a large portion of the money economy depended upon foreign trade, but toward the end of this period the size of the domestic economy grew rapidly, owing to immigration and abolition, which somewhat diminished the importance of the export sector, a development that has yet to be quantified. The figures shown in tables 4 and 5 do not take into account such factors as smuggling and the expenses of provincial governments; the latter represented a third of central government expenses.[8]

Comparing the size of the budget with the value of exports, we find that the government budgeted a sum equal to 46 percent of all exports in both 1840–1841 and 1845–1846. During the prosperous 1850s, exports grew faster than public expenditures. With the Paraguayan War, this tendency reversed itself so that in 1870–1871, government expenditures came to 49 percent of exports. High interest payments, public works, and drought relief kept this proportion around or above 50 percent until abolition. (The unusual 71 percent reached in 1885–1886 resulted from a sharp drop in export earnings.) After abolition, government expenses rose rapidly, pushing the percentage exceptionally high in 1889 and 1890. During the following two years, export earnings exploded in terms of the Brazilian currency, a result of devaluation and the growth of coffee and rubber sales, which caused the proportion to drop below 40 percent. In 1893 and 1894, it returned to 40 to 50 percent. Thus, over the period from 1840 to 1894, in spite of significant short-term oscillations, the successive governments proved able and willing to spend an amount of money equal to between 40 and 50 percent of the value of Brazilian exports. Today of course the government spends a sum that is a multiple, not a proportion, of exports, totally over a third of the entire gross national product. Before the recent privatizations, the role of the state had increased to include every activity from iron mines to telephone companies. Although less proactive than its contemporary successors, the imperial government can hardly be considered passive, since it succeeded in extracting substantial resources from a poor and dispersed economy.

Nathaniel Leff calculates that at the end of this period Brazil's exports equaled 16 percent of GNP and that the central government taxed 9.2 percent of the GNP.[9] These numbers are in line with the figures shown in tables 4 and 5, indicating public spending in excess of half of exports.

In comparison with other governments of its time, the empire may be considered reasonably active.[10] The United States on the eve of the Civil War had a population approximating 40 million, whereas Brazil in 1860 had fewer than ten million. Per capita income in the United States greatly exceeded that of Brazil, although we lack information on Brazil to make precise comparisons. The U.S. federal government budgeted $67 million in 1861, two and a half times Brazil's $26 million—so per capita central government spending in Brazil was higher than in the United States,[11] though U.S. state and local governments spent much more than the federal authorities did, whereas in Brazil the opposite was true. Nevertheless, the fact that the central government of such a poor country could outspend in per capita terms the globe's rising power seems worthy of note (see the Brazilian budgets in table 11 to compare). The breakdown of the U.S. budget reveals that the government in Washington spent almost nothing on "improvements" (such as railroads and ports), whereas the cabinet in Rio spent some 16 percent of its budget on improvements.[12] U.S. government expenditures for 1861, by departments, are shown in table 6.[13] These figures represent a peacetime budget; in 1865, the Union allocated fifty times more for the army than it did in 1861.

The American civil service consisted of the federal judiciary, the internal revenue service, and the post office; the other categories are self-explanatory (see table 6). Thus, U.S. federal expenses in 1861 resembled the Brazilian budgets of the earlier part of the century. Law and order were the principal objectives of the U.S. federal government at this time. In 1866, federal public works received a $4 million allocation, but by 1882 the U.S. government was spending $17 million on this item.[14] In 1882, in Brazil, the Ministry of Agriculture,

Table 6   United States Government
Expenditures for 1861 (Millions of
U.S. Dollars; $1 = 2 Milreis)

Civil service......................	6.1
Foreign service...................	1.1
Navy	12.4
Army........................	23.0
Pensions.......................	1.0
Interest	4.0
Total	47.6

Source: Paul Studenski and Herman Kroos, *Financial History of the United States*, New York, 1952, 152.

Commerce, and Public Works received $10 million; two years later its budget rose to $16 million. In absolute terms, the Rio government spent as much on "improvements" as its opposite number in Washington. In per capita terms, Rio spent far more.

Turning from the expenditure side of public finance to the income side, in 1861, virtually all of the United States' revenues came from import tariffs.[15] The situation in nineteenth-century Brazil was similar, except that Brazil also taxed exports. During the reign of Pedro II, import and export tariffs contributed three quarters of the state's income with the latter source representing approximately one fifth of the total customs. In the final years of the empire, sugar received a complete exemption from the export duties and other products had their tariffs reduced. Also during the last decade of the monarchy, the revenues under the heading "Interior" grew significantly. "Interior" included the stamp tax on documents, taxes on urban real estate, real estate transfers, and professions, and revenues from the postal service and the government-owned railroads. For the year 1888, import tariffs were 89,000 contos (approximately $45 million, or nearly £10 million), export duties were 15,000 contos, "interior" was 38,000, and other was 2,000; accordingly trade levies accounted for 72 percent of all revenue. For the years 1889, 1890, and 1891, this percentage dropped to 66, 62, and 58, respectively.[16] In 1892 a constitutional change gave the states the proceeds of the taxes on real estate and the professions, reducing the importance of the "interior" rubric to the federal government. That year, although the states also won the revenues produced by export tariffs, import tariffs alone provided 71 percent of federal resources. From 1893 to 1896, this percentage remained around 76. Clearly, the central government of the Republic was no less dependent on tariff revenues than the empire had been.

As both the empire and the military regime looked to import duties for the greater part of their income, these governments lacked flexibility in the use of tariffs for developmental ends. In her brilliant study, *A luta pela industrialização do Brasil* (The Fight for the Industrialization of Brazil), Nicia Vilela Luz demonstrates the swings between relatively protectionist and relatively free trade tariffs that occurred throughout the period from 1844 to 1914. Both excessively high and excessively low tariffs would have choked off the government's income, so rate policy had to keep tariffs within an intermediate band. Luz feels that the military governments, especially Deodoro's, were no more protectionist than their monarchist predecessors had been.[17] The Paulista presidents, from 1894 to 1906, although committed to "free trade" and the international financial system, maintained and even increased tariff schedules.[18]

The nineteenth-century world knew three other important sources of revenues besides tariffs: property taxes, excise taxes, and income taxes. The Brazilian elite would not hear of a tax on land, although urban real estate rates constituted a major source of revenue for municipalities. The Liberal government of Prime Minister Sinimbú, which assumed power in 1878, did include a land tax in its platform; within a few weeks of taking office, however, he discarded this idea. Six years later, Prime Minister Dantas raised the land tax issue again, also without success.[19] Under the Republic, President Campos Sales, innovating in his attempts to balance the budget, raised the domestic excise tax—primarily on alcohol and tobacco— thus demonstrating that there existed at least a partial alternative to customs revenues. However, even in 1901, the excise tax provided only a tenth of government revenue. One of Campos Sales's supporters proposed an income tax at this time but was overruled, as Congress considered such a tax uncollectable.[20] The empire had an income tax during the Paraguayan War, which had been levied only on government employees. By comparison, the United Kingdom instituted its first peacetime income tax in 1842, while the United States had to wait until 1913 for a constitutional amendment to do so.[21] Brazilian governments of this time therefore remained dependent upon trade tariffs for most of their income.

Throughout the nineteenth century, Brazil's governments had greater expenditures than receipts, and the public debt grew. The foreign debt went from less than £4 million in 1850 to £30 million by the end of the empire.[22] The internal debt expanded from some 40,000 contos at mid-century to 324,000 by 1878, and declined somewhat thereafter.[23] Given that the milreis fluctuated between one ninth and one eleventh of a pound sterling during this period, the magnitudes of the internal and foreign debts were quite similar. We have somewhat more precise data on debt service than on the debt itself, as the annual budgets contain figures on the servicing costs (see table 7). In general most of the debt service consisted of interest; amortizations took place at or around 1 percent per annum when they took place at all. Debt service throughout this period consumed between a quarter and a third of total government resources, representing a heavy though not unbearable burden on public finances.

The public debt increased little during the more or less peaceful decade of the fifties but it tripled during the sixties as a result of the Paraguayan conflict. After the war, indebtedness

Table 7   Brazil's Total Annual Debt Service for Six Years, from 1850 to 1895 (in Contos)

	1850	1860	1870	1880	1888	1895
Foreign	2,798	3,649	8,057	12,499	25,210	26,745
Internal	3,479	3,460	15,269	26,338	19,090	23,364
Total	6,277	7,109	23,326	38,837	44,300	50,107

Source: *Leis e Decretos do Brasil* and the *Relatórios da Fazenda* for the relevant years.

continued to grow as the result of public works expenses, railroad interest guarantees, and interest payments on the outstanding loans. From 1860 to 1880, the service of the debt absorbed an increasing percentage of the national budget (see table 8).

In fact, service of the external debt proved to be more onerous than first appears from table 8. When the exchange rate fell below par, 27 pence per milreis, the government charged the additional cost of service—in terms of milreis—to an account called "exchange difference" rather than including this cost directly in debt service, as would be done today. In 1870 and 1880, exchange difference added approximately 20 percent to the cost of the debt service as expressed in milreis. In 1888, with the exchange rate at par, the "exchange difference" was negligible. But the milreis fell continuously after the proclamation of the Republic, and the "exchange difference" increased rapidly, reaching a sum equivalent to foreign debt service by 1895 (see table 9).

During the Paraguayan War and again during the seventies, successive governments made much more extensive use of internal borrowings than external ones. The onerous terms of foreign loans as well as the availability of domestic capital dictated this policy.[24] In the eighties, this situation reversed itself. Foreign bankers offered Brazil funds at ever more attractive rates, while, internally, planters who could not borrow money mounted a campaign to force investors to turn their funds from government bonds into agricultural and commercial loans.[25] Under this pressure, the finance ministers of the eighties increased their overseas borrowings to the point where foreign debt service surpassed domestic. The figures for 1888 (table 9) reveal that internal debt service actually declined from the level of 1880. In 1887, interest on domestic bonds had been decreased from 6 to 5 percent per annum to make these instruments less attractive as investments and to save funds for the treasury. As the imperial bonds consistently traded over par, this reduction was certainly justified by

Table 8   Annual Debt Service (Largely Interest) as a Percentage of Brazil's Budget for Six Years, from 1850 to 1895 (in Contos)

	1850	1860	1870	1880	1888	1895
External	10	7	9	10	18	10
Internal	13	7	16	22	13	8
Total	23	14	25	32	31	18

Source: *Leis e Decretos do Brasil* and the *Relatórios da Fazenda* for the relevant years.

Table 9   Debt Service (Largely Interest), Including "Exchange Difference" as a Percentage of Brazil's Budget

	1850	1860	1870	1880	1888	1895
External	10	7	11	12	18	20
Internal	13	7	16	22	13	8
Total	23	14	27	34	31	28

Source: *Leis e Decretos do Brasil* and the *Relatórios da Fazenda* for the relevant years.

market conditions. The numbers imply that the government also succeeded in reducing the volume of the internal debt outstanding.[26]

The enormous inflation and devaluation that took place during the military government caused a violent contraction in internal debt service. By 1895, with the milreis worth only one third of par, bondholders were losing two thirds of their income while their capital depreciated accordingly. At this time, the internal debt consumed only 8 percent of the federal budget while foreign debt service reached a high point in real terms that ate up 20 percent of the budget.

The key points to remember concerning the structure of Brazil's nineteenth-century finances are the following: The Brazilian state depended upon trade tariffs for revenues. Perhaps as an extension of its colonial past, when the export levy of one fifth on gold mined and sent to Portugal yielded an important source of income, Brazil had export tariffs in addition to those for imports. At the end of our period, excise taxes began to contribute significantly to public finance, as did revenues from government-owned companies. The latter income, however, was more than offset by the expenditures of these same companies. Throughout this period, the state had ample opportunities to borrow both internally and externally and took advantage of these opportunities.

On the expense side, the government used most of its funds to maintain law and order until the middle of the century. From 1850 on, the state devoted an increasing share of its resources to public works and public companies, which consumed 40 percent of the budget by 1893. The service of the national debt continuously absorbed between a quarter and a third of the budget, while the portion of funds devoted to defense declined from 40 percent in 1850 to less than 20 percent at the fall of the monarchy. Although Floriano's war caused the government to again devote almost 40 percent of its resources to the army and navy, by 1900, the military's share of national spending once more fell below 20 percent.

Education never received more than 6 percent of the budget during the period under discussion. Regarding education, an interesting comparison may be made with Italy. After unification, in 1861, the Italian cabinet had nine ministers, two more than the Brazilian one. Under the monarchy, both the Italian and the Brazilian governments were headed by a "president of the council of ministers" who also held one of the portfolios. Six ministries common to both countries were finance, foreign affairs, interior, justice, army, and navy. The Italian cabinet had a ministry of agriculture and a ministry of public works, whereas the Brazilian government combined these two ministries. Significantly, Italy had a separate ministry for education throughout this period. The Brazilian monarchy never established such a ministry, and the Republic maintained one for only a few months during its first year.

Liberal historians are often accused of assigning too much importance to education. This charge notwithstanding, educational statistics serve as a convenient index of development. There was no higher education in Brazil during the colonial period. Pedro I founded the first civilian institutions of higher learning immediately after independence: the law schools of São Paulo and Recife, and the medical schools of Rio de Janeiro and Bahia. During Pedro II's minority, the regency established a high school named after him that educated many Brazilian men of letters and soon achieved a prestige almost equal to that of the professional schools. But Pedro II, hailed as the father of Brazilian culture, founded no new faculties at all.

Although he sought to enhance the prestige of education, he understood little about this matter, and most of the concrete accomplishments of his reign in the field of education were the acts of individual ministers. On the initiative of the War Ministry, the polytechnical school was separated from the military academy to become the Escola Polytecnica, the empire's school of engineering, in 1874. In 1878, the minister of the empire, Leoncio de Carvalho, created a normal school that for a while had a status between high school and college. The following year, Carvalho passed a law liberalizing education and permitting private individuals to organize professional schools and colleges (*faculdades livres*).[27] Only after the fall of the empire did various groups take advantage of this legislation. The empire's only other new endeavor was the Escola de Minas (school of mines) in Ouro Preto, which barely survived until the Republic. The number of students enrolled in higher education increased considerably during the last years of the empire (see tables 10A and 10B).

The figures in tables 10A, B, derived from successive reports of the ministers of the empire end the republican ministers of justice, are somewhat unreliable, especially those of 1865, which seem out of phase with those of neighboring years. Total matriculations seem to have stagnated between 1855 and 1874, but almost doubled between 1874 and 1880. Apparently enrollment peaked around 1886. The statistics for the Republic show, unsurprisingly, that attendance dropped drastically as a result of the civil war. It took a decade after the return of peace, in 1895, for university matriculations to surpass those of the best years of the empire.

The rising number of students at the end of the empire indicates that the elite began to have more respect for education and to perceive that more opportunities were becoming

Table 10A   Enrollment in Professional Schools: The Medical Schools of Bahia and Rio and the Law Schools of São Paulo and Recife

City	1855	1865	1874	1880	1886	1889	1895	1905
Bahia	239	133	284	411	777	400	141	360
Rio	253	161	503	587	535	463	270	815
São Paulo	264	430	151	385	510	473	120	536
Recife	320	396	284	466	932	887	197	434
Total	1,076	1,120	1,222	1,989	2,754	2,223	728	2,145

Table 10B   Enrollment in Other Higher Education, including the Polytechnical Institute, the School of Mines of Ouro Preto, and the Private Professional Schools "Faculdades Livres"

Type of School	1880	1886	1889	1895	1905
Polytech	264	209	181	27	182
Mines	—	24	59	161	28
"Faculdades Livres"	—	—	—	283	740
Total (Tables 10A and 10B)	2,253	2,987	2,463	1,199	3,045

Source: Reports of the imperial ministers of the empire and republican ministers of the interior.

Table 11   Brazilian National Budgets, by Ministry, for Fiscal Years from 1845–46 to 1899, from *Leis e Decretos* (in Thousands of Contos)

Ministry	1845–46	46–47	47–48	48–49	49–50	50–51	51–52	52–53	53–54
Total	24.8	24.1	Same	Same	26.8	26.3	Same	27.5	29.6
Empire	2.8	2.9			3.3	3.3		3.7	3.7
Justice	1.6	1.6			2.2	2.0		2.2	2.3
State	0.6	0.6			0.4	0.5		0.5	0.5
Navy	3.1	3.4			3.4	3.2		3.6	4.1
War	6.9	5.8			7.4	7.5		7.5	7.3
Finance	9.8	9.8			10.0	9.9		10.0	11.7

Ministry	1854–55	55–56	56–57	57–58	58–59	59–60	60–61	61–62
Total	31.2	32.4	33.8	35.5	40.1	48.3	Same	51.3
Empire	4.7	4.8	5.3	5.8	7.4	9.8		11.0
Justice	2.4	2.7	3.0	3.1	3.7	4.8		5.1
State	0.6	0.6	0.6	0.6	0.7	0.9		0.9
Navy	4.1	4.3	4.5	4.6	5.0	7.0		7.2
War	8.0	8.4	8.7	9.5	11.0	11.8		12.8
Finance	11.4	11.6	11.7	11.9	12.3	14.1		14.3

Ministry	1862–63	63–64	64–65	65–66	66–67	67–68	68–69	69–70
Total	Same	53.9	Same	58.9	Same	68.5	Same	Same
Empire		4.7		5.1		5.0		
Justice		3.2		3.1		3.3		
State		0.9		0.8		0.8		
Navy		7.5		7.5		8.1		
War		11.6		13.2		14.4		
Finance		17.7		20.1		25.1		
Agriculture		8.3		9.0		11.9		

Ministry	1870–71	71–72	72–73	73–74	74–75	75–76	76–77	77–78	78–79
Total	83.3	85.7	Same	98.3	Same	105.0	106.9	105.9	Same
Empire	5.0	5.3		7.1		7.7	7.7	7.6	
Justice	4.0	4.0		5.1		6.1	6.2	6.5	
State	0.8	0.8		1.0		1.2	1.1	1.1	
Navy	8.9	9.8		10.7		11.3	11.4	10.4	
War	13.5	12.9		15.8		15.4	16.8	14.9	
Finance	39.6	39.9		41.9		45.0	45.8	49.0	
Agriculture	11.6	13.0		16.6		18.3	17.8	16.4	

Table 11   (*Continued*)

Ministry	1879–80	80–81	81–82	82–83	83–84
Total	115.5	Same	Same	Same	Same
Empire	8.0				
Justice	6.5				
State	0.8				
Navy	10.3				
War	13.5				
Finance	57.2				
Agriculture	19.1				

Ministry	1884–85	85–86	86–87	1888	1889
Total	138.3	Same	137.6	141.2	Same
Empire	9.2		8.9	8.9	
Justice	6.8		6.4	6.4	
State	0.8		0.9	0.9	
Navy	11.1		10.9	10.8	
War	14.9		14.7	14.6	
Finance	63.4		61.7	64.4	
Agriculture	32.5		34.2	35.2	

Ministry	1890–92	1893	1894	1895	1896
Total	Missing	197.3	250.5	275.7	343.5
Justice and Interior		13.6	14.5	15.6	16.8
Exterior		1.6	1.8	1.9	2.0
Navy		15.7	17.8	17.8	25.3
War		28.8	30.0	36.7	52.8
Industry, Transportation, and Public Works		67.5	100.7	104.0	113.1
Finance		70.0	85.6	99.6	129.8

Ministry	1897	1898	1899
Total	329	325	346
Justice and Interior	16	16	16
Exterior	2	2	2
Navy	28	27	26
War	55	52	46
Industry, Transportation, and Public Works	99	88	89
Finance	129	139	166

Note: For the years 1888 to 1896 we present the figures actually expensed by the government. These data come from the *Orçamento da Receita e da Despesa* for the respective years, which may be seen in the library of the Ministry of Finance in Rio.

available within the liberal professions. These figures also suggest that the elite expanded to the point where many of its sons were forced off the land and into the professions. Some graduates felt that the imperial political leadership barred the way to their advancement, and so they tended to sympathize with the Republican Party.

At independence, there were no government high schools. Secondary education was conducted in a few church schools and in the homes of elite families who had private tutors. Between independence and 1850, local governments and private individuals established high schools in most of the provincial capitals. Thereafter educational opportunities expanded steadily, if not spectacularly. According to the minister of the empire's report of 1874, there were 3,593 secondary and 11,797 primary school students in Rio in 1874, a rather small fraction of the total school-age population. Provincial school attendance ranged from over 1,400 secondary and 20,000 primary students in Minas Gerais to no secondary school and 1,500 primary school students in Piaui. By comparing educational and demographic figures, one can deduce that only about 10 percent of the population could read and write at this time.

Unfortunately, the quality of available education is not easy to determine. It appears that Brazilian education was rather weak in comparison with that of Western Europe, the United States, or Argentina. The position of primary school teacher became a political reward in Brazil. Teachers' salaries remained pitifully low and often were paid months late. But since women had few other means of earning money, they and their families competed furiously for primary school positions. The viscount of Taunay wrote that when he became president of the province of Paraná in 1886, an adviser presented him with a proposal for educational reform consisting of transferring all primary teachers belonging to the opposing party to different towns so that they would be obliged to separate from their families or resign their positions, which could be awarded as political patronage.[28] Though many powerful imperial statesmen such as the viscount of Ouro Preto, the viscount of Taunay, and Leoncio de Carvalho understood the necessity of expanding and improving education, lack of funds prevented them from achieving major reforms.

In conclusion, Brazil's imperial and republican governments proved both willing and able to spend an amount equal to approximately half of total national exports. Revenues were dependent on tariffs, and public expenditures grew proportionally with trade. The Brazilian state mobilized as much of its society's resources as did other Western governments of its time and mobilized a considerably greater portion than did the United States.[29]

Notes

CHAPTER 1: INTERESTS OF THE ELITE

1. Nabuco, *Abolicionismo,* 143.
2. For an analysis of the political elite, see Carvalho, *Construção.*
3. Frank Colson, personal communication.
4. Haber, *How Latin America.*
5. Prado Junior, *Historia econômica,* 346.
6. Two important studies question the idea of dependence on Europe. They characterize the elite and the state as active, independent agents. See Leff, *Underdevelopment,* and Topik, *Political Economy.*
7. Luz, *Luta,* 24.
8. For example, the law of 1882, which liberalized the organization of limited-liability corporations, determined that foreign-owned firms still required a specific act of the legislature in order to incorporate.
9. Mello, "Economics."
10. On the land law of 1850, see Costa, *Da monarquia,* 139–161.
11. Dean, *Rio Claro;* Franco, *Homens livres;* and Stein, *Vassouras.*
12. Instituto Histórico, Conde d'Eu Collection, box 276, document 19.
13. The viscount of Taunay was the president of the Central Immigration Society and participated in the politics of Santa Catarina, the province where immigrant small farmers played a significant role.

14. Congresso Agrícola de 1878, 101, 132–134, 245.
15. *O Militar,* October 26, 1854, and April 25, 1855, and *Tribuna Militar,* March 5, 1882. These newspapers can be found at the National Library in Rio de Janeiro.
16. Stein, *Brazilian Cotton Manufacture,* chapter 6.
17. Dean, *Industrialization,* chapters 1 and 2.
18. Congresso Nacional, *Meio circulante,* 160, 192.
19. See chapter 4.
20. Journalists at the *Rio News* saw the coming of abolition as a real opportunity to reshape Brazilian society. For example, see the article of January 15, 1888, an excerpt of which appears as an epigraph to this volume. By 1901 the editor had become thoroughly discouraged and despaired of reform. See the March 19, 1901, issue. The officer corps also viewed the coming of emancipation as a necessary measure in order to modernize Brazil. With the fall of Canudos, the military had also lost its hope of changing Brazil in the short run. See Schulz, *Exército.*
21. Sodré, *Formação,* 322.
22. Prado Junior, *Historia econômica,* 215.
23. Ibid., 199 and 215.
24. *Gazeta de Notícias,* May 13, 1892.
25. For example, see Prado Junior, *Historia econômica,* 228 and 275, and Sodré, *Formação,* 335.

CHAPTER 2: THE INTERNATIONAL FINANCIAL SYSTEM

1. Repeated references to the foreign debt and the need to defend the country's creditworthiness can be found in the parliamentary minutes, the finance ministers' reports, and the press. See, for example, Alfredo, *Relatório da Fazenda,* 1888, 11.
2. See Roover, *Rise and Decline of the Medici Bank,* and Hunt, *Medieval Super-Companies.*
3. Clapham, *Bank of England,* I, 167.
4. Davies, *History of Money,* 251.
5. Clapham, *Bank of England,* I, 162.
6. Bagehot *Lombard Street,* 83.
7. Clapham, *Bank of England,* II, 19.
8. Kindleberger, *Financial History,* 64–66.
9. Clapham, *Bank of England,* II, 78.
10. Vilar, *History of Gold and Money,* chapter 35.
11. Originally a trade transaction, which is simply the sale of any merchandise, consisted of the seller's presenting a draft to the buyer payable at some time in the future, commonly ninety days. The draft states "You owe me." The buyer recognizes his debt by signing the draft and returning it to the seller. The seller then can discount the draft at his bank. The bank discounts ninety days of interest and gives the seller the remainder in cash. Both the seller and the buyer are liable for the type of draft that is called "two-name" paper. Rather than give the seller gold, the bank may deliver its banknotes to him. In this manner, a trade transaction produces an issue of banknotes. The banknotes may be retired when the buyer discharges his draft. On the other hand, if no one presents

the banknotes to the bank, these instruments will continue to circulate independent of the liquidation of the original transaction.

12. Deane, *First Industrial Revolution,* 199.

13. Clapham, *Bank of England,* II, 183.

14. Hammond, *Banks and Politics,* 79–82.

15. Ibid., 228–247, 466–480, and 712.

16. Ibid., 596.

17. Conant, *History of Modern Banks of Issue,* 350.

18. Ibid., 328.

19. Ibid., 123.

20. Ibid., 328.

21. Davies, *History of Money,* 482. Bonnet, *Crédit et les banques,* 91, notes that by 1874, banks in New York held a volume of deposits equal to ten times their issues of notes. This relationship of deposits to notes was apparently not yet typical of the country as a whole.

22. Conant, *History of Modern Banks of Issue,* 373.

23. Ritter, *Goldbugs,* 131–136.

24. Gide, *Curso de economia política,* 342–343, and Kindleberger, *Financial History,* 131.

25. The South Sea Bubble was a short but violent speculative movement on the London exchange, largely with the papers of the South Sea Company. This bubble has generally been considered a classic example of irresponsibility mixed with corruption and greed. An interesting recent publication that explains and almost defends the speculative movement is Neal, *Rise of Financial Capitalism.* On the foundation of the London capital market, see also Carruthers, *City of Capital.*

26. Sayers, *Lloyds Bank,* 218.

27. Ibid., 222.

28. Clapham, *Bank of England,* II, 311.

29. Ibid., I, 205.

30. Ibid., I, 114.

31. Ibid., I, 80, 91, 95.

32. Braudel, "The Perspectives of the World," 246–248.

33. Cameron, *Banking,* 151–182.

34. Clapham, *Bank of England,* II, 94. For a detailed account of the 1825 crisis, see Dawson, *First Latin American Debt Crisis.*

35. Studenski and Kroos, *Financial History,* 118.

36. See Marichal, *Century of Debt Crisis,* and Feis, *Europe: The World's Banker.*

37. Castro, *Empresas estrangeiras,* 61–67. A part of the equity attributed to the foreign companies appears to have functioned more as long-term debt with guaranteed interest. In 1889, guaranteed interest remitted by the government reached £0.8 million. Rates generally were between 5 and 7 percent, implying total debt outstanding of £13 million. If private unguaranteed debt reached £3 million, as Castro states, the total in 1889 for medium-term debt of companies must have been around £16 million.

38. Sweigart, "Financing and Marketing Brazilian Export Agriculture," 116.

39. The current account includes the commercial account (exports of good less imports of goods); the services account, which covers payments and receipts of interest, dividends,

insurance, freight, and tourism; and other current or short-term capital flows, including workers' remittances. Contemporaries saw their increasing public and private indebtedness as a sign of this current-account deficit. The *Rio News* of April 15, 1879, estimated the average trade surplus for the years 1875–1878 at 27,000 contos. Net external interest payments amounted to somewhere between 25,000 and 30,000 contos. This newspaper put workers' remittances at 20,000 contos and private bank interest at 10,000 contos, leaving a deficit on the current account of some 33,000 contos. Unlike other observers, the *Rio News* went on to state that if net smuggling plus understatement of exports (to avoid export duties) plus the export duty itself are counted, Brazil actually enjoyed an average current surplus of 17,000 contos. The editor's estimate of net smuggling appears to be sanguine.

40. Carreira, *História financeira*, II, 741, and Correia, *Problema econômico,* 69.
41. Data obtained from Carreira, *Historia financeira,* II, 639, 648, 726–741.
42. Alfredo, *Relatório da Fazenda,* 1888, 11.

CHAPTER 3: CREDIT AND CRISES, 1850 TO 1875

1. Bagehot, *Lombard Street,* 140–141, demonstrates that contemporaries perceived this phenomenon.
2. There are of course substantial differences between the oil crisis and the wheat crisis of the early nineteenth century. Petroleum is an exhaustible resource whereas wheat is not. A failed harvest could be general, making all countries poorer, whereas the oil crisis effectively transferred wealth from certain regions to others. Finally, the contemporary financial system is more sophisticated and capable of intervening to affect the course of a crisis.
3. Joslin, *Century of Banking,* 67–68.
4. Ibid., 68–73.
5. Ibid., 73.
6. The viscount of Mauá authorized his branch manager in Rio Grande do Sul to pay 6 percent per annum for deposits in slack times and as much as 8 percent during the harvest season. See the Mauá Collection at the Instituto Histórico e Geográfico Brasileiro, box 513, document 11, Mauá–Ricardo José Ribeiro, September 11, 1859.
7. Mauá, understanding that the opportunity cost of idle funds was much higher in Brazil than in Britain, managed his idle cash reserves at a level below the English rule of thumb, which was one third of liabilities. Instituto Histórico, box 513, document 10, Mauá–Ricardo José Ribeiro, February 20, 1861.
8. Bernardo de Souza Franco, *Bancos,* 27–31.
9. Nabuco, *Estadista,* 132.
10. Viana, *Banco do Brasil,* 320–321.
11. Ibid., 324–327.
12. Ibid., 327.
13. *Consultas do conselho de estado,* Seção de Fazenda, 1856–1860, 220.
14. Viana, *Banco do Brasil,* 335.
15. Wileman, *Brazilian Exchange,* 10, 135.

16. *Consultas do conselho de estado,* Seção de Fazenda, 1856–1860, 258.

17. Carreira, *Historia financeira,* II, 729–731.

18. Viana, *Banco do Brasil,* 346.

19. Ibid., 406.

20. Cavalcanti, *Resenha financeira,* 169, cites a speech of the viscount of Ouro Preto shortly after the crisis of 1875. The judicious use of banknotes to replace gold in times of crisis was used in industrial countries to good effect. When France had to pay large reparations to Germany after the Franco-Prussian War in 1870, the government insulated the local economy from a potentially disastrous deflation by issuing banknotes equal in value to the gold removed from circulation. See Gide, *Curso de economia política,* 360.

21. *Leis e Decretos do Brasil,* August 31, 1857.

22. See table 1, in this chapter.

23. Viana, *Banco do Brasil,* 356.

24. Ibid., 359.

25. *Consultas do Conselho de Estado,* Seção de Fazenda, 1856–1860, 213–214.

26. Viana, *Banco do Brasil,* 17, 27–29.

27. Ibid., 397.

28. Ibid., 416.

29. Joslin, *Century of Banking,* 71.

30. In October, the coffee-export season brought the exchange rate up to par. Instituto Histórico, box 513, document 10, Mauá–Ricardo José Ribeiro, October 4, 1860. In a letter dated December 21, contained in the same document, Mauá noted that the secession of the Confederacy in the United States had forced the Brazilian exchange rate well below the gold point in anticipation of lower coffee sales to the U.S., Brazil's major market.

31. Cavalcanti, *Resenha financeira,* 65, blames the law of 1860 for this crisis.

32. Goldsmith, *Brasil 1850–1984,* 44.

33. Carreira, *Historia financeira,* I, 415.

34. The figures for banknotes and paper money in circulation up to 1889 were taken from Cavalcanti, *Resenha financeira,* 333; the numbers for the years 1890–1894 come from the *Relatórios da Fazenda.* The figures for exports may be found in Carreira, *Historia financeira,* II, 726–741.

35. Instituto Historico, box 513, document 9, Mauá–Ricardo José Ribeiro, October 5, 1862.

36. Ibid., September 20, 1862.

37. Ibid., December 8, 1862.

38. Ibid., Document 8, March 9, 1864.

39. Clapham, *Bank of England,* II, 259–260.

40. For more information on the Paraguayan War, see Holanda *História geral,* vol. 6, 235–258.

41. Viana, *Banco do Brasil,* 433.

42. Ibid., 428–432. In addition to the fraudulent practices revealed during the liquidation process, the process itself occasioned further abuses. The former prime minister Zacarias de Gões e Vasconcelos accused the liquidators of graft and favoritism to the government's friends among the creditors. Anais do Senado, June 10, 1865.

43. Clapham, *Bank of England,* II, 261–270.
44. Joslin, *Century of Banking,* 73. Writing to his manager in Rio Grande do Sul, Mauá revealed that the Overend, Gurney affair was merely a pretext for aborting his merger with the London and Brazilian Bank. In fact, after fewer than four years in Brazil, the British institution had become technically insolvent as a result of uncollectable loans. Instituto Histórico, box 513, document 7, letter of December 6, 1866.
45. Nabuco, *Abolicionismo,* 123.
46. Ibid., 38, and Conrad, *Destruction,* chapter 6.
47. Nabuco, *Abolicionismo,* 74.
48. Nabuco, *Estadista,* 636.
49. Ibid., 635–637.
50. See table 1, this chapter.
51. Azevedo, *O mulato,* 73.
52. Carreira, *Historia financeira,* II, 735–737.
53. Clapham, *Bank of England,* II, 289–297.
54. In fact the exchange rate, which approached parity in May of 1873, declined to 26 pence in June. This movement occurred not because merchants feared a fall in demand from the consuming countries but rather because they perceived that Brazil's coffee harvest would be poor and therefore export volume would be inadequate to sustain the milreis. Instituto Histórico, box 513, document 3, Mauá–Ricardo José Ribeiro, June 4, 1873.
55. Holanda, *Historia geral,* VII, 171–172.
56. Mauá followed conservative lending practices. He wrote to his manager in Rio Grande do Sul that loans should be made exclusively to finance legitimate trade transactions. Both the drawer and the endorser of the drafts should be men of substance and character. Drafts should be for no more than ninety days and should not have to be renewed. Excessive concentration of risk should be avoided. Instituto Histórico, box 513, document 10, Mauá–Ricardo José Ribeiro, September 16, 1861. Unfortunately, given the lack of liquidity on the part of the ultimate borrowers, Mauá was not always able to follow his own rules.
57. See Joslin, *Century of Banking,* 54, and Faria, *Mauá,* 356, 494–497.
58. The Instituto Histórico e Geográfico Brasileiro in Rio de Janeiro has an extensive collection of Mauá's correspondence. My thanks to Marcia Naomi Koshiashi for calling my attention to these documents. Judging from Mauá's letters to his managers, foreign exchange constituted the bank's major source of income. Starting in the 1850s, Mauá had three branches in Rio Grande do Sul, three in São Paulo, and several in Uruguay and Argentina, in addition to his headquarters in Rio de Janeiro and his affiliates in London, Manchester, and Paris. After the crisis of 1864 he opened branches in Recife and Belem. He also had agents elsewhere in the Plate and in other towns of Rio Grande. Often he could arbitrage as much as 4 percent between Rio Grande and the capital, the exchange rate being 25 pence in Rio and 26 in the south, for instance. He also engaged in continuous arbitrage operations with the currencies of the Plate countries. Mauá even arbitraged among the money markets of London, Paris, and Lisbon. The instrument he used was the international bill of exchange. The tenor of these instruments were typically ninety days. He would generally draw against his European affiliates and correspondents while simul-

taneously purchasing drafts from his commercial customers. Often he either drew heavily before covering his position, in the expectation that the exchange rate would appreciate, or purchased drafts on Europe in the expectation that the milreis would fall. He also used British, Brazilian, and Platine gold coins to arbitrage among the various markets, transporting the coins to the city that valued them most highly. Gold coins also served as a vehicle for speculating on the exchange. See Instituto Historico, box 513, document 10, letters of January 8, 1860, and January 20, 1861. Mauá keenly felt the competition of the two British banks that began to do business in Brazil in 1863. On February 20, 1864, he complained to Ricardo José Ribeiro, his trusted branch manager, that the English banks were ruining the exchange market by buying drafts to earn a mere 2 percent. The exchange activities of the foreign banks became a subject of much controversy a little later on.

59. Faria, *Mauá,* 482–493. See also Caldeira, *Mauá, o empresário do império,* which provides an excellent assessment of Mauá and his role in the modernization of Brazil.

60. See *Relatórios da Fazenda* of this period.

61. The financial statements of these banks may be found in the appendix of the minutes of the Agricultural Congress of 1878.

62. Although he had had no prior banking experience, Sinimbú presided over the Banco Nacional, which had entered into restructuring at the same time as the Banco Mauá and which also went into final bankruptcy in 1878. *Rio News,* April 5, 1879. Rio Branco was the state-controlled Banco do Brasil's first vice president and second president. See Peláez and Suzigan, *Historia monetaria,* 81. Itaborahy, Cotegipe, and Dantas were later presidents of this bank, and João Alfredo and Ouro Preto became involved with privately owned banks after the Republic terminated their political careers.

CHAPTER 4: COFFEE PLANTERS

1. See Sweigart, *Financing and Marketing Brazilian Export Agriculture.*

2. Congresso Agrícola de 1878, 149.

3. Ibid., 149–150, and Sweigart, "Financing and Marketing Brazilian Export Agriculture," 192.

4. Kilbourne, *Slave Agriculture,* 38.

5. Levi, *The Prados.*

6. Kilbourne, *Slave Agriculture,* 38.

7. Ibid., 127.

8. On the other hand, Sweigart, *Financing and Marketing Brazilian Export Agriculture,* 146, notes that bank mortgages provided a significant volume of financing for planters in certain privileged regions.

9. See for example Dean, *Rio Claro.*

10. Prime Minister Ouro Preto discovered how tenuous land titles were in 1889 when he tried to grant mortgages rapidly in order to appease the ex-slaveholders. In the introduction to *Auxílios à lavoura* (Rio de Janeiro, 1889), the manual for rural lending, Ouro Preto acknowledged the difficulties of proving deeds.

11. Congresso Agrícola de 1878, page 74.

12. Viana, *Banco do Brasil,* 459–461.

13. Congresso Agrícola de 1878, 155.

14. *Relatório da Fazenda* of 1889, 67.

15. See Evanson, "Liberal Party."

16. Congresso Agrícola de 1878, 125.

17. As late as 1888, three fifths of Brazil's coffee exports were shipped through the port of Rio de Janeiro. See Delfim Netto, *O problema do café,* 17.

18. Congresso Agrícola de 1878, 161–162.

19. Ibid., 163–164.

20. Ibid., 155.

21. Ibid., 121.

22. Ibid., 74

23. See Hall, "Origins," and Davatz, *Memórias.*

24. Congresso Agrícola de 1878, 75–76.

25. See Dean, *Rio Claro,* and Costa, *Da senzala à colônia.*

26. Congresso Agrícola de 1878, 139.

27. Ibid., 164.

28. Ibid., 97.

29. Ibid., 101.

30. Ibid., 245–246.

31. Ibid., 164. See also, for example, the future viscount of Ouro Preto's (Afonso Celso de Assis Figueiredo) speech of May 4, 1877, against expenses on armaments, in the *Anais da Câmara de Deputados* of that year.

32. Congresso Agrícola de 1878, 139.

33. Ibid., 132.

34. Ibid., 74.

35. Cavalcanti, *Resenha financeira,* 71, and *Relatorio do Ministerio da Agricultura,* 1889, appendix. Before the fall of the monarchy, eighty-seven guarantees totaling 60,300 contos were granted, although few mills were actually built and relatively little of this money was disbursed. My thanks to Roberta Meira of the University of São Paulo for clarifying this point.

36. Congresso Agrícola de 1878, 78.

37. Ibid., 132.

38. Ibid., 112.

39. Ibid., 113.

40. Ibid., 69.

41. Ibid., 105, 224.

42. Ibid., 60.

43. Ibid., 226, 240.

44. Ibid., 131–132.

45. Ibid., 134.

46. Sweigart, "Financing and Marketing Brazilian Export Agriculture," 66–99.

47. Pinho, *Cartas de Francisco Otaviano,* 130.

48. Ibid., 113

49. Congresso Agrícola de 1878, 60, 150, 226

50. Ibid., 240.
51. Ibid., 60.

CHAPTER 5: ABOLITION

1. *Rio News,* February 15, 1888.
2. Ibid., May 14, 1879.
3. Ibid., November 24, 1879. This article is one of a number that compare Brazil and the United States. Carvalho, *Teatro de sombras,* 99, notes that Dantas made an attempt to introduce a land tax in 1884.
4. Congresso Agrícola de 1878, 139.
5. *Rio News,* October 7, 1889. See also Holloway, *Immigrants,* chapter 4.
6. For the hostility of the officer corps toward the elite, see Schulz, *Exercito,* 38–51 and 86–90.
7. See table 1, in chapter 1; Cavalcanti, *Resenha financeira,* 156; and *Leis e Decretos do Brasil,* April 15 and June 20, 1878.
8. See Evanson, "The Liberal Party."
9. Cavalcanti, *Resenha financeira,* 71–72.
10. Carreira, *Historia financeira,* II, 764.
11. Holanda, *Historia geral,* VI, 128–129.
12. Carreira, *História financeira,* II, 765.
13. Viana, *Banco do Brasil,* 513.
14. Holanda, *História geral,* VI, 247–248.
15. Although many northeastern slave owners complained bitterly about emancipation without indemnity, in fact abolition did not cause them any real hardship. See Eisenberg, *Sugar Industry,* chapter 7.
16. Nabuco, *Abolicionismo,* 221.
17. Law of December 17, 1886, in *Leis e Decretos do Brasil.*
18. Law of October 20, 1887. For an excellent study of the relationship between the northeastern elite and the imperial government at this time, see Evaldo de Cabral de Mello, *O norte agrário.*
19. Sweigart, *Financing and Marketing Brazilian Export Agriculture,* 200.
20. Viana, *Banco do Brasil,* 513, states that in 1887 almost half of the Banco do Brasil's mortgage portfolio was more than two years past due. For this reason, bankers must have considered rural mortgages poor credit risks. The Banco da Bahia's new mortgages at this time were also secured by urban real estate. See Azevedo and Lins, *Banco da Bahia,* 165.
21. *Relatório da Fazenda* of 1887, 21.
22. Ibid., 21–23.
23. At 95, with interest at 5 percent. Carreira, *Historia financeira,* II, 598.
24. Ibid., 603
25. *Relatório da Fazenda* of 1887, 21.
26. See Hall, "Origins."
27. *O Paiz,* July 6 and September 22 and 26, 1887.
28. Colson, "Death of Expectations," 56, letter of March 19, 1888.

29. See for instance the *Gazeta de Notícias* for the first ten days of March 1888.

30. Carreira, *História financeira*, II, 208.

31. *Relatório da Fazenda* of 1888, 11.

32. Ibid., 11.

33. *Rio News*, January 24, 1888.

34. Colson, "Death of Expectations," 56–70.

35. Barbosa, *O papel*, 117–118.

36. See Fernandes, *The Negro in Brazilian Society*, and Ianni, *As metamorfoses do escravo*.

37. *Cidade do Rio*, July 10, 1888.

38. *Gazeta de Notícias*, January 5, 1889.

39. Ibid., June 17, 1888.

40. Carreira, *Historia financeira*, II, 670 and *Relatório da Fazenda* of 1889, 29.

41. *Relatório da Fazenda* of 1889, 29.

42. Cavalcanti, *Resenha financeira*, 43. See also contemporary newspapers, particularly the *Gazeta de Notícias*. The increased availability of capital in Europe, especially Britain, at this time was a necessary precondition for foreign investment. Confidence in Brazil and its government was an equally essential factor. Contemporary Argentina attracted an even greater flow of investment capital than did Brazil, whereas other Latin American countries, offering fewer interesting opportunities, received much less investment. Europeans perceived Brazil as the second best market to invest their funds in Latin Amrica. For figures, see Feis, *Europe, the World's Banker*, 23.

43. Cavalcanti, *Resenha financeira*, 43, and Stein, *Brazilian Cotton Manufacture*, chapter 7. On January 24, 1888, the *Rio News* observed, "The increasing number of cotton mills has largely supplied the demand for coarser fabric."

44. Viana, *Banco do Brasil*, 529.

45. Franco, *Reforma monétaria*, 66–71.

46. Viana, *Banco do Brasil*, 569.

47. *Rio News*, January 7, 1889, criticizes João Alfredo for insisting upon large minimum sizes for banks of issue, 5,000 contos in Rio and 2,000 in provincial capitals, observing that U.S. banks of issue could have much smaller capital bases. See also *Gazeta de Notícias*, May 6, 1889.

48. *Relatorio da Fazenda* of 1888, 11.

49. The other Latin American country that encouraged the use of banknotes at this time, Argentina, foresaw only issues backed by bonds in its law of November 1887. Gold-backed banknotes appeared to be unviable. See Cortés Conde, *Dinero, deuda y crisis*, 201. In Brazil, the 1860 Law of Obstacles, which obliged banks to redeem banknotes in gold, caused the institutions founded during Souza Franco's ministry to renounce their right to issue banknotes. See also Cavalcanti, *Resenha financeira*, 128–130.

50. Franco, *Reforma monétaria*, 66–71, reaches similar conclusions.

51. Law of November 24, 1888, in *Leis e Decretos do Brasil*.

52. *Gazeta de Notícias*, May 1, 1889.

53. *Rio News*, May 13, 1889.

54. *Gazeta de Notícias*, May 2, May 6, and June 3, 1889.

55. Ibid., June 8 and June 10, 1889.

56. Ibid., May 6, 1889.
57. Schulz, *Exercito,* 108–120.
58. Ibid., 89–93.
59. See, for instance, the *Cidade do Rio* of July 4 and July 7, 1888, which describes the antagonism between freedmen who became monarchists and former slave owners turned republicans.
60. *Gazeta de Notícias,* June 12, 1889, and *Rio News,* June 17, 1889.

CHAPTER 6: THE ENCILHAMENTO

1. *Gazeta de Notícias,* June 12, 1889.
2. *Rio News,* June 17, 1889.
3. By 1889, the provincial income of São Paulo was 94 percent that of Rio de Janeiro. See Cavalcanti, *Resenha financeira,* 280–281. Within a few years, the income of São Paulo would in fact far surpass that of its declining neighbor.
4. *Gazeta de Notícias,* June 8, 1889.
5. *Gazeta de Notícias,* June 10, 1889, and Monteiro, *Pesquisas e depoimentos,* 216–219.
6. On the enthusiasm of the Commercial Association of Rio de Janeiro for the viscount of Ouro Preto, see Ridings, *Business Interest Groups,* 315.
7. Schulz, *Exercito,* 133–140, and *O Paiz,* October 11, 1889.
8. Individual politicians such as Quintino Bocayuva played barracks politics; most of the press, including even the liberal *Gazeta de Notícias,* helped create an atmosphere conducive to military intervention. See *O Paiz, Cidade do Rio,* and *Correio Paulistano.*
9. Cavalcanti, *Resenha financeira,* 257.
10. Castro, *Empresas estrangeiras,* 56–67.
11. Viana, *Banco do Brasil,* 569.
12. Decree of July 7, 1889, in *Leis e Decretos do Brasil.*
13. Cavalcanti, *Resenha financeira,* 57–60, 84.
14. Viana, *Banco do Brasil,* 538.
15. Ibid., 579.
16. Auxílios à Lavoura, 53.
17. Ibid., page 75, and Cavalcanti, *Resenha financeira,* 87.
18. Auxílios à Lavoura, 75.
19. *Rio News,* July 1, 1889.
20. Ibid., July 8, 1889.
21. Ibid., August 26, 1889.
22. Cavalcanti, *Resenha financeira,* 355. Nonindustrial stocks also dominated the British stock market at this time. Most of the volume consisted of rails and utilities. See Crouzet, *Victorian Economy,* 334.
23. *Rio News,* March 31, 1890.
24. Cavalcanti, *Resenha financeira,* 50.
25. Congresso Agrícola de 1878, 60, 150, 226.
26. Orçamento da Receita e da Despesa of 1889.
27. See the Orçamento da Receita e da Despesa of 1891.

28. Carreira, *História financeira,* II, 847.
29. Ibid., 716. Ouro Preto's conversion of the debt was undertaken at 90. He increased the principal of the debt by some 11 percent to save 1 percent per year over thirty years.
30. Cavalcanti, *Resenha financeira,* 336.
31. Ibid., 60.
32. Ibid., 57.
33. *Gazeta de Notícias,* October 7, 1889. A little earlier, on August 25, 1889, the same paper remarked that Ouro Preto tried so hard to win business support that there was no one left on the Rua do Ouvidor who had not been made at least a lieutenant in the National Guard.
34. See, for example, *Gazeta de Notícias,* September 5, 1889, and *Cidade do Rio,* September 17, 1889.
35. For details on the constitution, see Roure, *Constituinte republicana.*
36. See *Almanaques Militares* in the archives of the Ministry of War in Rio de Janeiro as well as Schulz, *Exercito,* 121–140.
37. *Rio News,* March 17, 1890. By this date, another 14,000 contos of aid to agriculture had been disbursed beyond the 26,000 of Ouro Preto's tenure. The aid to agriculture program ended in May 1890. See Viana, *Banco do Brasil,* 614.
38. Franco, *Reforma monetaria,* 97.
39. British Foreign Office, box 658, letter of December 23, 1889, from Wyndham to Salisbury.
40. So it seemed in the months following the coup. See for instance the *Rio News* of January 27, 1890.
41. Ibid., December 2, 1889.
42. Franco, *Reforma monetária,* 98, thinks that in fact Barbosa gave the ultimatum to the banks so that he could eliminate convertible notes. Before the ninety-day period expired, Barbosa produced his proposal for nonconvertible "gold-backed" notes.
43. The *Rio News* supported Ruy Barbosa prior to the decree of January 17. In a lengthy article dated December 2, 1889, this paper advocated adopting bond-backed notes, as the United States had done. For a more favorable view of Ruy Barbosa's intentions, see Peláez and Suzigan, *História monetária,* 141–145.
44. Cavalcanti, *Resenha financeira,* 65.
45. Franco, *Reforma monetária,* 107.
46. Ibid., 125.
47. Law of March 8, 1890, in *Leis e Decretos do Brasil.*
48. Viana, *Banco do Brasil,* 593–594.
49. Sayers, *Lloyds Bank,* 222.
50. Taunay, *O Encilhamento,* 4–6.
51. Abranches, *Governo provisorio,* 80.
52. Ibid., 102.
53. Ibid., 91.
54. The *Rio News* of January 27, 1890, noted that mass defaults had occurred on the stock exchange even before November 15 as wary investors refused to pay in capital they had already subscribed. According to this source, by December 31, "no one paid anyone."

55. *Gazeta de Notícias,* March 16, 1892.

56. The law of March 8, 1890, was not meant to be temporary.

57. Letter of June 16, 1891, from Ruy Barbosa to Mayrink, in the archives of the Casa de Ruy Barbosa in Rio de Janeiro.

58. *Rio News,* August 18, 1890. According to Magalhães Júnior, *Rui: O homem e o mito,* 82, the minister declined the offer of this house at the urging of his mother-in-law. Magalhães notes that Barbosa accepted other pecuniary rewards from Mayrink and his friends.

59. Viana, *Banco do Brasil,* 614.

60. Taunay, *Ensaios,* 263, provides figures on incorporations by month during the *Encilhamento.*

61. *Rio News,* November 3, 1890.

62. Taunay, *Encilhamento,* 234.

63. *Rio News,* November 17, 1890.

64. Ibid., January 6, 1891.

65. Ibid., December 29, 1890, and January 6, 1891.

66. British Foreign Office, box 666, letter of February 20, 1890, Wyndham to Salisbury.

67. Abranches, *Governo provisório,* 367–369.

68. *Rio News,* July 28, 1890, *Gazeta de Notícias,* October 9 and December 3, 1890.

69. Castro, *Empresas estrangeiras,* 56–68.

70. Franco, *Reforma monetária,* 44–50.

71. The *Rio News* of March 10, 1891, noted that "a few of the shrewdest speculators are now transferring their gains into pounds sterling and sending them abroad."

72. Hanley, *Native Capital,* discusses the history of the São Paulo stock exchange. On page 190 she describes Barbosa's relationship to this institution: "Ironically, a stock market was not envisioned by the government policymakers."

73. See the respective appendices of the reports of the ministers of finance.

74. Abranches, *Governo provisório,* 286.

75. British Foreign Office, box 675, letter of February 27, 1891, from Adams to Salisbury.

76. *Gazeta de Notícias,* February 5, 1891.

77. Ibid., October 9, 1890.

78. *Rio News,* June 30, 1890.

79. British Foreign Office, box 675, letter of January 23, 1891 from Adams to Salisbury.

80. *Rio News,* February 17, 1891.

81. Ibid., March 17, 1891.

82. A law of 1875 authorized the government to guarantee a return of 7 percent to investors in modern sugar mills. The total capital so guaranteed by the fall of the monarchy reached 60,300 contos. In April 1891, Lucena suspended 22,000 contos of these guarantees covering a number of projects that had not yet been started. Few central sugar mills were actually built under the guarantees. See Relatorio do Ministerio da Agricultura of 1890 and 1891, appendices.

83. British Foreign Office, box 677, letters of November 8 and November 20, 1891, from Wyndham to Salisbury.

84. *Rio News,* October 29, 1891.

85. *Gazeta de Notícias,* November 24, 1891.
86. Rothschild Archive, XI 65 8A, Rothschild to Lucena, November 9, 1891.
87. Rothschild Archive, XI 65 8B, article of December 1, 1891.
88. For the role of the *Encilhamento* in the early history of industrialization, see Stein, *Brazilian Cotton Manufacture;* Topik, *Political Economy;* Luz, *Luta;* Castro, *Empresas estrangeiras;* Franco, *Reforma monetária;* and Tannuri, *O Encilhamento.*
89. Luz, *Luta,* 49–66.
90. Ibid., 168–177.
91. Taunay, *Ensaios,* 265, provides figures on shares in the different activities.
92. *Rio News,* January 27, 1890.
93. See Topik, *Trade and Gunboats.*
94. *Gazeta de Notícias,* February 20, 1891, noted particularly the potential effect of this treaty upon furniture manufacturers.
95. Ibid., December 19, 1892, reported that comparing a fourteen-month period, from April 1891 to May 1892, to the fourteen months before, exports increased from $95 million to $135 million, and imports from the United States went from $16 million to $17 million.
96. Ouro Preto, although a member of the opposition, was called upon by João Alfredo to help draft the law of November 24, 1888, which reestablished banks of issue. *Relatório da Fazenda,* 1888, 11, João Alfredo argued that a commodity exporter such as Brazil could not have a metal-based currency.
97. Joslin, *Century of Banking,* 54–56, notes the similar difficulties with convertible currency experienced by Uruguay.
98. Even that advocate of tight money, Finance Minister Leopoldo de Bulhões, writing after the fact, admitted that the payment of wages made it necessary to expand the circulating medium from 200,000 contos to between 250,000 and 300,000. This increase, though nothing like the growth of the circulating medium during the Encilhamento, would nevertheless have been significant. See Bulhões, *Perfis parlamentares,* 302, speech of August 2, 1893.

CHAPTER 7: ORTHODOX REACTION: THE UNSUCCESSFUL PHASES

1. *Rio News,* April 19, 1892.
2. Ibid., January 19 and 26, 1892. See also the *Gazeta de Notícias* for these weeks. In a telegram of February 3, 1892, Industry Minister Serzedello Correia advised the Rothschilds that the government unsuccessfully attempted to impose Francisco Rangel Pestana as president of the Banco da República in place of Mayrink's close associate, viscount Guahy. Rangel Pestana came from the PRP and opposed inconvertible banknotes. See Rothschild Archive, XI 65 8B.
3. *Rio News,* February 9, 1892.
4. Ibid., February 16, 1892.
5. Ibid., December 15, 1891.
6. *Gazeta de Notícias,* January 5, 1892.
7. Lobo, *História do Rio de Janeiro,* 445–469.
8. Congresso do Brasil, *Meio circulante,* 338.

9. Correia, *Problema econômico,* 97.
10. Grandi, "Aquisição da Rio Claro," 71–85.
11. *Rio News,* March 1, 1892.
12. Ibid., March 1 and March 15, 1892.
13. *Gazeta de Notícias,* July 4, 1892.
14. *Rio News,* March 8, 1892.
15. British Foreign Office, box 677, letter, December 7, 1891, Wyndham to Salisbury.
16. Azevedo and Lins, *História Banco da Bahia,* 160. In a communication to the Rothschilds dated June 19, 1892, Rodrigues Alves reiterated his intention not to issue banknotes and praised the Banco da Bahia for surrendering its privilege. Rothschild Archive, XI 65 8B.
17. For a discussion of the conspiracy, see the *Rio News* of April 12, 19, and 26, 1892. See also Ventura, *Euclides,* 105–108.
18. *Rio News,* April 12, 1892.
19. Ibid., May 17 and May 31, 1892.
20. *Gazeta de Notícias,* May 13, 1892.
21. For further information on the struggle in Rio Grande do Sul, see Love, *Rio Grande do Sul,* 26–75, and Carone, *República velha,* vol. 2, 85–145.
22. Rodrigues Alves resigned because he wanted the government to assume responsibility for the outstanding banknotes immediately and without indemnities to the banks. *Rio News,* August 30, 1892. Furthermore, although he had actually gone so far as to propose issuing 60,000 contos of "aid to industry" bonds following the banking committee's recommendation (according to the *Rio News* of May 31, 1892), Rodrigues Alves strongly opposed all subsidies to industry (*Rio News,* August 6, 1892).
23. Congresso Nacional, *Meio circulante,* 160–174.
24. *Gazeta de Notícias,* July 27, 1892.
25. Congresso Nacional, *Meio circulante,* 160.
26. Ibid., 192.
27. Rothschild Archive, XI 65 8B, Rodrigues Alves to Rothschild, June 2, 1892.
28. Congresso Nacional, *Meio circulante,* 345–348.
29. Ibid., 340–351.
30. Ibid., 214. See Bulhões, *Perfis parlamentares,* 222–243, for the complete speech of October 25, 1892. Bulhões and his group proposed to cancel immediately all rights to issue banknotes; existing banknotes would become the responsibility of the federal government. They further proposed that the gold and government bonds serving as backing for these issues be taken over by the government as part payment for assuming the liability for the issues. The value of the gold would be calculated at the exchange rate of the day and the bonds would be valued at their market price on the day of the takeover. As the outstanding banknotes far exceeded the value of banks' gold and bonds, Bulhões accepted that the banks would have to repay the remainder of the issues to the authorities in installments, possibly without interest. He proposed, further, that the government sell the gold and bonds in order to redeem 100,000 contos of paper money within the first year. These fiscal conservatives wanted the government to borrow gold abroad to the extent necessary to return the exchange rate to parity. In view of the crisis, Bulhões and his allies conceded doubling the limit of 25,000 contos per bank for government loans under

the law of 1885, on condition that Congress specifically approved this limit and that the banks in fact delivered government bonds as security for these liquidity facilities.

31. Congresso Nacional, *Meio circulante,* 200. See also Bulhões, *Perfis parlamentares,* 257–308, for his address to the Congress on August 2, 1893. In this well-informed and interesting, if somewhat lengthy, lecture, Bulhões gives a summary of the financial experiences of England, France, the United States, and Russia as well as those of Brazil.

32. Congresso Nacional, *Meio circulante,* 278.

33. Ibid., 174. If this gold had been borrowed from the government, it had to be repaid in specie. Since it was the government's gold, there was no reason for the authorities to indemnify the bank for it.

34. Stein, *Brazilian Cotton Manufacture,* chapter 7.

35. Ibid., chapter 8.

36. *Rio News,* December 20, 1892.

37. Correia, *Problema econômico,* 95

38. Machado, *Um republicano,* 84.

39. Even the *Rio News,* which opposed Serzedello on "aid to industry," conceded (December 7, 1892) that after a year of Rodrigues Alves and Serzedello, the economic situation had improved significantly.

40. Interestingly, this credit proved to be a balance-of-payment loan as the government helped itself to the gold. At least so it seemed to the *Rio News* of April 25, 1893.

41. *Rio News,* February 7, 1893.

42. Freire, *História da Revolvção,* 32–37.

43. For a vivid description, see Love, *Rio Grande do Sul.*

44. A contemporary view of this violence may be found in Afonso Lima Barreto's novel *O triste fim de Policarpo Quaresma,* first published in 1911.

45. British Foreign Office, box 706, letter of October 18, 1893, Wyndham to Rosebury.

46. Topik, *Trade and Gunboats.*

47. Rothschild Archive, XI 65 8B, Rothschild to Felisbelo Freire, November 8, 1893.

48. British Foreign Office, box 705, letter of September 10, 1893, Wyndham to Rosebury.

49. British Foreign Office, box 724, letter of February 19, 1894, Wyndham to Rosebury.

50. *Gazeta de Notícias,* November 18, 1894.

51. See for instance *Gazeta de Notícias,* January 18, 1897.

52. See budget figures in the appendix.

53. Castro, *Empresas estrangeiras,* 61–73.

54. Viana, *Banco do Brasil,* 649 and 656. In his ministerial report of 1899, Joaquim Murtinho provides somewhat different figures, which indicate that the circulating medium expanded under Prudente, after only one year of contraction. See Luz, *Idéias econômicas de Joaquim Murtinho,* 181.

55. Wileman, *Brazilian Exchange,* 264.

56. Ibid., 227, and *Rio News,* January 1, 1896.

57. Wileman, *Brazilian Exchange,* 172 and 264.

58. Ibid., 39.

59. Ibid., 175.

60. Ibid., 167.

61. Ibid., 163.
62. Ibid., 46–47.
63. Ibid., 138.
64. *Rio News,* May 19 and October 6, 1896.
65. Rothschild Archive, XI 65 9B, October 13, 1896.
66. Vitorino's reference to the "liquidation of the *Encilhamento*" appears in the *Rio News* of January 5, 1897, and Mayrink's link to Vitorino comes from the *Gazeta de Notícias* of March 2, 1897.
67. *Gazeta de Notícias,* January 16, 1897.
68. Schulz, *Exercito,* 197–202.
69. For a discussion of the Jacobins, see Queiroz, *Os radicais da República.*

CHAPTER 8: STABILIZATION

1. Marichal, *Century of Debt Crisis,* 49, 104.
2. Rothschild Archive, XI 65 10A, Bernardino de Campos to Rothschild, November 27, 1897.
3. Rothschild Archive, XI 65 10A, Rothschild to Bernardino de Campos, February 28, March 1, March 4, March 21, 1898.
4. *Anais da Câmara de Deputados* of 1898. On the eve of Brazil's resumption of interest payments in 1901, Senator Arthur Ríos castigated Murtinho for treating the foreign creditors much more generously than he treated the Brazilians. Ríos declared, "We are nothing more than a colony of the Jews of the City!" (sic) *Jornal do Brasil,* May 28, 1901.
5. Castro, *Empresas estrangeiras,* 61–73.
6. Contemporaries perceived the relationship between the Encilhamento and the debt crisis. See *Rio News,* April 26, 1898.
7. *Gazeta de Notícias,* April 7, 1900.
8. Luz, *Idéias econômicas de Joaquim Murtinho,* 190.
9. *Rio News,* September 25, 1900.
10. Ibid., September 4, 1900. Though advocating a balanced budget, the foreign commercial community resented the zeal of the excise-tax collectors—a sign that taxes were being imposed effectively.
11. Viana, *Banco do Brasil,* 706.
12. Guanabara, *Presidência Campos Sales,* 191.
13. Viana, *Banco do Brasil,* 667–693.
14. Guanabara, *Presidência Campos Sales,* 273.
15. Joslin, *Century of Banking,* 144–145.
16. Guanabara, *Presidência Campos Sales,* 192.
17. *Jornal do Brasil,* September 17, 1900.
18. *Cidade do Rio,* September 11, 1900.
19. *Gazeta de Notícias,* September 15, 1900.
20. This cash did not in fact exist. *Rio News,* September 18, 1900.
21. *Jornal do Brasil,* September 11, 1900. The most violent attack upon Petersen came from José do Patrocinio's newspaper *Cidade do Rio,* which on September 11 not only called

for Murtinho's resignation but also placed a detailed description of the German occupation of Paris in 1871 on the front page next to the denunciation of the German banker. The *Rio News* condemned the appointment of Petersen as well. Its American editor felt that this decision represented Murtinho's favoring German interests over those of Britain. He noted, on November 27, 1900, that Petersen had sold a doubtful loan of 2,400 milreis from the Brasilianische Bank to the Banco da República, a highly improper transaction because Peterson was a director of both institutions.

22. Rothschild Archive, XI 65 10C, Joaquim Murtinho to Rothschild, September 26, 1900.
23. *Jornal do Brasil,* November 29, 1900.
24. Ibid., September 13 and September 18, 1900.
25. *Gazeta de Notícias,* September 15, 1900.
26. Ibid., September 25, 1900.
27. Ibid., October 26 and October 31, 1900.
28. Guanabara, *Presidência Campos Sales,* 191. Murtinho's own institution, the Banco do Rio e Matto Grosso, founded during the Encilhamento, made unrealizable loans, suffered during the crisis of 1900, and was liquidated shortly thereafter. Luz, *Idéias econômicas de Joaquim Murtinho,* 29.
29. *Gazeta de Notícias,* October 25, 1900.
30. Azevedo and Lins, *História do Banco da Bahia,* 60–61 and 195.
31. *Gazeta de Notícias,* September 26, 1900.
32. Ibid., November 5, 1900.
33. The crisis caused a good deal of capital flight by both Brazilians and foreigners. *Rio News,* October 16, 1900. As the situation returned to normal, funds began to flow back to Brazil.
34. *Gazeta de Notícias,* November 16, 1900. Ouro Preto's loan of 1889 traded at 58½ on November 15, 1899, and at 61 exactly one year later, while the loan of 1895 rose from 65 to 70 and the Funding Loan improved from 83 to 84¾.
35. Peláez and Suzigan, *História monetária,* 146–147.
36. *Jornal do Brasil,* October 26, 1900, citing an article in *The Times* of the previous day. See also *Gazeta de Notícias* of March 4, 1901, commenting on an article in *The Economist.*
37. Correia, *Problema econômico,* 43–46.
38. Ibid., pages 19–26. When Murtinho resumed payment of the external debt, it was Serzedello who proposed that the Chamber of Deputies give the minister a vote of congratulation. *Jornal do Brasil,* July 2, 1901.
39. Topik, *Political Economy,* chapter 4.
40. Guanabara, *Presidência Campos Sales,* 151.
41. Topik, *Political Economy,* chapter 4.
42. Luz, *Idéias econômicas de Joaquim Murtinho,* 277.
43. Ibid., 278.
44. Ibid., 277–278.
45. *Rio News,* October 23, 1900.
46. See, for instance, Luz, *Idéias econômicas de Joaquim Murtinho,* 270, 341–520, on Vieira Souto's attack on Murtinho.

47. Murtinho made available 100,000 contos in bonds, 60,000 in sterling, 50,000 of the renegotiated loan, 25,000 in paper money, and the 10,000 deposit, for a total of 245,000 contos, compared to a circulating medium of less than 700,000.

48. Luz, *Idéias econômicas de Joaquim Murtinho,* 274.

49. Ibid., 288.

50. Ibid., 275–276

51. *Rio News,* February 5, 1901.

52. Ibid., January 18, 1898.

53. Ibid., June 11, 1901.

54. Ibid., March 12 and March 19, 1901.

55. *Cidade do Rio,* June 15, 1901.

56. *Rio News,* September 10, 1901.

57. Viana, *Banco do Brasil,* 712.

58. Ibid., 726–730.

59. For a discussion of public finance in the period from 1906 to 1930, see Fritsch, *External Constraints.*

60. A conservative textbook of 1911 praised valorization as a creative way of defending an economy from the effects of overproduction. See Gide, *Curso de economia política,* 160. For a further discussion of valorization see Delfim Netto, *Problema do café,* and Fritsch, *External Constraints.*

CHAPTER 9: REFLECTIONS ON INFLATION

1. Cavalcanti, *O meio circulante nacional, 1808–1835,* first published in 1893, is still the best financial history of this period. For a political account, see Barman, *Brazil: The Forging of a Nation.*

2. Vilar, *Gold and Money,* chapter 36.

3. Goldsmith, *Brasil 1850–1984,* 29–35.

4. Ibid., 30–31.

5. See Schulz, *Exercito,* 211–212, for complete salary tables as well as an explanation of the components of officers' remuneration.

6. Vilar, *Gold and Money,* chapters 24, 25, 30, and 31.

7. Cortés Conde, *Diñero, deuda y crisis,* 50.

8. Gide, *Curso de economia política,* 362.

9. Ibid., page 390.

10. For a discussion of the effects of nineteenth-century crises upon the United States, see Sobel, *Panic on Wall Street,* 32–272.

APPENDIX: PUBLIC *FINANCE* IN BRAZIL

1. In fact, in seventeenth-century England, customs and land taxes each contributed almost half of state income. During the following century, the excise tax came to be as important as either of these two sources of revenue. See Brewer, *Sinews of Power.*

2. Furtado, *Economic Growth of Brazil,* demonstrates the significance of 1850 as a turning point.

3. Cavalcanti, *Resenha financeira,* 130. The literature often mentions guaranteed "interest." In most cases, the revenues of the railroads failed to provide the guaranteed returns, so this capital was treated as a loan, usually at 7 percent, of which 5 percent came from the imperial government and 2 percent from the provincial government. In the case of the São Paulo Railway, earnings exceeded the 7 percent level, and investors received higher dividends. The imperial treasury did not have to pay anything once the 7 percent threshold had been reached.

4. Ibid., page 156. The laws sanctioning the credit of 70,000 contos may be found in the *Leis e Decretos do Brasil,* April 15 and June 20, 1878.

5. Greenfield, "Migrant Behavior," 69–86.

6. Figures obtained from successive *Relatórios da Fazenda.* On immigration, see Holloway, *Immigrants,* and Hall, "Origins."

7. Leff, *Underdevelopment,* I, 37, cites Contador and Haddad, "Produto real, moeda e preços."

8. Leff, *Underdevelopment,* II, 105. See also José Murilo de Carvalho, *Teatro das sombras,* 26.

9. Leff, *Underdevelopment,* I, 195.

10. Around 1890, Argentina's government spent between 12 and 14 percent of the country's GNP, Italy's, around 10 percent, and the United States federal government, 3 percent. See Paolera, "How the Argentine Economy," 72.

11. Studenski and Kroos, *Financial History,* 152.

12. We have taken the sum allocated to the Ministry of Agriculture, Commerce, and Public Works as the resources budgeted for "improvements" in Brazil.

13. Studenski and Kroos, *Financial History,* 152.

14. Ibid., 165.

15. Ibid., 152.

16. In 1891, the published figure was 54 percent. Adjusting "exchange difference" owing to the gold tariff in force that year, we arrive at 58 percent.

17. Luz, *Luta,* 161–162, 169.

18. Ibid., 180–188, Topik, *Political Economy,* chapter 5.

19. On Sinimbú, see *Rio News,* May 14, 1879. Dantas's attempt is cited in Carvalho, *Teatro de sombras,* 99.

20. Guanabara, *Presidência Campos Sales,* 197.

21. Deane, *First Industrial Revolution,* 205.

22. Carreira, *História financeira,* II, 718–719. For an excellent discussion of the debt in particular and public finance in general, see Abreu and Lago, *Property Rights.*

23. *Congresso Agrícola de 1878,* 226. Figures presented in Goldsmith, *Brasil 1850–1984,* 72–73, show the internal debt increasing rather than decreasing during the decade of the 1880s.

24. The foreign loan of 1865 was made at 74—that is, at a 26 percent discount. See Carreira, *História financeira,* I, 435. The annual interest rate was 5 percent. The foreign loan of 1886, also at 5 percent interest, was placed at 95 (that is, at a discount of only 5 percent.) Ibid., II, 598.

25. *Congresso Agrícola de 1878,* 240.

26. Since debt service decreased by 25 percent between 1880 and 1888 while the interest rate declined by 18 percent and the amortization rate remained constant, the volume of the debt must have contracted.

27. Barros, *A illustração Brasileira,* 274–277.

28. Taunay, *Memórias,* 418.

29. Paolera, "How the Argentine Economy," 76, notes that the U.S. federal government spent only 3 percent of that country's GNP, whereas Leff, *Underdevelopment,* I, 195, calculates that the Brazilian government of the late nineteenth century spent 9 percent.

Glossary

accepted draft: A draft that the payer has acknowledged and signed. The draft can be discounted once it has been accepted.

authorized capital: The total capital that a corporation is authorized to issue.

backing: The asset, usually gold or government bonds, that served as security for the banknotes issued.

bank of issue: A bank that issues banknotes.

banking house: A bank in which the partners had unlimited liability. This institution was roughly equivalent to the private bank in nineteenth-century Britain.

banknote: An obligation of a bank, in bearer form, which circulated until presented for payment at the issuing bank. In the nineteenth century, the notes of privately owned banks circulated widely; these instruments became worthless if the issuing bank failed. Today, only banknotes of central banks circulate, so the term has become synonymous with paper money.

bill of exchange: Originally an accepted draft covering an export, payable in the importer's currency.

bimetallic: In the nineteenth century, term meaning that a currency was convertible into two metals, gold and silver, at a fixed rate for both metals.

bond: A long-term obligation of a government or a corporation; it may or may not be secured.

circulating medium: The total money in circulation, including metal, government paper money, banknotes, and other instruments accepted as money for payment.

commercial bank: A bank whose principal business is taking deposits and lending money.

commission merchant; factor: A merchant who acted as a planter's agent, selling his coffee, purchasing his supplies, and obtaining financing, all on a commission basis.

conto: One thousand milreis. At parity, the milreis was worth 27 English pence, so one conto was worth £111, or just over $500.

convertible: A currency that can be exchanged for gold and other currencies at a fixed rate; also, a banknote that can be exchanged for gold.

debasement: The reduction of the metallic content of coins.

debenture: A bond that is a general obligation of the issuer and for which no specific assets have been pledged.

debt peonage: A system whereby a worker can never repay his debts to his employer and consequently is forced to continue to labor for him, usually for extremely low wages.

discount: The interest a banker charges for financing a draft, taken upfront, or "discounted." For instance, a banker who delivers 97 percent of the value of the draft to its owner and collects 100 percent at maturity has taken a 3 percent discount.

draft: An instrument issued by the seller of a good that says, in effect, "You owe me." The buyer shows that he accepts this debt by signing, or "accepting," the document. Once the draft is thus "accepted," it can be "discounted."

Encilhamento: Literally, "girthing or saddling up." The period of intense speculation in Brazil from June 1889 to November 1891.

endorse: To sign an instrument on its back. When a draft is discounted, the seller endorses it, making himself responsible to pay the banker if the buyer fails to do so. Bills of exchange, promissory notes, and other instruments can also be endorsed.

fiscal policy: The government's actions regarding its income and expenditures.

forced circulation: The situation in which a government declares that instruments such as paper money and banknotes are to be accepted at face value regardless of the relationship of the currency to gold.

funding loan: A loan that provides funds to repay previous obligations. In 1898, Brazil obtained a funding loan from the Rothschilds sufficient to pay three years' interest on its entire external debt.

gold point: Under the gold standard, the point where it became profitable for merchants to discharge their obligations by transporting gold rather than purchasing a bill of exchange.

gold standard: A system in which currencies are fixed to the price of gold.

inconvertible: A currency or banknote that cannot be exchanged for gold and other currencies at a fixed rate.

investment bank: A bank that underwrites stocks and bonds and then sells them to its clients (places them) and trades these securities. Investment banks do not take deposits or make loans, as commercial banks do.

limited liability: Said of a company whose shareholders are responsible only to the extent of the capital they have invested in the company, so that a shareholder's maximum loss is his original investment.

limited partnership: A partnership in which the "limited partners" have limited liability and the "general partners" have unlimited liability.

merchant bank: A bank that undertakes the activities of both an investment and a commercial bank, usually emphasizing the former. This type of institution existed in the United Kingdom in the nineteenth century and exists today. During the nineteenth century, the Rothschilds were the most important merchant bankers.

milreis: Unit of Brazilian currency from independence in 1822 to 1942. At parity, it was worth 27 English pence or half a U.S. dollar.

monetary policy: The government's actions that affect the volume of money in circulation and the ease or difficulty of obtaining credit.

money supply: The circulating medium plus deposits of the banking system.

monometallic: In the nineteenth century, said of a currency that was convertible into one metal, gold or silver.

moratorium: A legally authorized period of delay in the performance of a legal obligation or the payment of a debt. A moratorium may apply only to the payment of principal or may apply to payments of both principal and interest.

mortgage: The pledging of a property as security for a loan. Usually the term refers to a pledge of land but it may also be applied to slaves, animals, and equipment (a so-called chattel mortgage), or to flows of income such as customs receipts.

note; promissory note: A financial instrument issued by a government, company, individual, or bank, usually for a relatively short period of time. The note may be secured by specific assets or be an unsecured general obligation of the issuer. Unlike the draft, the note does not arise from an underlying trade transaction and is in the form of an "I owe you."

paid-in capital: The amount of capital that has actually been paid into a company's treasury.

paper money: Instruments issued or guaranteed by a government that circulate as money.

private bank: In the nineteenth century, usually meant a bank in which the partners had unlimited liability. Today, a private bank usually is an institution that administers its clients' funds; however, there are still a few private banks in the nineteenth-century sense of the term.

reserved liability: A nineteenth-century arrangement whereby a shareholder was liable to the full extent of the shares he subscribed but he paid in only a fraction of this amount. If the company went bankrupt, the shareholder had to pay the difference between the subscribed and paid-in capital or see his goods sold in public auction.

sharecropper: An agricultural worker who is paid with a fraction, usually half, of what he produces in lieu of a salary.

squatter: An individual who holds land without a title; generally the term refers to those who lack the means to legalize their claims.

subscribed capital: The stock a shareholder has made a commitment to purchase, regardless of whether or not he has actually paid for these shares.

underwrite: Of an investment or merchant bank, to commit to purchase stocks or bonds. The bank is at risk between the time it underwrites a security and the time it sells the security to its clients. In 1890, Barings, a major merchant bank, became insolvent because it could not place (sell) Argentine bonds that it had underwritten.

Bibliography

Abranches, João Dunshee de. *Atas e atos do governo provisório.* Rio de Janeiro, 1953.

————. *O golpe de estado—atas e atos do governo Lucena.* Rio de Janeiro, 1954.

Abreu, Marcelo de Paiva, and Lago, Luiz Aranha Corrêa do. *Property Rights and the Fiscal and Financial Systems in Brazil: Colonial Heritage and the Imperial Period.* Rio de Janeiro, 1977.

Alfredo, João (João Alfredo Correia de Oliveira). *Relatórios da Fazenda.* Rio de Janeiro, 1888.

Azevedo, Aluizio de. *O mulato.* Belo Horizonte, 1980; first published, 1881.

Azevedo, Thales de, and Lins, E. Q. *História do Banco da Bahia, 1858–1958.* Rio de Janeiro, 1969.

Bagehot, Walter. *Lombard Street.* London, 1874.

Barbosa, Ruy. *O papel e a baixa do câmbio.* Rio de Janeiro, 2005; first published in 1892.

Barman, Roderick. *Brazil, the Forging of a Nation.* Palo Alto, 1988.

————.*Citizen Emperor Pedro II and the Making of Brazil, 1825–91.* Palo Alto, 1999.

Barreto, Afonso Henrique de Lima. *O triste fim de Policarpo Quaresma;* first published Rio de Janeiro, 1911.

Barros, Roque Spenser Maciel de. *A illustração Brasileira e a idéia de universidade.* São Paulo, 1959.

Bergad, Laird. *Slavery and the Demographic and Economic History of Minas Gerais, Brazil, 1720–1888.* Cambridge, 1999.

Bethell, Leslie. *The Abolition of the Brazilian Slave Trade.* Cambridge, 1970.

———— et al. *Brazil Empire and Republic, 1822–1930.* Cambridge, 1989.

Bonnet, Victor. *Le crédit et les banques d'émission.* Paris, 1875.

Braudel, Fernand. *The Perspectives of the World.* New York, 1984.

Brewer, John. *The Sinews of Power: War, Money and the English State, 1688–1783.* New York, 1989.

Bulhões, Leopoldo. *Perfis parlamentares de Leopoldo Bulhões.* Brasília, 1979.

Caldeira, Jorge. *Mauá, empresário do império.* São Paulo, 1995.

Cameron, Rondo. *Banking in the Early Stages of Industrialization.* New York, 1967.

Cano, Wilson. *Raízes da concentração industrial em São Paulo.* São Paulo, 1981.

Cardoso, Fernando Henrique. *Capitalismo e escravidão no Brasil meridional.* São Paulo, 1962.

Carone, Edgard. *A República velha.* São Paulo, 1971.

Carreira, Liberato de Castro. *História financeira e orçamentária do império no Brasil.* 2 vols. Brasília, 1980; first published, Rio de Janeiro, 1889.

Carruthers, Bruce G. *City of Capital.* Princeton, 1996.

Carvalho, José Murilo de. *A construção da ordem: A elite política imperial.* Rio de Janeiro, 1980.

———. *Os bestializados: O Rio de Janeiro e a República que não foi.* São Paulo, 1987.

———. *Teatro de sombras: A política imperial.* Rio de Janeiro, 1987.

Castro, Ana Celia de. *As empresas estrangeiras no Brasil.* Rio de Janeiro, 1979.

Cavalcanti, Amaro. *O meio circulante nacional (1808–1835).* Brasília, 1983; first published Rio de Janeiro, 1893.

———. *Resenha financeira do ex-império do Brasil.* Rio de Janeiro, 1890.

Chernow, Ron. *The House of Morgan.* New York, 1990.

Clapham, John. *The Bank of England.* 2 vols. Cambridge, 1945.

Colson, Roger Frank. "The Death of Expectations: Abolition and Its Aftermath in Brazil." Unpublished manuscript kindly provided by the author.

Conant, Charles. *A History of Modern Banks of Issue.* New York, 1896.

Congresso do Brasil. *Meio circulante.* Rio de Janeiro, 1892.

Conrad, Robert. *The Destruction of Brazilian Slavery, 1850–1888.* Los Angeles, 1972

Contador, Claudio, and Haddad, Cláudio. "Produto real, moeda e preços: A experiência brasileira no período 1861–1970." *Revista Brasileira de Estatística* 36 (July 1975).

Correia, Inocêncio Serzedello. *Problema econômico no Brasil.* Brasília, 1980; first published Rio de Janeiro, 1903.

Cortés Conde, Roberto. *Dinero, deuda y crisis: Evolución fiscal y monetaria en la Argentina, 1862–1890.* Buenos Aires, 1989.

Costa, Emilia Viotti da. *Da monarquia á república: Momentos decisivos.* São Paulo, 1987.

———. *Da senzala à colônia.* São Paulo, 1966.

Crouzet, François. *The Victorian Economy.* London, 1982.

Davatz, Thomas. *Memórias de um colono no Brasil.* São Paulo, 1972; first published 1850.

Davies, Glyn. *A History of Money.* Cardiff, 1994.

Dawson, Frank G. *The First Latin American Debt Crisis, 1822–1825.* New Haven, 1990.

Dean, Warren. *The Industrialization of São Paulo, 1880–1945.* Austin, Texas, 1969.

———. *Rio Claro: A Brazilian Plantation System, 1820–1920.* Palo Alto, California, 1976.

Deane, Phyllis. *The First Industrial Revolution.* Cambridge, 1981.

Delfim Netto, Antonio. *O problema do café no Brasil.* Rio de Janeiro, 1978.

Eichengreen, Barry. *Golden Fetters: The Gold Standard and the Great Depression, 1919–1939.* Oxford, 1992.

Eisenberg, Peter. *The Sugar Industry in Pernambuco, 1840–1910.* Los Angeles, 1974.

Evanson, Phillip. "The Liberal Party and Reform in Brazil, 1860–1889" Unpublished Ph.D. Dissertation University of Virginia, 1969.

Faria, Alberto de. *Mauá.* São Paulo, 1958.

Faria, Fernando Antonio. *Os vicios da Re(s)publica.* Rio de Janeiro, 1993.

Fausto, Boris. *A Concise History of Brazil.* Cambridge, 1999.

Feis, Herbert. *Europe, the World's Banker, 1870–1914.* New York, 1961.

Ferguson, Niall. *The World's Banker: The History of the House of Rothschild.* London, 1998.

Fernandes, Florestan. *The Negro in Brazilian Society.* New York, 1969.

Ferns, H. S. *Britain and Argentina in the Nineteenth Century.* Oxford, 1960.

Fetter, Frank. *Monetary Inflation in Chile.* Princeton, 1930.

Figueiredo, Afonso Celso de Assis. *Perfis parlamentares do visconde de Ouro Preto.* Brasília, 1978.

Fogel, Robert William, and Engerman, Stanley R. *Time on the Cross: The Economics of American Negro Slavery.* New York, 1984.

Franco, Bernardo de Souza. *Os bancos do Brasil.* Brasília, 1984; first published 1848.

Franco, Gustavo Henrique Barroso. *Reforma monetária e instabilidade durante a transição republicana.* Rio de Janeiro, 1983.

Franco, Maria Silvia de Carvalho. *Homens livres na ordem escravocrata.* São Paulo, 1969.

Freire, Felisbello. *História da Revolução de 6 de Setembro de 1893.* Rio de Janeiro, 1896.

Fritsch, Winston. *External Constraints on Economic Policy in Brazil, 1889–1930.* London, 1987.

Furtado, Celso. *The Economic Growth of Brazil.* Berkeley, 1963.

Gide, Charles. *Curso de economia política.* Paris and Mexico, 1911.

Goldsmith, Raymond. *Brasil 1850–1984: Desenvolvimento financeiro sob um século de inflação.* São Paulo, 1986.

Government of Brazil. *Leis e Decretos*

Government of Brazil. *Orçamento da Receita e da Despesa.* Official Financial Records from 1845 on. Archived at the Library of the Ministry of Finance, Rio de Janeiro.

Graham, Richard. *Britain and the Onset of Modernization in Brazil, 1850–1914.* Cambridge, 1972.

———. *Patronage and Politics in Nineteenth-Century Brazil.* Palo Alto, 1990.

Grandi, Guilherme. "A aquisição da Rio Claro-São Paulo Railway pela Companhia Paulista." *Historia e Economia,* Vol. 2, 2006: 71–86.

Granziera, Rui Guilherme. *A Guerra do Paraguai e o capitalismo no Brasil.* São Paulo, 1979.

Greenfield, Gerald. "Migrant Behavior and Elite Attitudes: Brazil's Great Drought, 1877–1879." *The Americas 43,* no. 1(July 1986): 69–86.

Guanabara, Alcindo. *A presidência Campos Sales.* Brasília, 1983; first published 1903.

Guimarães, Alberto Passos. *Quatro séculos de latifúndio.* Rio de Janeiro, 1963.

Haber, Stephen H., ed. *How Latin America Fell Behind: Essays on the Economic History of Brazil and Mexico.* Palo Alto, 1997.

Hall, Michael. "The Origins of Mass Immigration to São Paulo, 1870–1914." Ph.D. dissertation, Columbia University, 1969.

Hammond, Bray. *Banks and Politics in America: From the Revolution to the Civil War.* Princeton, 1957.

Hanley, Anne G. *Native Capital: Financial Institutions and Economic Development in São Paulo, Brazil, 1850–1920.* Palo Alto, 2005.

Holanda, Sergio Buarque de, and Fausto, Boris. *História geral da civilização Brasileira.* Vols. 6–9. São Paulo, 1971–1978.

Holloway, Thomas. *Immigrants on the Land.* Chapel Hill, 1980.

———. *Policing Rio de Janeiro: Repression and Resistance in a 19th-Century City.* Palo Alto, Calif., 1993.

Hunt, Edwin C. *The Medieval Super-Companies.* Cambridge, 1994.

Ianni, Octavio. *As metamorfoses do escravo.* São Paulo, 1962.

Javari, Barão de. *Organizações e programas ministeriais.* Rio de Janeiro, 1962; first published, 1889.

Joslin, David. *A Century of Banking in Latin America.* London, 1963.

Karasch, Mary C. *Slave Life in Rio de Janeiro (1808–1850).* Princeton, 1987.

Kenwood, A. G., and Lougheed, A. L. *The Growth of the International Economy, 1820–1990.* London, 1992.

Kilbourne, Richard Holcombe. *Slave Agriculture and Financial Markets.* London, 2005.

Kindleberger, Charles P. *A Financial History of Western Europe.* New York, 1993.

———. *Manias, Panics, and Crashes: A History of Financial Crises.* New York, 1996.

Kynaston, David. *The City of London.* Vol. 2: *Golden Years, 1890–1914.* London, 1995.

Lacombe, Americo Jacobina. *Á sombra de Rui Barbosa.* Rio de Janeiro, 1984.

Leff, Nathaniel. *Underdevelopment and Development in Brazil.* 2 vols. London, 1982.

Levi, Darrell E. *The Prados of São Paulo: An Elite Family and Social Change, 1840–1930.* Athens, Ga., 1987.

Levy, Maria Bárbara. "The Banking System and Foreign Capital in Brazil." In Cameron Rondo and V. I. Bovykin, eds., *International Banking, 1870–1914.* Oxford, 1991.

———. *Historia da bolsa de valores do Rio de Janeiro.* Rio de Janeiro, 1977.

Lobo, Eulália. *História do Rio de Janeiro.* Rio de Janeiro, 1978.

Love, Joseph. *Rio Grande do Sul and Brazilian Regionalism, 1882–1930.* Palo Alto, 1971.

Luz, Nicia Vilela. *A luta pela industrialização do Brasil.* São Paulo, 1961.

———. *Idéias econômicas de Joaquim Murtinho.* Brasília, 1980.

Lyra, Heitor. *História da queda do império.* São Paulo, 1964.

Machado, Eurico Serzedello. *Um republicano: A vida de Inocêncio Serzedelo Correa.* Rio de Janeiro, 1972.

Magalhães Jr, Raimundo. *Rui: O homem e o mito.* Rio de Janeiro, 1965.

Manchester, Alan. *British Preeminence in Brazil.* London, 1933.

Marichal, Carlos. *A Century of Debt Crisis in Latin America.* Princeton, 1989.

Meira, Roberta Barros. "O processo de modernização da agroindústria canavieira" *História e Economia,* Vol. 3, 2007: 40–54.

Mello, Evaldo Cabral de. *O norte agrário e o império, 1871–1889.* Rio de Janeiro, 1984.

Mello, João Manoel Cardoso de. *O capitalismo tardio.* São Paulo, 1982.

Mello, Pedro Carvalho de. "The Economics of Slavery on Brazilian Coffee Plantations, 1850–1888." Ph.D. dissertation, University of Chicago, 1977.

————. "The Profitability of Brazilian Slavery." In Robert William Fogel and Stanley L. Engerman, eds., *Without Consent or Contract: Markets and Production*. New York, 1992.

Monteiro, Tobias. *Pesquisas e depoimentos para a história*. Rio de Janeiro, 1913.

Nabuco, Joaquim. *O abolicionismo*. Brasília, 2003; first published in 1883.

————. *Um estadista do império*. Rio de Janeiro, 1997; first published in 1897.

Naro, Nancy. *A Slave's Place, a Master's World: Fashioning Dependency in Rural Brazil*. London and New York, 2000.

Neal, Larry. *The Rise of Financial Capitalism: International Capital Markets in the Age of Reason*. Cambridge, 1993.

Oliveira, João Alfredo Correia de. *Relatórios da Fazenda*. Rio de Janeiro, 1888.

Paolera, Gerardo della. "How the Argentine Economy Performed During the International Gold Standard: A Reexamination." Ph.D. dissertation, University of Chicago, 1988.

Peláez, Carlos. *História econômica do Brasil*. São Paulo, 1979.

Peláez, Carlos, and Suzigan, Wilson. *História monetária do Brasil*. Brasília, 1981.

Pinheiro, Paulo Sergio and Hall, Michael. *A classe operária no Brasil, 1889–1930*. São Paulo, 1979.

Pinho, José Wanderley. *Cartas de Francisco Otaviano*. Rio de Janeiro, 1977.

Prado Junior, Caio. *Historia econômica do Brasil*. São Paulo, 1956.

Queiroz, Suely. *Os radicais da república Jacobinismo: Ideologia e ação, 1893–1897*. São Paulo, 1986.

Ridings, Eugene. *Business Interest Groups in Nineteenth-Century Brazil*. Cambridge, 1994.

Ritter, Gretchen. *Goldbugs and Greenbacks*. Cambridge, 1999.

Roover, Rupert de. *The Rise and Decline of the Medici Bank, 1397–1494*. Cambridge, Mass., 1963.

Roure, Agenor de. *A constituinte repúblicana*. Rio de Janeiro, 1920.

Saes, Flavio Azevedo Marques de. *Crédito e bancos no desenvolvimento da economia paulista, 1850–1930*. São Paulo, 1987.

Sayers, R. S. *Lloyds Bank in the History of English Banking*. Oxford, 1957.

Schulz, John. *O exército na politica*. São Paulo, 1994.

Shannon, Richard. *The Crisis of Imperialism, 1865–1915*. London, 1974.

Slenes, Robert W. "The Brazilian Internal Slave Trade, 1850–1888." In Walter Johnson, ed., *The Chattel Principle*. New Haven, 2004.

Smith, Tony. *The Pattern of Imperialism: The United States, Great Britain, and the Late-Industrializing World since 1815*. Cambridge, 1981.

Sobel, Robert. *Panic on Wall Street*. New York, 1968.

Sodré, Nelson Werneck. *Formacão historica do Brasil*. Rio de Janeiro, 2004; first published in 1962.

Stein, Stanley. *The Brazilian Cotton Manufacture: Textile Enterprise in an Undeveloped Area, 1850–1950*. Cambridge, Mass., 1957.

————. *Vassouras, a Brazilian Coffee County, 1850–1900*. Princeton, 1985.

Stern, Fritz. *Gold and Iron: Bismarck, Bleichroder, and the Building of the German Empire*. New York, 1979.

Studenski, Paul, and Kroos, Herman. *Financial History of the United States*. New York, 1952.

Summerhill, William R. *Order Against Progress: Government, Foreign Investment, and Railroads in Brazil, 1854–1915.* Palo Alto, 2003.

Sweigart, Joseph. *Coffee Factorage and the Emergence of a Brazilian Capital Market, 1850–1888.* New York, 1987.

———. "Financing and Marketing Brazilian Export Agriculture: The Coffee Factors of Rio de Janeiro." Ph.D. dissertation, University of Texas, 1980.

Tannuri, Luiz Antonio. *O Encilhamento.* São Paulo, 1981.

Taunay, Afonso. *Ensaios de história econômica e financeira* in *anais do Museu Paulista.* Vol. 16. São Paulo, 1962.

Taunay, Alfredo (Visconde de). *O Encilhamento.* São Paulo, 1923; first published 1893.

———. *Memórias.* São Paulo, n.d.

Topik, Steven. *Political Economy of the Brazilian State, 1889–1930.* Austin, Texas, 1987.

———. "Revolução burguesa no Brasil." *Revista Brasileira de Historia,* number 28, 1994.

———. *Trade and Gunboats: The United States and Brazil in the Age of Empire.* Palo Alto, Calif., 1996.

Toplin, Robert B. *The Abolition of Slavery in Brazil.* New York, 1972.

Triner, Gail D. *Banking and Economic Development: Brazil, 1889–1930.* New York, 2000.

Triner, Gail D., and Wandschneider, Kirsten. "The Baring Crisis and the Encilhamento, 1889–1891: An Early Example of Contagion Among Emerging Capital Markets." *Financial History Review,* October 2005.

Ventura, Roberto. *Euclides.* São Paulo, 2003.

Viana, Victor. *O Banco do Brasil.* Rio de Janeiro, 1926.

Vilar, Pierre. *A History of Gold and Money, 1450–1920.* London, 1976.

Vilela, Andre Arruda. "The Political Economy of Money and Banking in Brazil, 1850–1870." Ph.D. dissertation, London School of Economics, 2003.

Wileman, J. P. *Brazilian Exchange: The Study of an Inconvertible Currency.* Buenos Aires, 1896.

Williams, John. *Argentine International Trade Under Inconvertible Paper Money, 1880–1900.* Cambridge, Mass., 1920.

Young, George. "Anglo-German Banking Syndicates and the Issue of South American Government Loans in the Era of High Imperialism, 1885–1914." Monograph from the Bankhistorisches Archiv. *Zeitschrift fur Bankgeschichte,* 1990, 3–38.

Index

abolition: army and, 62; banking system and, 65–70; civil rights and, 6; coffee and, xiv, 45, 48, 97; in Cuba, xiii, 48; enactment of, ix–x, xiii–xiv, 64–65; immigration and, 73, 97; indemnification for, 65, 73; Isabel and, 63; labor and, 60, 62, 64–65, 73, 97; monetary policy and, 7–8; movement for, 6, 40, 59–60, 62–63; in New York, 40; Paraíba Valley and, 65; planters and, 45, 48; in Portugal, 40; public finance and, 7–8, 65–70; Rio de Janeiro Province and, x, 64–65; *Rio News* and, 152n. 20; São Paulo Province and, 48, 62, 65; in United States, x, xiii, 2–3, 40, 60

accepted draft, 172

Agricultural Congress, 48–54

agriculture: Agricultural Congress, 48–54; Banco da Bahia and, 66; Banco do Brasil and, 5, 49, 66; banking system and, 21–22, 45–54, 57–59, 65–70; banknotes and, 51–52, 54, 61–62, 66–68, 74, 76–78; bonds and, 52–53, 67–68, 76–78; capital for, 49–54, 65–66; credit for, 52–53, 65–66, 74–78, 79, 96, 100–101, 128; elite and, 5–6; during Encilhamento, 91–92; foreign trade and, 5, 68–69; in France, 6, 56; gold standard and, 61–62, 63–64, 67–68, 78; in Great Britain, 21–22; immigration and, 6, 49, 55, 56, 68–69; inflation and, 51–52, 68; labor and, 49–50, 54, 55–58, 62; monetary policy and, 51–55, 61–62, 63–64; mortgages and, 50–51, 52–53, 54, 61, 74, 76; public finance and, 50–54, 57–59, 60–62, 63–64, 65–70; railroads and, 21–22, 24–25; taxation and, 56; in United States, 6, 56. *See also* planters; *individual products*

20; in Germany, 20, 23, 30, 42, 67; gold standard in generally, 17–18; in Great Britain, 15–18, 20–23, 27–28, 30, 31, 38–39, 40; industrialization and, 81; inflation and, 16, 17–18, 35, 68; interest bearing accounts in, 16, 28; limited liability in, 20–21, 30; Lucena and, 133; Mauá in, 29–30, 36, 40, 42–43, 49; in Minas Gerais Province, 80; monetary policy and, 33; of Netherlands, 22; Ouro Preto and, 66, 68, 74–78, 96, 132–33; in Paraná Province, 80; planters and, 45–54, 57–59, 65–70; regulation of, 34; reserved liability in, 34–35; in Rio de Janeiro Province, 43–44, 46, 80, 122; in Santa Catarina, 80; in São Paulo Province, 80, 82, 84, 89; Souza Franco and, 32–35, 67–68; stabilization and, 100–102, 105–9, 119–23, 125–26; stock market and, 75–76; in United States, 18–20, 30, 33, 42, 46–47, 66, 106, 153n. 21. *See also* banknotes; *individual banks*

banknotes: agriculture and, 51–52, 54, 61–62, 66–68, 74, 76–78; in Argentina, 160n. 49; of Banco da República, 113, 114; of Banco do Brasil, 28, 31–32, 33, 35–36, 39–40, 41–42, 43; of Bank of England, 16, 17–18, 31; Barbosa and, 79–81, 82–84, 86–87; in Brazil, 27–34; coffee and, 51–52, 54, 61–62; definition of, 172; during Encilhamento, 74, 79–81, 82–84, 86–87, 92–93, 96–97; in foreign trade, 15–16, 17–18, 42; inflation and, 17–18, 31–32, 51–52; Lucena and, 92–93, 96–97; in monetary policy, 17–18; Ouro Preto and, 74, 76–78; planters and, 51–52, 54, 61–62, 66–68, 74, 76–78; private banks issue, 15–16, 42, 67; stabilization and, 101–2, 105–9, 113, 114; in United States, 18–20, 66. *See also* banking system

Bank of England: banknotes of, 16,

17–18, 31; credit issued by, 21; discount rate at, 38, 40, 42; formation of, 15; in monetary policy, 17–18; in stock market, 22

Bank of the United States, 18–19, 46

banks of issue: Barbosa and, 79–81, 82, 87, 97; definition of, 172; establishment of, 34–35, 44; Lucena and, 97; Oliveira and, 66, 69–70, 77; Ouro Preto and, 66, 74, 97; planters want, 54; Sousa and, 61; stabilization and, 106

Banque de France, 42, 67

Banque de Paris et de Pays-Bas, 77, 79

Barbosa, Ruy: army and, 88; banking system and, 79–87, 96, 102, 133; banknotes and, 79–81, 82–84, 86–87; bonds and, 80, 101; civil war and, 110; Constituent Assembly and, 88; during Encilhamento, 79–89, 94–96, 97; financial policy of, xv; historiography on, 9–10, 35, 79; industrialization and, 94; labor and, 65; public finance and, 79–87, 96; in Senate, 99; stock market and, 84–87

Bardi bank, 15

Baring crisis, 9

Barings bank, 88, 90, 108

Bastos, Coelho, 65

bills of exchange, 14–15, 172

bimetallic standard, 16–17, 19, 20, 135, 172. *See also* gold standard

Bismarck, Otto von, 6, 40

Black Guard of the Princess, 65

Blaine-Mendonça Treaty, 95

Bocayuva, Quintino, 161n. 8

bonds: agriculture and, 52–53, 67–68, 76–78; Alves and, 101–2; in banking system, 33, 35, 44, 52; Barbosa and, 80, 101; in Brazil, 33; coffee, 52–53; definition of, 172; deflation and, 80; gold and, 76–77; in Great Britain, 21–24; Lucena and, 101; Ouro Preto and, 76–78; planters and, 52–53,